Acclaim for *Beautiful Holiness*

During the nine years I spent in Mexico as Apostolic Nuncio, I discovered with wonder the extraordinary human personality of Conchita Cabrera de Armida and her unique mystical itinerary. I am sure that the present study by Kathleen Beckman will help many priests, religious, and laity to benefit from the witness of her life and from her spirituality of the Cross. Kathleen Beckman presents in a very attractive way the great figure of Conchita to English-speaking readers.

—**Archbishop Christophe Pierre**
Apostolic Nuncio to the United States

I have found Conchita's writings to be very personally formative and, I believe, critical for the people of today. Her reflections on the priesthood have greatly inspired me, and she is a must-read for every priest! Kathleen Beckman does an excellent job of capturing Conchita's thoughts, which ultimately come from the heart of God.

—**Msgr. Stephen Rossetti**
Author, *Diary of an American Exorcist*

Blessed Conchita is one of my favorite mystics! I have always found her insights into the Eucharist, the Sacred Heart of Jesus, Our Lady, St. Joseph, and the spiritual life to be profound and emanating from a place of deep prayer. I am delighted that Kathleen Beckman has written this inspired work on the mysticism of Blessed Conchita. The book will lead readers closer to the Heart of Jesus, our Savior.

—**Fr. Donald Calloway, M.I.C.**
Author, *Consecration to St. Joseph*

Wife, mother, widow, mystic, saint—if you want to know how a layperson can pursue and know holiness in the midst of the busy vocation of marriage and normal lay life, there is no better source than Conchita Cabrera and our eloquent guide to her life, Kathleen Beckman. If you pick up this book, you will not be able to put it down.

—Dan and Stephanie Burke
Divine Intimacy Radio and SpiritualDirection.com

We are all called to be saints! Blessed Conchita shows the way of sanctity with her breathtaking love of Jesus. Kathleen Beckman tenderly introduces us to her beautiful life in love with our Lord, guided by the Holy Spirit. This book is a gift. Drink it in on the journey to Heaven.

—Kathryn Jean Lopez
Senior Fellow, National Review Institute;
Director for the Center for Religion, Culture and Civil Society;
Author, A Year with the Mystics: Visionary Wisdom for Daily Living

In *Beautiful Holiness, A Spiritual Journey with Blessed Conchita to the Heart of Jesus*, Kathleen Beckman offers us a rich and valuable selection of texts from Conchita's *Diary* and other mystical writings. Kathleen complements these materials with wise personal commentaries, full of faith and love, and enlightens Conchita's spiritual doctrine with insight from relatives and from spiritual children in religious orders. I trust that in reading this book, you will receive an impulse to be holy and joyful.

—Fr. Domenico Di Raimondo, M.Sp.S.
Director of the House of Prayer for Priests, Orange, CA

Kathleen Beckman wrote in the preface of her book *Beautiful Holiness: A Spiritual Journey with Blessed Conchita to the Heart of Jesus* that "there are others in Conchita's spiritual family who would do a finer work." I disagree. Kathleen has done a stellar job of presenting the life and spiritual legacy of Blessed Conchita Cabrera de Armida,

Mexican wife, mother, mystic, and foundress. The exquisite title says it all. You will not be disappointed. You will be captivated, drawn in, and enthralled by Blessed Conchita as she leads you in your spiritual journey to the Heart of Jesus.

—**Sr. Timothy Marie Kennedy, O.C.D.**
Carmelite Sisters of the Most Sacred Heart of Los Angeles;
Author, *In the Face of Darkness: The Heroic Life and Holy Death
of Mother Luisita* and *Unleashing Hope: The Biography of Venerable
Maria Luisa Josefa of the Most Blessed Sacrament*

Belonging to the blood family of Blessed Conchita; having met her sons, daughters, and grandchildren; and being a witness to the process of canonization, I have been blessed. It's a privilege to contribute my memories and knowledge about Conchita, a holy wife and mother, mystic and apostle. Kathleen Beckman has done a great work in presenting Blessed Conchita's life and spirituality to the English-speaking world. In reading this book, you will discover Conchita throughout these pages, and thus, you will find Jesus speaking to you.

—**Sr. Guadalupe Labarthe, R.C.S.C.J.**
Relative of Blessed Conchita Cabrera

Beautiful Holiness will assuredly contribute to the spiritual life of the Church. I believe this work will inspire readers already familiar with the mystic Blessed Concepción Cabrera de Armida to appreciate her in a deeper way and will open new possibilities for spiritual growth to those who are not yet acquainted with this wife and mother known as Conchita. Kathleen Beckman offers insightful reflections on Blessed Conchita's mystical writings, making this book a joy to read and study.

—**Msgr. Stephen S. Doktorczyk, J.C.D.**
Vicar-General for Legal and Canonical Affairs, Diocese of Orange;
Pastor, St. Martin de Porres Church, Yorba Linda, California

Beautiful Holiness

Kathleen Beckman

Beautiful Holiness

A Spiritual Journey with
Blessed Conchita to the Heart of Jesus

SOPHIA INSTITUTE PRESS
Manchester, New Hampshire

Nihil obstat: Reverend Joseph Son Nguyen, M.Div., MA, BCC, S.Th.D., *Censor librorum*

Imprimatur: Most Rev. Kevin W. Vann, J.C.D., D.D., Bishop of Orange in California, November 3, 2022

Sophia Institute Press
Box 5284, Manchester, NH 03108
1-800-888-9344

www.SophiaInstitute.com

Sophia Institute Press® is a registered trademark of Sophia Institute.

paperback ISBN 978-1-64413-634-8

ebook ISBN 978-1-64413-635-5

Library of Congress Control Number: 2022951961

First printing

To the priests who have formed my
spiritual life over the past thirty years:
Fr. Raymond Skonezny, Msgr. Stephen Doktorczyk,
Fr. Charles Cortinovis, Fr. Thomas Nelson, O. Praem.,
Msgr. John Esseff, and Fr. Jeffrey Droessler

Contents

Foreword

Archbishop Gustavo García-Siller, M.Sp.S.

As a Missionary of the Holy Spirit who has lived much of his adult life in the United States, I am delighted to share a few thoughts on a book that introduces to the English-speaking world one of the figures I treasure and know the most: Blessed Concepción Cabrera de Armida, better known throughout the world as Conchita.

Conchita is a treasure to be known—especially now that she has joined the ranks of the saints recognized by the Church—and this book by Kathleen Beckman does a great job of introducing readers to her life, teachings, and spirituality.

As a member of one of the institutions that were established thanks to her apostolic zeal and one who has read her *Diary* cover to cover on several occasions, I recognize in *Beautiful Holiness* something very similar to what I have experienced in my relationship with God and Conchita over the years: a journey.

On the one hand, this book presents us with the journey that Conchita experienced from her years as a young girl—thirsty "for something very big which would fill (her) poor soul"[1]—to her final

---

[1] Richard Zimbrón Levy, M.Sp.S., *Priestly People* (self-publ., San Luis Potosí, Mexico, 2011), 12.

and full embrace of the spirituality of the Cross at the moment of her death. This journey took Conchita from an ever-growing desire for God (which we all have, even if we have not recognized that that is what it is) to the increasing knowledge of Him that turned her life into the love story you will find in these pages.

Her transformation was not exempt from material and spiritual difficulties, and this makes Conchita someone we can all relate to. Just like you and me, Conchita had to go through a conversion experience—resulting, in her case, from the tragic, unexpected death of her brother—that left in her a deeper desire for God and for the salvation of souls.

Kathleen Beckman's introduction to Conchita presents the multiple facets that made Conchita who she was and is today: a daughter, a wife, the mother of nine children, a widow, a mystic, an apostle, the most prolific writer of contemporary mystical literature, an active intercessor—as we read in the narration of the miracle that led to her beatification—and the first Mexican laywoman to be beatified.

Beckman's book also provides an accessible approximation to some of the most important aspects of Conchita's experience of the Christian faith: in her family life, in her prayer life, in her encounter with the Cross and her self-surrendering love, in her union with Mary, in her Eucharistic life, in her love of priests, in her obedience to her spiritual directors, and in her ability to love with the Holy Spirit. These are all important elements connected to one of the many gifts she received from God—namely, a Christocentric, Trinitarian, and Marian spirituality that was entrusted to her for the salvation of souls and is known as the Spirituality of the Cross.

Through all of this, Conchita is presented to us as a spiritual mother, one who allowed God's love to transform the whole of her existence and who wanted nothing but to guide others to the center and source of that love: Christ.

Beautiful Holiness describes the effects that the active and committed love of this woman had in the life of her family and in the lives of the many priests, prelates, and religious sisters and brothers she encountered throughout her life as well as a multitude of laypeople who, through her writings, her example, and the institutions she inspired, have discovered their own calls to holiness.

The descriptions of many of these effects and aspects of Conchita's life come from the testimonies of people who have studied her over the years, including Cardinal Raniero Cantalamessa, whose insights about Conchita are deeply valued by all of us.

On the other hand, this book is also a step in our own journey. From this perspective, I invite you to use it not only to learn more about an outstanding woman but to take advantage of all that Christ taught her to learn more about yourself and what He has in store for you.

Read this book in a spirit of prayerfulness. Pause to reflect on the questions the author shares at the end of each chapter.

Allow God to use the time you spend reading and reflecting on this book to make Himself present in your life and to transform you. If you do, I am sure that the author, Conchita, and our Father in Heaven will all be very, very happy.

"As he who called you is holy, be holy yourselves in every aspect of your conduct, since it is written, 'You shall be holy for I am holy'" (1 Pet. 1:15–16).

Preface

Over the past eighteen months, as I wrote about Blessed Conchita (1862-1937), recurring thoughts came to me: This wife, mother, and mystic is an antidote to mediocre discipleship. Holiness is very attractive. It is good to be Catholic. Yet Christ and the Church are mocked and despised by not a few people around the world today. Yes, the Church has difficulties, her faithful people are sometimes confused, and there have been failures. But to the Catholic Church Jesus entrusted the undiluted "words of eternal life" (cf. John 6:68). The Heart of Jesus will never cease to draw people to Him. Even if Christ were to have more enemies than friends, His friends would ceaselessly proclaim the glory of the Lord, raise up His Cross, and kneel down in Eucharistic adoration.

In leading international retreats over the past two decades, I've noted in practicing Catholics an authentic thirst for God and a deep desire for mentoring in the spiritual life. The Holy Spirit is powerfully gathering, restoring, and equipping His faithful friends. Yes, Jesus has His friends, public and hidden, on earth and in Heaven. These are His faithful priests, nuns, religious communities, families, and youth who are more enlivened now. Rooted in Christ, established in love, we cannot be "canceled." The Holy Spirit has anointed us to be Christ's living word, "sharper than any two-edged sword, piercing to the division of soul and of spirit, of joints and of marrow, and discerning the thoughts and intentions of the heart" (Heb. 4:12).

Now the Lord is raising up an acclaimed mystic, a saintly wife and mother of nine children, Blessed Conchita, who is an icon of Love Crucified. Conchita challenges us to examine our hearts to discover seeds of heroism. Saints are the embodiment of heroic virtue. We need heroes of the Faith. We want to go forward courageously. We look to the holy ones on earth and in Heaven to show us the way to radiate Christ's Heart and draw souls to Him. How did Jesus attract disciples? How were you drawn to Him? He offered something mysterious and glorious, a better vision, and perfect charity. He offered His Heart to be pierced on the Cross. And people were drawn to Him.

Conchita urges us to climb to the heights of loving God. But our ascent must be through the Cross. Our hallmark must be Love Crucified. In her vision of the Cross, Conchita saw that the Holy Spirit dominated the Cross. This means that the same Holy Spirit who compelled Jesus to the Cross will compel us to union with Him.

In practice, what does this look like? Conchita invites us to love more sacrificially; to serve loved ones more perfectly; to choose more ascetical practices, away from the comforts we enjoy; to look deeper and do more for the care of souls—ours and others'; to fear not where Jesus leads; to rejoice and laugh much; to gather souls; to nurture virtue; to pray unceasingly; never to cease growing but to reach for more. She would have us begin in our families and proceed outward to priests and the Church. Conchita would exhort us to anticipate all the grace we need from Jesus, Mary, and the Holy Spirit, and the Father's plan for good.

Preface

Conchita had a little saying: "Let yourself be done and undone by Jesus." I have now experienced the meaning of these words. In my eighteen months of research and writing, there have been too many difficulties, sicknesses, crises, and spiritual attacks to count. Throughout that time loomed the temptation to quit, as I could not possibly do justice to the remarkable mystic. Her essence was so profound, her influence so vast, her writings so numerous that it was challenging to synthesize her life and legacy for this book.

Her advice that I let myself be done and undone by Jesus was real—and uncomfortable. Then, when I was in a position of being undone, Jesus did something quite beautiful. So many special graces moved this work forward, helping me to present judiciously the keynotes of Conchita's spiritual itinerary. There are others in Conchita's spiritual family who could do a finer work. The writing of this book fell to me for reasons you'll know when you reach the end of it.

This book begins with the story of a miracle and ends with Conchita's family remembrances of spiritual warfare. The miracle story forms an arc over the entire work to point to the interventions of God in the life of this ordinary laywoman. At the end, the account of Conchita's spiritual battles reminds us to be vigilant. Conchita knew how to make the devil flee.

Spiritual warfare is the topic of my previous book, and many know that I serve in the Church's ministry of deliverance and exorcism. On the exorcist's team, I witness a very real battle between good and evil; I know the tragic stories of how people fall into sin and evil. I can testify to the power of divine love, the efficacy of faith and holiness. Real authority lies with Jesus, His Church, and disciples called to holiness.

Beautiful Holiness

This book is organized so that at the end of each chapter, individuals or groups may ponder a scriptural text, discuss three questions, and pray one of Conchita's prayers.

In reading, may you discover the seeds of heroic virtue within you. I trust that Blessed Conchita will imprint a special word of God upon your heart as you ponder these writings.

Kathleen Beckman

September 14, 2022

Feast of the Exaltation of the Cross

Acknowledgments

A debt of gratitude is owed many people for assisting in this humble work on Blessed Concepción Cabrera de Armida, known as Conchita.

Fr. Domenico Di Raimondo, M.Sp.S., you made this book possible by your inspiration, editing, translations, expertise, and dedication. I'm deeply grateful that you have been my professor on the life and spirituality of Blessed Conchita. You invested much of your time and talent in this book. Your loving devotion as a priest son of Blessed Conchita radiates throughout these pages. May God richly reward you and the Missionaries of the Holy Spirit priests.

Thank you to the Sisters of the Cross of the Sacred Heart of Jesus of Modesto, California, for your spiritual contribution and writings you generously provided.

I'm grateful to Conchita's living relatives who graciously answered my inquiries on her family life. May God reward you: Sr. Guadalupe Labarthe, Religious of the Cross of the Sacred Heart of Jesus, and Maria Teresa Madero Lafarga.

To Conchita's spiritual family of clergy, religious sisters, and lay communities, I'm indebted for your prayers, and I ask your indulgence for any imprecision in my presentation of your spiritual mother.

Beautiful Holiness

Thank you, Charlie McKinney, president of Sophia Institute Press, for accepting my proposal for this book. I'm humbled to work with the fine team at Sophia.

Msgr. Stephen Doktorczyk, I'm deeply grateful for your counsel and review of this book. Thank you for your encouragement and constancy in prayer for me and Fr. Domenico.

Fr. Charlie Cortinovis, I hope you realize how much I counted on your prayerful intercession, discernment, humor, and friendship.

My beloved family, thank you for allowing me the silence and solitude that this book required. May you be blessed forever.

Holy Spirit, Our Lady, and Blessed Conchita, for the little signs and big graces bestowed upon me, and for entrusting this work to a poor servant, I'm deeply grateful.

Beautiful Holiness

1

Of Mystics and Miracles

With men this is impossible, but with God all things are possible.

—Matthew 19:26

Within these pages are stories of the many facets of human and divine love, the kind that embrace deepest joys and sorrows; relationships that make life's journey a very rich adventure. The preeminent love story in this book is the ancient one of the gift of God: Christ's incarnational love for the human family. It is this love that captured Blessed Conchita. Her communion with Christ only deepened her love for her husband and her children. The Lord conformed this simple laywoman to His Heart, to His Cross, and to His Mother. It was from these vantage points that she learned to love as Jesus asked.

María Concepción Cabrera de Armida (1862–1937), the wife, mother, and Mexican mystic known as Conchita, was a woman in love with Jesus Christ. Over her lifetime of seventy-four years, the Lord confided to her many secrets of His Heart. I think that no one was more surprised by the Lord's abiding presence and proposals than Conchita.

Upon seeing Jesus in a dream at six years of age, Conchita was captivated by the fact that He was "full of life." From that encounter, Conchita perceived that she was the object of Christ's love. This little girl grasped what we each need to discover and believe about Jesus. He lives! He is full of life and reveals Himself to us. He wills that we have abundant life in communion with Him. Conchita's dream planted seeds of wonder and awe in her soul. But she would grow up as an ordinary girl among the lively haciendas of her wealthy family in San Luis Potosí, Mexico.

Jesus called Conchita to the vocation of marriage and motherhood. Within these exquisite vocations, Christ adorned an ordinary woman with a glorious garment of grace.

> The Lord Himself has announced to her that she would be a model wife and mother, but that her mission would extend far beyond to make shine the sanctifying might of Christ and of the Holy Spirit "in all states of life." Yes, indeed she is a model wife, mother, teacher, but she is also one of the greatest mystics of the Church leading souls to consummation in the Unity of the Trinity. Her message calls the entire laity, married men, and women, to the highest sanctity.[2]

Conchita is a witness to the creative beauty of family life, from which all vocations are derived. Her love of God grew within her family and infused her husband and her nine children. But her love of God was so vast that it radiated far beyond the walls of her family home.

Conchita's legacy of mystical writings continues to inspire bishops, priests, nuns, and laity to strive ardently for holiness. The preacher to the papal household, Cardinal Raniero

---

[2] M. M. Philipon, O.P., *Conchita: A Mother's Spiritual Diary* (Staten Island, NY: St. Paul's, 2014), 244.

Cantalamessa, O.F.M. Cap., likened Concepción Cabrera de Armida's mystical life to that of St. Teresa of Ávila. Conchita did ask St. Teresa to help her to pray well and to love God more.

This daughter of the Virgin of Guadalupe stands in radical contrast to the lethargy of mediocre discipleship. Conchita's zeal for God and for the salvation of souls inspires the most committed among us to grow in soul-stretching faith, in heart-expanding selflessness. Learning of the interaction between the Holy Trinity and Conchita can provide formation on what it is to be fully human according to God's will.

Witness to the Laity's Call to Holiness

Conchita, an ordinary laywoman, embodied the dignity of the lay vocation, living it with joy and sacrifice. We know this because her *Diary* captures the essence of her life and spirituality. She wrote in obedience to her wise spiritual directors. Thankfully, the priests did not allow her to destroy her writings. She wrote well of the triune God and articulated holiness of life. She wrote of mystical realities that quicken the laity's baptismal call to be priest, prophet, and king. And her mystical writings on the ministerial priesthood are breathtaking, as discovered by many clergy.

Christ's disciples are called to holiness — called to conform ourselves to Jesus. We must walk in His footsteps and follow Him at each stage of life. In my thirties, I finally internalized this call when, in the gaze of St. John Paul II's eyes, I perceived Christ looking at me. I understood that I was known and loved by Him and that holiness is very attractive. Each saint witnesses to something uniquely beautiful about the call of God in our lives.

Saintly people simply radiate the loving, holy Heart of Jesus. Our triune God is the eternal Holy One who forms His children to mirror the beauty of His holiness. Even nonbelievers recognized the attractiveness of St. Teresa of Calcutta and St. John Paul II, who each dramatically changed the world for the good.

We need new saints to contribute to the renovation of our morally deteriorating, post-Christian society. Christ looks to you and me. We are poor, but He endows us. Conchita was exceedingly simple, humble, and unashamed of her spiritual poverty. Whatever our stage of life, vocation, or spiritual itinerary, Blessed Conchita models a loftier pursuit of sacrificial love and service. She presents a new vista of holiness rooted in the Cross and enveloped in love. As Fr. M. M. Philipon, O.P., wrote:

> The entire laity, married men, and women are called to the highest sanctity through the transfiguration of daily life, the sanctification of the profane, by love of the spirit of sacrifice in ordinary life. And the greatest holiness, the transcendence of the message of the Cross. Even the most banal actions are made of value to the infinite by the offering of love in union with the Cross.[3]

Sometimes, the lives of saints, the greatest mystics in the Church, can overwhelm, intimidate, and inspire us at the same time. This is how I felt at the suggestion that I write a book about Blessed Conchita.

A Providential Encounter

It was February 11, 2021, the feast of Our Lady of Lourdes, which, to me, is profoundly meaningful. In 1994, at Mary's shrine in France, I experienced a transformative conversion. Almost three decades later, I was eager to attend Mass to thank God for the life-changing Lourdes graces. I never expected to encounter a priest of

[3]   *A Mother's Spiritual Diary*, 244–245.

the Missionaries of the Holy Spirit, the order of clergy initiated by Blessed Conchita.

Fr. Domenico Di Raimondo, M.Sp.S., was the celebrant of the weekday Mass at my parish. I had not met Father, but I knew of his good work at the diocesan House of Prayer for Priests and that he once was the postulator for Conchita's cause.

Following Mass, Father and I met and conversed for a while. Then I blurted out, "Father, why don't you write a book about Blessed Conchita since few people in the U.S. know about her?" Father gently smiled and said, "Let's pray together." Pray together we did, and the Holy Spirit was very tangible. Afterward, Father stunned me, "*You* should write the book about Conchita."

"No, Father, I am not the expert!"

Father gently replied, "I'll be at your side as you write. I'll help you."

We decided to pray and discern this proposal, but a seed had been planted. Later that week, Fr. Domenico again celebrated the Mass at my parish. Afterward, I went to the adoration chapel to pray as usual. Soon, Fr. Domenico entered the chapel and silently handed me a beatification card with Conchita's picture and a flash drive. I placed them in my handbag.

A week later, I inserted the flash drive into my computer and observed a narrated video of a series of photos taken by eyewitnesses that reveal the miraculous healing of Jorge Guillermo Treviño, who had specifically asked the intercession of Conchita for that intention. Her photograph rested upon his chest throughout the healing. His was the medical miracle that Pope Francis approved for Conchita's beatification.

My heart was moved by these events. I was compelled to accept Fr. Domenico's invitation to write a book about Blessed Conchita.

Beautiful Holiness

Thus, he and I began to meet regularly at his office to collaborate on this work.

On my desk, books of Conchita's writings were piled high, awaiting exploration. In Fr. Domenico's office, the huge red volumes given to Vatican investigators of Conchita's cause were stacked nearly floor to ceiling. Her writings filled sixty-six large volumes of diaries, not to mention her many published books (written in Spanish; few are translated into English). Conchita's mystical writings amount to a library at least as vast as St. Thomas Aquinas's works. And yet, greater works by renowned theologians will be written about Conchita whose mystical life and spirituality will be mined for generations.

Saints inspire us to aim higher, to love harder, and to grow always. We need saints in the trenches to motivate us to resist and renounce our selfishness, the spirit of the world, and the devil. God works through saints. They are His team, His army, His ambassadors.

In learning of the vastness of Conchita's maternal heart; her writings, her influence, and her charisms; her mystical union with Jesus; and the tremendous joys and breathtaking sorrows of her family, I was captivated by God's actions and by Conchita's generous responses. It's humbling to reflect on the magnitude of Conchita's yes to God. And hers was a big yes! The fruits of her *fiat* are tremendous.

Uniquely, Conchita's yes to God was given one moment, one hour, one day at a time—*not* enclosed in a convent but rather, while attending to her vocational duties. As Fr. Philipon wrote of her:

> She fulfilled all the vocations of woman: fiancée, wife, mother, widow, grandmother, and even by a special indulgence of Pius X, without ever being deprived of her family

status, died canonically as a religious in the arms of her children.[4]

All her duties were enveloped in a singular, magnanimous love of God. Her cloister was Christ. The Lord took Conchita to the pinnacle of union with Him.

Our reflection on the multifaceted life of Blessed Conchita begins with the miracle that made possible her beatification on May 4, 2019. This starting point sets a foundation for how Christ worked in and through the life of Conchita, interweaving her ordinary life with extraordinary grace, bringing forth a plentitude of fruitfulness for the Church.

Miracles in the Church

In the miracles of Jesus Christ so richly articulated across the pages of the Gospels, we encounter a supernatural mercy that speaks to the human heart: "See how I love! See that nothing is impossible for me." God works miracles for His glory and for our edification. Some Catholics are incredulous regarding miracles, signs, and wonders.

Personally, authenticated miracles bring me joy and hope because they tell the truth: that God intervenes in time and place. God's power and presence are gratuitously manifested in ordinary lives. He prompts a response of wonder, awe, and gratitude. Discipleship is a journey of faith, and most will not see documented miracles like those attributed to saints. Yet it is magnificent when God works miracles of reconciliation and healing. We stand firmer in faith for having a glimpse of His supernatural hand.

On earth, Jesus Christ worked many miracles. And He said, "Truly, truly I say to you, he who believes in me will also do the

---

[4]   *A Mother's Spiritual Diary*, x.

works that I do; and greater works than these will he do, because I go to to the Father" (John 14:12). The Lord works miracles *through* His apostles. After Jesus ascended to the Father, and the Holy Spirit descended on Pentecost, the Lord's disciples worked miracles in His name. These were proofs that Jesus is who they said He is.

Later, the saints worked miracles that testify to Christ's Lordship. As the Holy Father said during his homily at the Mass for Conchita's beatification:

> Miracles submitted in the process of canonization are an excellent example of primary and secondary ends of miracles. A miracle of healing associated with the intercession of one of God's servants gives glory to God and manifests His saving mercy. These are primary ends. The beneficiary is given a temporal grace (secondary to eternal salvation) of better health. The miracle testifies to the sanctity of the intercessor and provides a clear sign of God's intercession.[5]

The intercession of the saints in Heaven is dynamic. We on earth are the beneficiaries of graces that sometimes are miraculous. Such was the case for a young husband and father named Jorge Guillermo Treviño, whose miracle was approved by Pope Francis on June 8, 2018. As you ponder this miracle through the intercession of Blessed Conchita, consider asking her intercession for you and your family. She has proven to be a powerful intercessor for spouses, children, religious sisters, and priests.

Mystics and miracles strengthen our faith, hope, and love and encourage deeper trust in Providence. God and His saints intervene with so much love and power to heal us. Perhaps as you read about Jorge Treviño's physical affliction and his need for divine

---

[5] *A Mother's Spiritual Diary*, x.

intervention, you might consider your life and where you are in need of God's healing mercy.

The Miracle: Jorge Guillermo Treviño

What is shared in this transcript of the miraculous healing of Jorge Treviño is from the official documentation submitted to and approved by the Holy See.

Jorge Guillermo Treviño was born in Monterrey, Nuevo Leon, Mexico, on December 7, 1960, to a devout Catholic family. He lived a normal childhood and young adulthood, and on July 26, 1984, he married Cecilia Plancarte Gonzalez. Jorge was an athletic man who often played tennis with his wife. He was short in stature (five foot three) and had a thin build (139 pounds). He and Cecilia had two children: Jorge and Gabriel. Despite being healthy his whole life, in 1986, at the age of twenty-six, he began suffering from severe gastritis. Doctors controlled Jorge's condition through diet and the prohibition of tobacco use, as he had smoked excessively.

In 1989, he contracted hepatitis and was isolated for thirty days. Beginning in 1990, he went through a great deal of instability at work, ultimately requiring him to sell his home and his vehicle. These were extremely stressful events, and he was diagnosed with hypertension.

In 1993, despite being thirty-three years old, Jorge began to grow taller (up to six inches) and to gain weight. During this time, his muscles would involuntarily contract during physical activity and even at rest. During this year, and despite strict medical supervision, Jorge began suffering from various symptoms without knowing their cause. These included acid reflux, heartburn, high blood pressure, fainting, general weakness, cardiac spasms, headaches, numbness of the limbs, excessive sweating, and above all, muscular contractions and intense cramps, accompanied by torn muscles and sprained ligaments in his legs. From 1996 to 2004, his symptoms became more frequent and severe. His cramps, muscle contractions, and strains would happen at any time during the day, regardless of what he was doing, even while he slept. The episodes at this point lasted hours, days, or even months. This was a particularly painful situation for him and his wife because there was nothing they could do to control these recurring crises.

In January 2004, Jorge contracted pneumonia; he was taken to the emergency room and spent a week in the hospital. Moreover, his muscle cramps, torn muscles, and contractions increased in intensity, pain, and duration; his left hand began to close involuntarily so that he could not use some of his fingers. His right hand also started to cramp when used even in daily tasks. At one point, he was diagnosed with multiple sclerosis, and the appropriate medical treatment was prescribed. In the absence of any improvement, this diagnosis was eventually discarded.

In January 2005, he contracted pneumonia again, and the muscular problems became more severe than the previous year. Starting in August of that year, the muscular contractions, accompanied by cramps and pain, became permanent. His left arm was twisted across his chest, and the muscles of his left leg were drawn tight. When he tried to stretch his leg, the pain sharpened, muscle tears occurred, and bruises appeared. It was then that Dr. Manuel De La Maza Flores, a neurologist, ordered a battery of tests. Jorge's condition was deteriorating with every passing day. In January 2006, he was hospitalized again with his entire left side contracted, including his mouth and neck. His doctors administered potent muscle relaxants, analgesics, and even morphine without any result. Several tests were performed: electromyography, encephalograms, MRIs, and multiple lab tests. No diagnosis was indicated.

Several of his spinal discs were found to have protrusions, and as Jorge was beginning to be paralyzed, a surgeon operated on one of the four damaged discs. No improvement was obtained from this intervention.

In August 2006, Jorge was again hospitalized because of allergies and because the contractions were now affecting the abdomen. By the end of 2006, the contractions worsened, extending from his left to his right side. Jorge and Cecilia felt hopeless in the face of Jorge's acute and painful condition, which was relentless night and day, and his poor response to medical treatments, examinations, hospitalizations, and so forth.

As Jorge's woes continued, he regularly went to the hospital for therapy and lab tests with no positive results. The muscle relax-ants and sedatives left him frequently drowsy, his doctors seemed unable to do anything, and there was still no diagnosis. In August 2007, they decided again to operate on Jorge to remove another cervical disc and to attach a plate in his spine. Before the surgery, Jorge met the Missionaries of the Holy Spirit for the first time. This second surgery again failed to improve his condition. Jorge received occupational therapy, hydrotherapy, and other treatments. Three months later, this protocol was discontinued because the muscle pain, contractions, and cramps were more intense. Because of all these medical procedures, as of January 2008, Jorge was very weak; a splint was placed on his left foot. Using a cane, and with the help of another person, Jorge could walk only a few steps. Generally, he spent his time in a wheelchair or lying down. The situation was getting worse, and Jorge was deteriorating every day without any kind of medical diagnosis. Jorge's family and friends feared the worst would happen.

That February, Marcela Morales, a friend of the couple from their youth with whom they had reconnected in 2006, gave Jorge a picture of Conchita, a short biography of her, and the Cross of the Apostolate founded by Conchita. Marcela also talked to Jorge about the headquarters of the Missionaries of the Holy Spirit, Jesus Maria, in San Luis Potosí, as a place of peace and prayer. Upon receiving the picture, Jorge told his wife that he loved the way Conchita's image gazed at him. Since Jorge had this picture of Conchita, he remembers asking her to intercede for his health.

The disease continued, and because of the lack of diagnosis, a neurologist offered to take Jorge's case, which was exceptionally well documented, to different neurology congresses to consult with specialists from the United States, Europe, and Canada. By this means, it was hoped, some light would be found for Jorge's rare sufferings. Meanwhile, this neurologist continued performing tests and studies on Jorge. All the tests came back negative.

Journey to "Jesus Maria" and Petition of Health

On May 15, 2008, with permission from his doctor, Jorge decided to go to Jesus Maria with Cecilia and their friend Marcela, who offered to take them both from Monterrey to San Luis Potosí (a trip of about 335 miles). They stayed at the house of the Missionaries of the Holy Spirit, who are dedicated to research into the spirituality of the Cross. Jorge was in bad condition after the trip. During dinner, he told all those present the intention of his trip: to ask, through the intercession of Conchita, for his health. The superior of the community, Fr. Carlos Francisco Vera, M.Sp.S., after hearing the story of Jorge's illness and knowing the intentions of his journey to Jesus Maria, asked each of those present if they had faith in such intercession. Each one clearly answered yes, including Fr. Carlos himself. Then he invited them to believe strongly that the goal of the pilgrimage would be achieved. He told them that Conchita, as a mother herself, favored families with her intercession.

Jorge, Cecilia, and Marcela's stay in Jesus Maria was organized into several visits: after visiting the house of the Missionaries of the Holy Spirit, they went to the house of the Religious of the Cross of the Sacred Heart of Jesus, where the mother superior, knowing about the purpose of their visit, told them that the community would pray to Conchita for such an important favor. The mother superior then led Jorge to the chapel of the community, where Jorge prayed before the Blessed Sacrament and asked for the miracle of his healing. Jorge then visited Conchita's garden and a small museum dedicated to her. He was in the place where the first Cross of the Apostolate was erected by Conchita in 1894. Here, Fr. Rafael Ledesma, M.Sp.S., prayed with Jorge and asked God that if it was His will, Jorge's health would be restored through Conchita's intercession.

Later, Jorge made other visits, such as to the house of the Guadalupan Missionaries of the Holy Spirit, whom he invited to join in his intention. From that stay in Jesus Maria, Jorge remembers with deep emotion that despite his difficulty walking, he wanted to walk the Stations of the Cross in "Conchita's Garden" and that he finished exhausted. He also remembers his visit to the Cross of the Apostolate, where he prayed and where a relic of the Cross was given to him.

God's Ways

The pilgrims returned to Monterrey on Saturday, May 17, and during the trip, perhaps because of the effort and the emotion, Jorge felt bad. By Monday, he was hospitalized due to a sharp rise in his blood pressure and elevated blood glucose—in addition to the muscle contractions, cramps, and torn muscles from his medical crisis. After being anesthetized—because his muscle contractions prevented him from staying still—he underwent a CT scan and an MRI. Unable to control his pain, or lower his blood pressure and glucose, his doctor decided to apply a treatment using Botox, a palliative treatment that relaxes the muscles but is not a permanent cure. The idea was that easing Jorge's pain would, in turn, lower his blood pressure and glucose. He did not seem to like this proposal because he felt that this would be a deception; the situation made him depressed. In response to the pleading of his wife, however, Jorge agreed to carry out the treatment with general anesthesia. It was scheduled for Saturday, May 24, and the operating room was reserved. But as we shall see, it was not needed.

On Thursday, May 22, 2008, at about 7:00 p.m., Jorge, Cecilia, and two other friends (Marcela Morales and Consuelo Sada) were in the hospital room. Jorge asked his wife for the image of the Cross of the Apostolate and the holy card of Conchita that Marcela had given him earlier. They invited Consuelo to join the prayer chain asking, through the intercession of Conchita, for Jorge's health. Consuelo did not know who Conchita Cabrera was, so Jorge briefly told her about Conchita's life. Then he fell asleep, and Consuelo left the room. Marcela and Cecilia began to see that Jorge, while asleep, opened his left hand, which had not been open for years. It was nearly 7:10 p.m. when Jorge, still sleeping, began to move. The women thought that perhaps, as on other occasions, he was having muscle contractions, but his facial expression was calm and his muscles were relaxed. Cecilia, thinking that Jorge would not believe that he had opened his hand and moved his feet while he was asleep, took some pictures of Jorge with her cell phone camera. Marcela did the same. Jorge began to move his hands, arms, and legs; he stretched and lifted his limbs. He ran his left hand, which had been paralyzed, over his face. He then touched his neck and his left leg, which was also paralyzed. His facial expression was one of peace and happiness, completely relaxed—something they hadn't see in him for years. Hearing him mumbling something in his dream, the women approached and realized that he was reciting the Our Father.

At that moment, Cecilia's two adult nieces and a child entered the room. They were all astonished at what was happening: Jorge moved his arms and legs; he opened his hand, which had been stiff for more than five years. He gently passed it over his face and neck. He looked relaxed and happy. The four women were moved to tears. Jorge had on his chest the image of Conchita throughout this process, and there it remained. The family doctor and specialty internist came into the room. Looking at Jorge's legs, straight and without contractions, and his arms over his chest and moving normally, the doctor stared for a moment and then ordered the cancellation of further treatment, including the planned Botox. He left the room excited and saying, "Blessed be God!" It was 7:25 p.m. on Thursday, May 22, 2008. Later, they realized that this was the Thursday after Corpus Christi. At that same hour, a Mass praying for the health of Jorge was being celebrated in Jesus Maria, in the Sanctuary of the Cross of the Apostolate.

A New Reality

Jorge woke up at 11:40 p.m. By that time, his parents, siblings, sons, and nephews and nieces were present. All were aware of the healing and wanted to see for themselves what had happened. His wife told him, "Jorge, look at your hands." He could not believe it; he was amazed and asked his wife, "Have I gone through surgery?" He thought that the Botox treatment had been done. "No," she said. "Today is Thursday, and your surgery was scheduled for Saturday."

Beautiful Holiness

Incredulous, Jorge said, "You're lying to me." His wife reiterated the date of his scheduled surgery. Jorge's father and his sister Patricia told him that the Botox treatment had not been applied.

Jorge was moved to tears; he could not believe it. He checked his entire body: hands, legs, feet, neck, and face. Then, to the astonishment of all, he rose to his feet by himself and went to the bathroom without any assistance. After the rest of the visitors had gone, Cecilia asked Jorge what had happened while he was asleep. She asked him if he had had a dream and to tell her what it was.

She drew near to him, and Jorge said, "I was with Conchita. I saw her about twelve inches away from me. I cried, and I asked her to listen to me. She then approached me and asked, 'Were you looking for me? What do you ask from me?' And I said, 'I do not want to see my wife and my children suffering because of me. Please help me!' She told me, 'Let's pray,' and she began to pray the Our Father, but I, crying, interrupted her saying, 'I cannot take it anymore; I do not want to see my wife and children suffering!' At that point, she told me, 'Do me a favor: receive Communion daily and pray for priests.' She then continued praying the Our Father and the Hail Mary. After praying, she caressed my face; I then tried to touch her, but I think that at that moment she disappeared." After narrating this to his wife, Jorge fell asleep.

The next day, Jorge was able take a shower without assistance; he wanted to make sure that what he had experienced was not just a dream. He was completely cured. He then began to cry again.

Jorge personally announced his healing to the Missionaries of the Holy Spirit priests, Fr. Carlos Francisco Vera Soto and Fr. Rafael Ledesma, and to his doctors, Pedro Mario Gonzalez and Manuel De La Maza Flores. He walked out of the hospital without any assistance.

Jorge's Thanksgiving

On Friday, June 6, 2008, Jorge and Cecilia went to Jesus Maria to thank God for the miracle of his health and Conchita for her intercession. At the foot of the Cross of the Apostolate, a Mass of thanksgiving was held. In the garden of the Sisters of the Cross of the Sacred Heart of Jesus, better known as "Conchita's Garden," Jorge identified the place where he encountered Conchita in his dream. The next day, another Mass was celebrated in the convent of the Sisters of the Cross of the Sacred Heart of Jesus, and there they gave testimony of Jorge's healing.

Jorge has become a great devotee of Conchita. He speaks of her as one speaks of an affectionate and caring mother. He is still in perfect health. He shows no signs of his old disease; his manner is cheerful and positive. The grace received from God through Conchita was for him, at the same time, a commitment and a splendid gift.

Conchita's Message concerning Priests

During the miraculous encounter, Jorge reported, "She told me, 'Do me a favor: receive Communion daily and pray for priests.'" Since Conchita is now in Heaven, it is telling that she maintains profound concern for the holiness of priests. Spiritual maternity of priests is a pillar of her mission. In her message to Jorge, she refers to the Eucharist and to priests because she was exceedingly devoted to both.

Jesus spoke to Conchita about her intercession for the holiness of priests.

Remember how many times I asked you to offer yourself as a victim for My beloved Church? Don't you see you are all hers since you are Mine, and you are Mine because you are all hers? Precisely on account of this special union which links you to My Church, you have the right to participate in her anguish, and the sacred obligation to console her by sacrificing yourself for her priests (*Diary*, September 24, 1927).[6]

This previews Conchita's revelations on the priesthood, which we will study in another chapter.

The Beatification of Blessed Conchita

Conchita's canonization process was begun in 1959 (twenty-two years after her death) by the archbishop of Mexico City, who presented two hundred volumes of her writings to the Congregation for the Causes of Saints. After her writings had passed the scrutiny of the Church, Pope John Paul II declared Conchita Venerable in 1999.

Since her beatification in 2019, her cause for canonization has been progressing. Presently, twenty miracles are being reviewed, one of which will be chosen. The *Catechism of the Catholic Church* (CCC) describes the role of miracles as divine validation thus: "Miracles strengthen faith in the One who does his Father's works; they bear witness that he is the Son of God" (548).

The solemn Mass and Rite of Beatification of Blessed María Concepción Cabrera de Armida occurred on May 4, 2019, at the Basilica of Our Lady of Guadalupe in Mexico City. Two hundred priests concelebrated the Mass with the prefect of the Congregation for the Causes of Saints as the principal celebrant. The Mass was attended by an estimated ten thousand people. Blessed Conchita was the first Mexican laywoman to be beatified. During the Mass, her portrait hung near the famous tilma of St. Juan

---

[6]   *A Mother's Spiritual Diary*, 208.

Diego. Conchita's portrait was unveiled as her granddaughter, Sister Consuela Armida, and Jorge Guillermo Treviño, carried a relic of Conchita and a blood-stained bandage to the main altar.

The Collect for the memorial Mass for Blessed María de la Concepción Cabrera de Armida's feast day, March 3, reads:

O God, who called Blessed María de la Concepción to live in the world as wife and mother in intimate union with you and great apostolic zeal, grant us, through her merits and intercession, that, faithfully following your Son, we may consecrate ourselves this day to building your Kingdom. Through our Lord Jesus Christ, your Son, who lives and reigns with you in the unity of the Holy Spirit, one God, for ever and ever.

In declaring Conchita Blessed, the Church confirms her heroic virtue and prophetic mysticism. In these pages, you will discover a holy friend, a mentor for the interior life, an encourager, a loving mother who will help you to love God above all and to wrap your heart around all that Jesus loves. Her spiritual *Diary* will be our central guide throughout this work.

It is my intention, rather than to write another historical biographical sketch of Conchita, to approach her as a master of the interior life, an ideal mentor for marriage and family life, a prophetic voice heralding God's vision for all vocations. In practical and lofty ways, her example inspires holiness, and she makes it applicable to ordinary daily life. Desire is the first step toward sanctity. Conchita's fascination with Jesus can quicken our desire to know and love Him much more.

Our sanctification is a work of the Holy Spirit. What do the Church and her saints mean by holiness? From the *Catechism* we learn the following:

Beautiful Holiness

"The Church on earth is endowed already with a sanctity that is real though imperfect" (*LG* 48 § 3). In her members perfect holiness is something yet to be acquired. "Strengthened by so many and such great means of salvation, all the faithful, whatever their condition or state—though each in his own way—are called by the Lord to that perfection of sanctity by which the Father himself is perfect" (*LG* 11 § 3). (825)

Next, we learn the heart of holiness: "Charity is the soul of the holiness to which all are called: 'it governs, shapes, and perfects all the means of sanctification'" (*LG* 42) (826).

In Conchita's writing we discover her idea of what it is to be fully human—namely, man is explained only through God. Therefore, in modeling the Lord, we discover the very joy that God expressed in creating us in His image and likeness. His beauty and holiness are meant to shine through earthen vessels such as you and me. Blessed Conchita's witness is proof that holiness is not only desirable and possible but also essential.

INDIVIDUAL OR GROUP REFLECTION

Ponder

"So we know and believe the love God has for us. God is love, and he who abides in love abides in God, and God abides in him" (1 John 4:16).

Engage

1. Jorge asked Conchita to pray for his healing. Consider asking Conchita to pray for the healing you need.
2. How do you pursue holiness in your vocation—mother or father, son or daughter, religious or lay?
3. Are you or your family in need of a miracle? Speak to Jesus about this now.

Pray

Jesus, we want to empty our life into You. We want to be able to pour all our tenderness into Your Heart. We want to be consumed by Its fire, as a holocaust for love of You. We will no longer hesitate to make any sacrifice. Give us, O Lord, that union with You that we so desire. Give us a love for You that is so pure, so holy, so devoid of self-love, so full of charity toward our neighbor and so much Your own that we will only concern ourselves with pleasing You and consoling You. Amen.[7]

---

[7] *A Mother's Spiritual Diary*, 53.

2

Love Story: Portrait of a Wife, Mother, Widow, Mystic

She gave all that she had.

—See Mark 12:44

Blessed Conchita's life stirs the Catholic imagination. Her authenticity is refreshing, her mysticism Marian. Her suffering mystifies; her joy attracts. As the mother of a family of nine, her feet were planted on earth, but her soul seemed to bridge Heaven and earth. The walls of her home would tell a love story much like that of the holy house in Nazareth.

Allow me to unveil this exceptional woman of God. Here, I have abbreviated the biographical details since these topics are developed in subsequent chapters. Fr. Domenico and I chose to allow *Conchita's voice* to permeate this book since her writings are exquisite reflections.

María Concepción Cabrera was born on December 8, 1862, to Octaviano Cabrera and Clara Arias in the city of San Luis Potosí in North-Central Mexico. She was the seventh of twelve children in a wealthy family with many haciendas.

Conchita was baptized within two days of her birth and received her First Holy Communion on December 8, 1872, at the age of ten. From childhood she had a natural inclination to love Jesus:

> She spent her childhood and adolescence in the haciendas and ranches, sailing in a boat along the streams, jumping into the water or pushing her companions and her father's employees into the water, laughing heartily, mingling with everyone, passionately fond of music and song, endowed with a fine voice.... She is young, jolly, fascinating and will have, down through her last years, a tremendous influence on everyone about her.[8]

Conchita is described as a charming child with an exuberance for life, love, and laughter. Throughout her life, people seemed drawn to her. We'll see God's hand upon this child, forming her for His exalted purpose. God leads us where He wants us to go, on paths we may not have chosen. But He leads us to the place of greatest spiritual fruitfulness.

Conchita recalls that her education was elementary:

> *I only attended three schools: as a tiny child, at the home of some little old servants, named Santillana. Later, but only for a short time, at Madama Negrete's; finally at a school run by the Sisters of Charity. When they were expelled, I was still very young, being only eight or nine years old. My mother did not want to send me anywhere else. Some teachers came to the house to instruct us and teach us music* (Aut., 1, 23).[9]

Despite a lack of formal education, Conchita proved to be a very intelligent lady. Her writings make this evident. The Lord

---

[8] A Mother's Spiritual Diary, 3.
[9] A Mother's Spiritual Diary, 3.

schooled Conchita throughout her life. And in her adult life, she was taught by priest spiritual directors, including bishops. She showed herself to be a gifted lifelong pupil of Jesus and His Church.

Child

I spent long hours on the flat roof of my house contemplating heaven and wished I could penetrate it with my heart. I was athirst for something very big with which to fill my poor soul, a thirst that longed for the Supreme Good.... Nature and music have always drawn me to God. Almost without my even knowing it, Lord, I felt your presence, your beauty, your power, and goodness within me. But I was very bad, and I quickly forgot you and tossed those sentiments, those interior touches of the Holy Spirit, on the ground.[10]

From youth, Conchita was sensitive to God's presence; her soul longed for something greater than herself. In her childhood, her inconsistencies and faults were typical of youth. Her mother raised an exceptional young lady to be a very hard worker. As Conchita once recalled:

My mother taught us how to run a household: from scrubbing the floor to embroidery. At the age of twelve I was already put in charge of the expenditures of the house. At the hacienda—farm—the cows had to be milked, the dough kneaded, and meals prepared. My mother never let us be idle. She was very watchful and insistent we keep busy. We surely did: mending, darning, all kinds of sewing, preparing hors d'oeuvres, sweets, and pastries. Besides my mother taught us ever to be humble and not to give way to vanity.... Poor

[10] Levy, *Priestly People*, 12.

momma labored beyond belief to train us properly and made every effort possible to teach us not to be selfish. Quite a few Sundays, inviting us to take a walk, she brought us to the hospital to see the dead and the dying. From my earliest years, as soon as one of our friends fell seriously ill, we had to watch over and take care of that friend in every possible way. She also had me attend men, women, children, rich and poor when they were dying and this taught me not to be afraid, but rather to help them by my prayers, clothe them and keep them neat and clean.[11]

Fiancée

Given the time and custom of her culture, it's not unusual that Conchita was courted from the age of thirteen. Physically beautiful and charming, she had many suitors, influential and wealthy. *"The young governor of the State liked to talk with me and courted me,"* she remembered. *"As for me, I told him stories and was at a loss what else to say. How naïve!... At this time and while I was riding, the man who was to be my husband, as he himself later on told me, met me for the first time."*[12]

Francesco Armida (called Pancho) was the love of her life, her only boyfriend. Conchita's brother introduced her future husband to her at a dance:

We were engaged for nine years before we married. I must gratefully say that Pancho never took advantage of my simplicity. As a fiancé he was always correct and respectful. On my part, from the very first letter, I strove to raise him up to God. I had the satisfaction of seeing him ever inclined to piety. I spoke to him about his

[11] A Mother's Spiritual Diary, 6.
[12] A Mother's Spiritual Diary, 8.

religious duties, about the love of the Blessed Virgin. He, in turn, sent me prayers, religious poems, and a copy of the Imitation of Christ *packaged in a very pretty case.... I urged him to frequent the sacraments as much as possible. Later, I never stopped being concerned about his soul* (Aut., 70–72).

My betrothal never troubled me as an obstacle to my belonging to God. It seems to me so easy to combine them both! When I went to bed and was alone, I thought of Pancho, then of the Eucharist which was my greatest delight. I went to Communion every day and it was on those days that I saw him going by. Thinking of him did not hinder me from praying. I made myself look as lovely as I could, and I dressed myself elegantly to please him. I would go to the theatre, to dances for the sole purpose of seeing him. Nothing else did I care for. But amid of all this I never forgot God. I dreamed of Him constantly as I could, and He drew me to Him in an indescribable way.[13]

Wife

On November 8, 1884, a month prior to her twenty-second birthday, she married Francesco. She wrote, "*To be a wife and mother was never a hindrance to my spiritual life.*"[14]

I remember that at the wedding banquet, when toasts were being made, I got the idea to ask him, who was now my husband, to promise he would do two things for me: allow me to receive Communion every day and never to be jealous. Poor soul! He was so good that many a year later, he stayed home with the children waiting for me to come back from church. During his last illness

---

[13] A Mother's Spiritual Diary, 10.
[14] A Mother's Spiritual Diary, 15.

he asked me whether I had gone to receive Our Lord. God must have rewarded him for this favor which made up my whole life. Many priests assured me that God has chosen him for me as an exceptional favor. He was a model husband; a man of virtue (Aut., 1, 111).[15]

Conchita offered this intention for her husband:

I will make every effort not to lose his trust in me but rather increase it more and more. I will keep myself informed about his business; I will ask God for light to make some sage suggestions. . . . I will act in such a way that he will find in me consolation, holiness, sweetness, and total abnegation. Equanimity will be evident under all circumstances, to such a point that he will see God working through me for his spiritual profit. Never in any way will I speak ill of his family, I will always excuse them, I will keep silent, and trust they will respect me.[16]

Mother of Nine

Conchita is an exemplary model of motherhood. She solicitously watched over her children's physical and spiritual lives. The care of their souls was foremost for Conchita, who was very respectful of their unique personalities.

She was a prolific letter writer to her sons and daughters. While we enjoy e-mailing and texting our children, these can't compare to a handwritten letter filled with sentiments that encourage closeness to God.

The following lovely letter was written to her eldest son, whom she calls "Pancho," like his father:

---

15   *A Mother's Spiritual Diary*, 17.
16   *A Mother's Spiritual Diary*, 34.

Pancho, my beloved son: not only one but a thousand blessings would I tenderly send your way today, enveloping you in them and in all the blessings of heaven.... You have been a model son, and I hope you will also be a husband as Christian, as honorable, as loving, and noble as your father: in that way you will make Elisa truly happy, as she, with great devotion and first love is going to unite her life to your own. I had always prayed that the Lord would give you a wife who would understand you, who, with her virtues, would sweeten your character, who would cultivate your religious feelings, who could be your companion in this exile, who would wipe away your tears, who would help you endure life's sorrows and appease your grief and help you to remove the thorns in your path. God has listened to my humble prayers for He never fails to hear a mother's plea, and so you have this ideal upon earth. You are going to receive her this day from the hands of the holy Church, she is a sacred gift: she is going to be the mother of your children. Respect her, love her and appreciate her, and then she will be whatever you wish her to be. Avoid the least quarrel and do not stop at any sacrifice to have peace in your home and with her family. It's better to bend than to break; with prudence, education and certain common sense, many troubles can be avoided. O my son! Never forget that everything that you are, all that you have and the happiness you now enjoy, you owe to good Jesus Who has loved you with such tenderness! From how many dangers He has delivered you!... Be grateful my son: recognize with gratitude the fatherly tenderness of God over you and demonstrate your gratitude by your actions, and never be ashamed of being a good Christian (Aug. 2, 1910).[17]

---

[17] Concepción Cabrera de Armida, *A Mother's Letters: A Vision of Faith in Everyday Life* (Staten Island, NY: St. Paul's, 2004), 15, 16.

Beautiful Holiness

Mother of Fr. Manuel, S.J.

The first child to leave her household was Manuel. She had dreamed that he would become a Priest of the Cross, the order she inspired. "But God is the master of vocations," she confessed, and instead, he entered the Society of Jesus at age seventeen.[18] Conchita prayed intentionally for Manuel's vocation to the priesthood.

> Monday, October 28, 1889, ... The Angelus bells were ringing. At that hour Jose Camacho, a priest, died; as soon as I learned this, I offered my little boy to the Lord to take his place before the altar. I really gave him with all my heart. He entered the Society of Jesus in 1906 at the age of seventeen (Autobiography I, p. 44)....
>
> I remember he must have been about seven years old when one day, at dinner time, as all the children were around him, their father told them to hurry and grow up soon so that they could help him with the household expenses, and Manuel quickly answered, "I will help you, yes, but in the spiritual part, in what touches the soul, because I was not born to earn money which is vanity and dust." Pancho and I looked at each other and were surprised at that response.[19]

Fr. Manuel was ordained in Spain and remained there his entire priesthood, a great sacrifice for the family. Conchita wrote fifty-eight letters to him with ample spiritual direction. Once Conchita wrote to Fr. Manuel, "I have no words or sufficient heart to thank you for the 80 masses that you offered for me and my intentions."[20] Mother and priest son drew special graces upon one another.

---

18 A Mother's Spiritual Diary, 81.
19 A Mother's Letters, 22.
20 A Mother's Letters, 69.

Conchita offered keen insights to Fr. Manuel: "*Keep your feet on earth but raise your soul, your life, and your whole heart up to heaven.*" "*Always love the Cross in whatever manner it comes to you, because it is always kind to the heart that sees the sacred will of God wrapped in its seeming ruggedness.*" "*Love is nourished by giving, by self-sacrifice, and with the holy fuel of suffering.*"[21]

More recently, in 2022, Cardinal Raniero Cantalamessa referenced Conchita's words to Fr. Manuel when preaching his second Lenten talk at the Vatican:

> The Mexican mystic Concepción Cabrera de Armida, familiarly called Conchita, who died in 1937 and who was beatified in 2019, writes to her son, who was a Jesuit as the date of ordination was approaching, "My son, remember that when you will have Jesus in your hands in the sacred species, you will not say, 'This is Jesus' Body, this is His Blood.' No, you will say, 'This is my body, this is my blood.'"

We can see how much Blessed Conchita has influenced the Church and the priesthood.

Mother of Sr. Teresa

Conchita's daughter Concha was a delightful child, considered to be the joy of her family. In her youth, it became evident that Concha's soul was very inclined to God and imbued in inviolable purity. She made a vow of virginity at fifteen years of age and spoke of entering the convent. She grew into a beautiful young lady whose personal charm attracted many. For a time, she changed her mind about entering the convent. Her heart, so full of love, was torn between two worlds. Respecting her daughter's decision,

---

[21] *A Mother's Letters*, 27, 31.

Beautiful Holiness

Conchita allowed her time and freedom. But Conchita prayed for her even more, asking the Lord to remove all obstacles to her vocation to the religious life if He so willed. On returning from a retreat, Concha exclaimed, "Mama, I have chosen Christ forever."

Mother and daughter began to share the interior life with each other. Conchita marveled that her daughter mirrored her intense love for God. They grew very close in the intimacy of prayer. Years later, after proper formation, Concha pronounced perpetual vows on October 23, 1916. She was now Sr. Teresa de María Inmaculada in the contemplative branch of the Religious of the Cross of the Sacred Heart of Jesus, founded by Conchita.

Conchita offered her daughter, too, a great deal of indispensable advice:

> Become a saint, Teresita. Fall in love with Jesus, give yourself to Jesus, and let yourself be done and undone by the One who loves you so much.

> Courageous and hardworking, no childishness. You were not born to be a sweet talker, but to cross a thousand worlds.

> Beware of that clinging heart!

> Let thy dealings be natural.

> Throw yourself headlong into an interior and perfect life, without losing your character.[22]

Widow

Conchita lived twenty-two years as a single woman, seventeen years as a wife, and thirty-six years as a widow. Francesco contracted

---

[22] *A Mother's Letters*, 85.

typhoid fever, and on September 17, 1901, with Conchita's loving assistance, he died a holy death.

I was already concerned with having him go to confession and receive Viaticum. I frequently recited the prayers of the dying and for the recommendation of his soul. I encouraged in so far as I could, by ejaculatory prayers, acts of contrition, acts of love, hope and faith, to give him strength and courage. I said them repeatedly with all my soul.

In this way I spent hours until he expired, my soul suffering with him during his terrible agony. But no, I was not alone in my suffering. God was with me and sustained me. My God! What my heart felt ... You alone, You alone know.

I fell right down on my knees and made to the Lord, with all my heart, the offering of perpetual chastity.... Oh! A night of solitude, of sorrow and of suffering.[23]

She was thirty-nine years old when she became a widow, left alone to raise eight children. One child had died while Francesco was living. "*The sound of the children crying over their father pierced my soul,*" she later recalled. "*My body is exhausted. Now it is that I feel wearied for I never was far from my husband while he was ill neither during the day or night, until he died. May the Lord sustain me with His cross*" (*Diary*, September 28, 1901).[24]

Later, after a visit to the cemetery, she recalled:

What a sad day for my heart, the heart of a wife and mother, was this day, my husband's birthday. Overcoming my feelings, I went to his tomb with my children, to spend the morning there, right near

---

[23] A Mother's Spiritual Diary, 50–51.
[24] A Mother's Spiritual Diary, 53–54.

his remains, praying and weeping. The soil that covers him whom
I loved so much, is still moist, and had been recently turned. My
children's and my own tears moistened this soil, this dust out of
which we have been formed and to which we shall return. There
passed through my imagination, in rapid flight, the years gone by
and the memories of them: sorrows, joys, and dreams. In an instant
all had vanished, like smoke at the breath of death.[25]

A Holy Death

Conchita died on March 3, 1937, at the age of seventy-four, mystically conformed to Christ crucified.

She had already established her international spiritual family.

Sixteen years prior to her death, Conchita wrote, "I must reproduce in me Christ Crucified" (*Diary*, September 16, 1921). In the last years of her life, this occurred through the multiplication of physical and spiritual sufferings. Dominican Fr. Philipon, who was both an investigator for Conchita's cause and the editor of published portions of her *Diary*, wrote about the final years of Conchita's life:

> After her last retreat at Morelia under her spiritual director, on "the perfect joy of suffering," Conchita returned to Mexico City. She spent the last three years of her life, now in bed, now in an armchair, undergoing atrocious suffering. She was afflicted by bronchial-pneumonia, erysipelas, and uremia.... She still performed corporal penances out of her ardent love for Christ and for men.... In her soul there was a feeling of despair. Her prayer sought refuge in Christ's words at Gethsemane. She shared in the feelings

---

[25] *A Mother's Spiritual Diary*, 51.

of the Crucified, abandoned by His Father. For her, her Beloved Jesus has wholly disappeared. "It is as if we had never known each other," she said again and again to her innermost self. Two of her children, Ignacio and Salvador, each taking one of her arms, raised up their mother to ease her breathing. "She might well have been said to be Christ in agony on the Cross." There was even at the moment of death a strange phenomenon to which her sons and Father Jose Guadalupe Trevino, M.Sp.S., have testified firmly. The same testimony was given also by other witnesses. The phenomena took place on the death of Conchita, imprinting on her, as the seal of God on her personal vocation and her mission for the Church, a concrete and amazing synthesis of the spirituality of the Cross. Conchita's appearance was seen to change. No longer was there the face of a woman but the Countenance of the Crucified.[26]

Conchita passed into eternal life leaving a lasting imprint on earth. In her *Diary*, she described how Jesus remained hidden from her at the end, that her Lord was silent or asleep, and that her memory of Him was her only keepsake. She prayed for God's mercy amid temptations that her spiritual life was all an illusion. She found peace only in the complete surrender of her will to God's will.

Once she even asked her spiritual director, "*Does Jesus love me?*" and "*Do I love Him?*" Have you ever asked the same piercing questions in your heart? I have. Yet I understand that the Lord asked the greatest sacrifice from Conchita to bring forth special graces for His priests—namely, that priests would not suffer alienation from Jesus. Conchita gave her yes to God to her last breath.

---

[26] *A Mother's Spiritual Diary*, 108, 109.

Beautiful Holiness

The Mystic

Conchita has been called one of the greatest mystics of our time and is one of the most prolific writers of contemporary mystical literature. A mystic may be described as one who encounters God through sacramental life and contemplation; one whose spiritual life progresses toward union with the triune God. The Church encourages us to become mystics like the saints.

Conchita's mystical itinerary is so central to her life and legacy that it warrants its own chapter to follow. But in this biographical sketch, we would be remiss not to mention the scope of her mystical experiences. These include visions, locutions, dialogues, and the highest stages of transforming union with Christ. For Conchita, this union was on the Cross.

As noted before, Conchita never received literary or theological formation. Her formal education was minimal. Yet she published forty-six books, and her *Diary* consists of sixty-six volumes. Her book *Before the Altar* numbered more than one million copies in different languages. Conchita was an avid reader of Scripture and spiritual books, and she learned to write by writing the words of Christ spoken in the silence of her heart.

A small sample of an interior conversation with Christ can aid our understanding of her mysticism.

> CONCHITA. *Oh Jesus, if such a distance separates us, if between this nothingness and Your immensity there is an impossible abyss, how is union possible between these two poles?*
>
> CHRIST. *Between these two poles, God and you, I am here. I, God made man, alone can join them very closely. No one arrives at the immensity of God, no one perceives My Divinity, without passing through Me. Likewise, without Me, no one can humble himself, nor be conscious of his*

> nothingness. I am the center, the gateway, the road, the
> light which gives self-knowledge and introduces to contem-
> plation. I am the point of encounter, the Redeemer, the
> Light, the Life, the Hearth of eternal perfection. Study
> this book, your Christ, and you will be a saint on imitat-
> ing Him.[27]

Ordinary and Extraordinary

Saints sometimes make self-sacrifice seem natural or easy, but it never is. Self-denial always costs the immolation of the will, naked-ness of the heart, and conformity to the Cross. Conchita allowed herself to be vulnerable to all the movements of grace. Outwardly it seemed natural, but inwardly it required the crucifixion of self. Such a cost is not without greater gain—that of the Holy Spirit birthing Christ in one's soul. Conchita's deepest desire was to magnify the Lord, whom she ardently loved.

The life of a saintly person is hidden in God. We can perceive the effects of personal holiness only through testimonies, writ-ings, and lasting fruit. Conchita's handwritten diaries spanning forty years capture the essence of a remarkable laywoman. Yet when Vatican investigators interviewed her children, asking, "Was your mother a saint?" one child responded that he didn't know if his mom was a saint, but she was a good mother and a very good cook. Indeed! She often offered hospitality in her family home, and her recipe book is now enshrined in the Museum of Jesus Maria.

Conchita endeared herself to me when she wrote, "*I am overly fond of sweets.*" She told her daughter Lupe that when she passed a jewelry store, it didn't attract her, but when she passed

---

[27] A Mother's Spiritual Diary, 144, 145.

a confectionary store, her mouth watered. Conchita was always authentic. And the following story from her *Diary* captures her determined nature, humor, and gusto for life:

> *Neither my father nor mother could stand affection. When I was only six, I got on a horse by myself. The horse was frightened, reared, and threw me off. Disregarding my tears, my father made me take a drink of water and then get back on the horse! In this way I no longer had any fear of horses. I was so proud I rode the most spirited ones, those which no one else could master. I have always been extremely fond of horses. How many times in Mexico, when my husband took me for a ride, the only thing I noticed was the horses! As for the people, they all looked alike.*[28]

By the age of thirty-five, Conchita made a defining decision— one that we are also called to make:

> *I want to be a saint. This aspiration without bonds never leaves me, despite the weight of my misery. I want an obscure sanctity; ... one which God alone might see. I want to be seen as something contemptible and common place ... that the world judge me as a worm.*[29]

In Conchita's *Diary* we discover a project of God. Originally called her *Account of Conscience*, it was written in obedience to her spiritual director, Fr. Alberto Cusco Mir, though sometimes she was tempted to stop writing:

> *I would like to stop writing, forget everything, turn the page, change my life. Such is, at this moment, the state of my spirit, submerged*

---

[28] *A Mother's Spiritual Diary*, 6.
[29] *A Mother's Spiritual Diary*, 39.

in temptations and sufferings. But I must control myself with God's grace. I renounce myself without pity, and keep on going, even though I may die in the struggle (Diary, March 26, 1897).[30]

These few lines written at the age of thirty-five reveal a person who struggles, and then renounces her will in favor of God's will. "Even though I may die in the struggle"—Conchita's resolve is evident and will serve her well in the pursuit of virtue.

"Momma always smiled," her children told Fr. Philipon, who visited her family as part of the Church's investigation of Conchita's sanctity. This comment about always smiling is important because often behind her smile was a sea of suffering reserved for God's eyes only.

Her secret? "Unbelievable love for Christ ... and daily life transfigured by faith."[31] Those who knew Conchita knew that she had fallen deeply in love with Jesus, to the enrichment of her vocation. They looked to Conchita for guidance, knowing that she was close to the Lord.

She Gave All That She Had

Jesus said, "This poor widow has put in more than all those who are contributing to the treasury. For they all contributed out of their abundance; but she out of her poverty has put in everything she had, her whole living" (Mark 12:41-44). This Scripture passage reflects Conchita's heart. Her long widowhood lasted from 1901 to 1937. Conchita consistently gave her all to God and to souls. And the Lord is not outdone in generosity. What would we be if

---

30   *A Mother's Spiritual Diary*, 117.
31   *A Mother's Spiritual Diary*, 38.

we held nothing back from God? In life, there comes a time when, like the poor widow, we must decide to give our all to Christ.

The crib and the Cross merged in the heart of this virtuous laywoman. Filled with the Holy Spirit, Conchita yielded to the divine will, taking Jesus and Mary as her models, placing her yes into their yes. Jesus fashioned her into a heroic victim of divine love. Her heart was pierced many times, and she would cling more to the Cross.

Conchita lived the abundant life with so much love to spill into others' lives. People were naturally attracted to her warmth and strength. Conchita recognized the closeness of Jesus in the most ordinary events, such as a loving glance from her spouse, the innocent inquiries of her children, the work of Providence in their business, and the daily fulfillment of her vocation in the family.

God reveals love in many ordinary moments. If only we were more attentive to the little signs of His abiding presence! Perhaps it's finding a holy card tucked into your Bible or journal with the needed Scripture or sentiment; or the unexpected text "I prayed for you today"; or the smell of a newborn baby; or being moved to tears on Good Friday; or the expectant joy of Christmas Eve. Christ is in the infusion of calm during a storm, a burst of strength when you're exhausted, or sudden awareness that you're capable of achieving the dream that God planted in your heart. Our Lord is in the details of ordinary life. Christ is a perfect lover and mover of our heartstrings.

Conchita learned to abide in His presence. This is no small thing. As Conchita herself wrote:

> I desire to always be with him, even in the midst of the crowds and all my daily duties. He has conquered me, and I have

overcome various obstacles with a smile on my face. This invasion by God has saturated me, as though I am thoroughly absorbed in him, like milk in coffee, like sugar in water. My soul continues to be absorbed in God. And with Him, I don't care about the sufferings, the rebuffs, and the humiliations. Jesus calls me day and night. He steals my heart, and I melt within Him, my All! He wants me to stay with Him, to speak about him, to do everything for Him.[32]

"He steals my heart." Conchita is incomplete without her Lord. Why would we look for fulfillment outside of the One who completes us? That Jesus is present in each moment of life changes the dynamic of living. Jesus gives value to everything; our sorrows and joys touch His heart. Ordinary moments become holy moments in Christ. In God's eyes, nothing is small; the humble ones elevate the ordinary.

The Garden of the Soul

Blessed Conchita's life and spirituality illumine a path of godly possibilities that most have not imagined. If we are brave enough to believe that we are made for the depths of union, and the heights of mystical life, we will discover a guide in Blessed Conchita. She is approachable and inviting. The little girl who loved Jesus matured into a woman of great spiritual stature who was able to wrap her arms around *Love Crucified.*

A moment's reflection on the words "Love Crucified" will help us to grasp the spiritual depth of Conchita, as Jesus had formed her. Her legacy is that of love that sacrifices everything for the sake of the Beloved. The Cross of Jesus was Conchita's

[32] Levy, *Priestly People*, 114.

signpost; the Crucified Lord was her model. For this time in the Church, Conchita is unveiled as a proclamation of the power of the Cross.

In reading Conchita's writings, it is easy to forget that she was a simple laywoman with a house full of children and a husband and business that demanded her time and attention. Yet Conchita knew how to care for the garden of the soul, tending to the seeds Jesus planted. Devoted to the humanity of Jesus, she saw the perfection of incarnational love in the God-Man. Her love would always be incarnational. Our imitation of Jesus should also be incarnational. We are to be present and available, ready to accompany and engage the people entrusted to us along the journey.

Conchita embraced suffering as a gift of love. Her crosses were many and heavy, but she didn't carry them alone. The Lord abided within her, and she knew it. Anyone who has passed through a time of heavy cross carrying knows that Jesus carries you. Pain, sorrow, tears, heartbreak, dark nights, and devilish torments visited this daughter of God. Conchita was not spared suffering, nor would she want to be spared anything that Jesus endured for love.

"He who abides in me, and I in him, he it is that bears much fruit, for apart from me you can do nothing" (John 15:5): this Scripture passage helps us to discover the foundation of Conchita's spirituality. This lovely Mexican laywoman knew herself to be the branch that simply could not be separated from the vine that is Jesus Christ. She understood that God had loved her first, that He initiated their union. She desired to reciprocate by lavishing as much love on Jesus as was humanly possible. His grace watered the garden of Conchita's soul so that many mystical flowers arose from her humble heart.

"Let Me Cry"

Four months after her six-year-old son died of typhoid fever, Conchita wrote in her diary:

> *The time for testing is now occurring. It has been a raw and very difficult experience for my weakened state of being. First, I had spiritual struggles, then economic difficulties and desolation. And then – Oh my Jesus, you yanked my son from my arms, tearing my heart apart. You have transplanted him to heaven, leaving behind a wound in my soul that will never heal. Who could have told me that my son would see so soon what I have not yet seen and have unveiled for him that which I myself cannot come to understand. I thank you for this separation but let me cry. Lord, gather these tears that do not spring from a rebellion against your holy will, but rather from this heart of flesh.*[33]

Conchita's heart surrendered to God's will, yet she implored Him, "Let me cry." Jesus understands that tears must flow to heal the aching wound from losing a child. He understands the language of tears. Jesus understood that Conchita's tears were an accompaniment to her surrender.

Conchita was the mother of nine children. I'm a mother of two. I know the number of tears I've shed for my sons. Imagine the torrents of tears that Conchita must have shed as a mother of nine!

So when it is necessary for you, let yourself cry. After all, tears moistened Christ's holy face at times (see John 11:35). Sometimes the soul surrenders itself unto God in the prayer of tears – as Our Lord's did in His Passion and death.

---

[33] Levy, *Priestly People*, 17–18.

Beautiful Holiness

Conchita placed herself and her family in the arms of Jesus. On one occasion when she was very ill and death seemed near, she wrote:

> At times fear came over me and one night, nestling myself in His arms, I said to the Lord: "I am afraid." He answered, "Do not be afraid." "Be calm." His words came true and from that moment on, I felt peace of soul and boundless confidence, with the certainty that I was not going to die" (Diary, April 21, 1898).[34]

Inviting Christ into our deepest fear allows Him to transform it. Sometimes nothing suffices like climbing into the arms of Jesus and saying, "I need Your love to uphold me, Lord." We may not understand the whys of suffering. But we can climb into the waiting arms of Jesus, who soothes and strengthens us.

Conchita wasn't born a saint. She struggled to follow Christ. She struggled to understand her mission and her vocation. Sometimes, she didn't understand at all what Christ was doing in her soul or in her life. She understood only that she was the unworthy object of God's design. She humbly yielded like a child. In the arms of Jesus, she was nurtured to the full stature of an apostle.

Conchita transitioned effortlessly from the heights of mystical prayer to preparing dinner, training children, and accompanying her husband to gatherings around town. Her family didn't place her on a pedestal or treat her like a saint on a shelf. Her children recall their mother writing, but they did not report seeing her in any extraordinary state of prayer.

At the age of thirty-two, Conchita wrote a rule of life:

---

[34] *A Mother's Spiritual Diary*, 38.

I propose to do ever what is most perfect. I propose in my actions to seek in all things Jesus and His Cross, in conformity to His holy will. . . . I will never be disquieted should circumstances prevent me from observing my Rule of Life. I will go on tranquilly. I will be flexible in the face of difficulties, humbly . . . then onward, ever onward!" (Extract from her "Rule of Life," Aug. 21, 1894).[35]

This is a preview of the love story that is Conchita's life. If we approach Conchita as a spiritual mother, she will teach us how to nurture that unique ray of God within us. "Ever onward" toward the "more" of God.

---

[35] *A Mother's Spiritual Diary*, 35.

INDIVIDUAL OR GROUP REFLECTION

Ponder

"Before I formed you in the womb, I knew you, and before you were born I consecrated you; I appointed you a prophet to the nations" (Jer. 1:5).

Engage

1. Are there parts of Conchita's love story that you identify with?
2. How do you relate to Conchita's family life?
3. How can you grow in virtue within your vocation?

Pray

Oh, my Jesus! I have seen my spirit strained by my ingratitude toward You, indifference toward my neighbor, and apathy toward myself. But now, Lord, I am truly repentant, and I love You – O yes! – with the lively anxiety of responding to your Goodness, sacrificing myself for You, and everyone else, in union with You! You are my life, my living and only delight in my exile! Pluck from my soul, not only my sins, vices, and defects, but also every worldly creature that can impede Your love.... My Jesus, today, more than ever, I want to consecrate myself to You forever: please be so kind as to accept this poor offering this miserable victim, through the hands of Mary. I want to be pure, obedient, and poor; increase my desires; confirm my promises, which I would defend with all my blood. I am completely Yours.[36]

---

[36] Concepción Cabrera de Armida (Conchita), *Holy Hours* (Staten Island, NY: St. Paul's, 2006), 98.

3

Family Life:
School of Sacrificial Love

*Beloved, let us love one another, for love is from God
and he who loves is born of God and knows God.*

—1 John 4:7

In 1981, Pope St. John Paul II wrote in *Familiaris Consortio*:

> At a moment of history in which the family is the object
> of numerous forces that seek to destroy it or in some way
> to deform it, and aware that the well-being of society and
> her own good are intimately tied to the good of the family,
> the Church perceives in a more urgent and compelling way
> her mission of proclaiming to all people the plan of God
> for marriage and the family.[37]

For the reasons that St. John Paul II mentions, Conchita's witness to marriage and motherhood is vital and timely. Thanks to her writings, we can enter the Armida household to observe the workings of grace in their midst.

---

[37] Pope John Paul II, post-synodal apostolic exhortation *Familiaris Consortio* (November 22, 1981), no. 3.

Beautiful Holiness

Blessed Conchita ties everything to the family, whom she loved passionately. She desired her loved ones to fall in love with Jesus, so they would know the joy of loving Him. The warmth of the Armida home centered on incarnational, sacrificial love. This quality of love formed the foundation upon which her family thrived. The heart of the home was the mother, who shone with virtue and wholesomeness.

Exceedingly pure of heart and with evangelical simplicity, Conchita was firm but quick-witted with a self-effacing humor. A family member, Maria Teresa Madero, shared that Conchita laughed easily, was very cheerful, sang, played the piano, and entertained at meetings in her house. Another family member, Guadalupe Labarthe, R.C.S.C.J., recalls that Conchita had a great sense of humor. There are many anecdotes about her sense of humor. Her son Ignacio shared, "She had written a notebook full of jokes and would bring them out most gracefully and naturally."[38] A sense of humor seems to be a hallmark of saintly people. Joy is the fruit of our communion with Christ. Conchita's family delighted in one another and in the Lord.

People were drawn to Conchita and gathered in her home. Ignacio shares:

> Mother was a very active woman. She received visitors all the time. There was nothing striking or unusual in her style of life. She had a very sweet character but was firm and energetic. When she had decided to act in a certain way, no human power could deter her. With her, one had to obey. This was also true of the works she undertook. She had her plan, her inspiration, her ideal and followed it through the end.[39]

[38] *A Mother's Spiritual Diary*, 96.
[39] *A Mother's Spiritual Diary*, 96.

Joyful, firm, and energetic—attributes that served her vocation well. One look at Conchita's intense blue eyes reveals a person of firm resolve.

The years of Conchita's marriage and young motherhood were formative for her spiritual life. She loved Jesus and let herself be loved by Him. A dynamic relationship with God, by its nature, radiates outward and appropriately fits one's vocation. Fr. Philipon comments about Conchita's practicality.

> It is interesting to analyze what she entitles her "retreat resolutions" she wrote at the end of her Spiritual Exercises, ten days from September 20 to 30, 1894. Conchita was thirty-two years old at this time. They were not resolutions of a nun but of a married woman, mother of a family, and mistress of a household. Her director advised her to divide them thus: seventeen points concerning her relations with her husband; twenty-three for her daily conduct with her children; and a final page, seven points, for orienting her attitude in justice, kindness, and charity toward the servants of the home.[40]

Simplicity, humility, prudence, and magnanimity made Conchita an exceptional housewife, as these virtues rendered her unencumbered. She was fully engaged in the moment. When she was doing housework, it was Heaven's work. When she was at prayer, her family was incorporated. Her son told Vatican investigators that when the family went to church, his mother was always present to them—not in some ecstatic state. The expansiveness of her love was inclusive of God, family, and souls.

---

[40] *A Mother's Spiritual Diary*, 34.

Beautiful Holiness

Loving Jesus as Much as Possible *with Family*

Aware that she wasn't singularly capable of loving Jesus as He deserved, she prayed to be married and to have many children, so that together her family would love Jesus more. This is a rather novel concept. Conchita magnifies her gift of self to God by attaching her family to the gift, as she explains in her *Diary*:

> I received and visited the Blessed Sacrament. I said to Jesus: "Lord, I feel so unable to love You, so I want to get married. Give me many children so that they will love you better than I." This did not seem out of place to me, rather a legitimate prayer to quench the thirst of my soul, my desire to love Him more and to see Him loved even better by beings proceeding from my being with my blood and my life (Aut., 27-29).[41]

Augmenting her gift of self to God by having a large family is a beautiful example of generosity and humility. Her love was communal; her heart was missionary; her instinct was motherly.

"Your Mission Is the Salvation of Souls"

Jesus told His pupil, "Your mission is the salvation of souls." It wasn't Conchita's idea. She was an instrument in God's hands, so her mission knew no bounds. She began by forming her husband and children in a life of holiness. The fruit of her marriage to Pancho is seen in their nine children. Those of us who are raising families can imagine the herculean task that Conchita faced. A few of her children presented problems because of their stubbornness. We know that some children are more difficult to raise than others! With her nine children, each with unique temperaments, she learned to nurture them according to God's grace and plan.

---

[41] *A Mother's Spiritual Diary*, 8.

If we keep God in the equation of raising our families, as did Conchita, it will go well.

A Child Formed by Her Parents' Example

It's striking to note the precision of Divine Providence, which creates and connects the details of Conchita's life. In our lives, Providence works with similarly amazing precision.

Conchita admires her mother:

> *My mother was a saint. She was an orphan when she was only two years old. She suffered much. She married when she was seventeen. She had twelve children: eight boys and four girls. My mother passed on to my soul love of the Most Blessed Virgin and of the Eucharist. She cherished me with all her heart and was quite broken-hearted when I got married. However, she told me that my husband was an exceptional person and that not everyone was like him. She performed a great number of hidden virtues, and her martyrdom was ever unknown to all.... I assisted her to die and then laid her in her coffin (Aut., 366).*[42]

Conchita extols the qualities of her father:

> *My father was very charitable to the poor. Any time that he saw someone in need he could not refuse to help them. He was so jolly and so frank. I helped him die a good death. And he himself was so brave. He himself prepared the altar for the Viaticum, begged pardon of his children for any bad example.... Then he took us into his arms one after another, kissing each one and gave each one a piece of advice. In his will he requested that we bury him without any commemorative plaque, without a tombstone, not*

---

[42] *A Mother's Spiritual Diary*, 5.

even with a name on the grave but only a simple cross. Despite the pain it caused us we carried out his dying wish (Aut. 365).[43]

Conchita's parents diligently formed their daughter by holy example. She was an observant, obedient daughter who imitated their virtues.

An Ordinary Girl

Conchita's youth was typical to children of her time and place: "*I got angry with my brothers,*" she recalled. "*I fought with them, disobeyed my parents, stole candy or fruit, and told lies – horrible, at times! I later made up for it, and then once again offended my Jesus.*"[44]

Some people with the messiest childhoods end up being the most virtuous adults thanks to God's grace. When the child Conchita offended her parents or Jesus, she quickly tried to improve. The Lord works wonders with the very raw material of our humanity.

The Tragic Death of Her Brother

The tragic death of her brother was a turning point in Conchita's youth. She was dramatically changed, and she matured emotionally and spiritually following this horrific experience.

> *A terrible blow took me away from the world and its vanities to bring me close to God. My brother Manuel, the eldest of all my dearly beloved brothers, was suddenly shot to death. His brains were blown out by a bullet while he was entertaining a friend, Don Pancho Cayo. Don Pancho insisted on wearing his gun to dinner. As he sat down at the table the trigger of his gun caught*

---

[43]   *A Mother's Spiritual Diary*, 5.

[44]   *A Mother's Spiritual Diary*, 3.

on something and the bullet passed through Manuel's cheek and came out of his head. It was a terrible tragedy but an accident. My brother fell down dead. He left behind his wife and three children.

As soon as we heard what happened we took the road to Jesús María. When my mother learned of the death of her son, she fell on her knees and prayed before giving way to her grief. The tragedy occurred at two o'clock in the afternoon and, around six o'clock I was close to the corpse.

My parents were almost out of their minds but resigned and accused no one. Don Pancho was in despair. My brother Primitivo, who was present when the accident happened, walked back and forth on the terrace, as thunder boomed and lightning flared, completely overcome. Then sprang his vocation. Good Lord, what a tragedy!

For me the blow was cruel but salutary for my poor soul, so confused and distraught. And this was true for the whole family. I returned home in sorrow, resolved to give myself wholly to God, to think more intimately about Him, to detach myself more fully from the trends which led me toward the vanities of the world.

I have always been afflicted by my extreme sensitivity. My soul is affected not only on the occasion of death but even by simply the absence of someone.... Yes, indeed, my soul has suffered much because of my sensitivity.[45]

The experience of premature, violent death—even an accidental one—robs us of our childhood innocence. We fast-forward from childhood to adulthood. It may take years to heal from such experiences. And we are forever changed by them. I know from

---

[45] *A Mother's Spiritual Diary*, 12.

personal experience. My father-in-law was beaten to death. He was unrecognizable due to blunt-force trauma to the head. Thirty-one years have passed, and I recall each horrific moment of that day. With such tragedies, something ruptures in the human heart. Only God can put it back together. Thankfully, He does.

Christ understands the trauma of violent death because He passed through it. A scriptural verse comes to mind: "We know that in everything God works for good with those who love him, who are called according to his purpose" (Rom. 8:28). The death of her brother accelerated Conchita's maturity.

Wife of Francesco Armida Garcia

Conchita's husband, Francesco Armida Garcia, was born in the city of Monterrey, Mexico, on March 17, 1858. He was nine years old when his parents, Idelfonso Armida Bermejo and Petra Garcia y Delgado, moved to San Luis Potosí. At a young age, Francesco began work in a commercial trading house, "El Moro," and was esteemed by all.

On January 16, 1875, he began his engagement with Concepción Cabrera, and nine years later they married, on November 8, 1884. In San Luis Potosí, Francesco started a trading house of his own. In October 1895, he and the family went to live in Mexico City, where he had very good job prospects. Conchita and family members acclaim his goodness and piety. He died on September 17, 1901, leaving a small inheritance for the family.

Conchita writes about her husband:

He was sensitive to any misfortune, affectionate with me, an
excellent father who had no other distraction than his children;
they were his happiness, and he suffered a great deal when
they were sick. He was very correct in his dress, very fine in his

dealings with me, a man of the home, very simple, respectful, and delicate. He had a strong, energetic character, which with time sweetened him. He had great confidence in me and often spoke to me about his business, taking my opinion even though it was worthless.[46]

Francesco valued her opinion in all things. Conchita could draw out the best in a person, and that is no small gift. Conchita's letters to her family reveal how well she could affirm, encourage, and coach them to be virtuous and faithful to God. And Pancho had his role in helping his wife.

My husband followed a schedule for leaving and returning home from work. I took advantage of this for speaking to my Jesus, for spiritual reading and for doing penance, removing my haircloth belt at the moment he was about to arrive. Once he noticed it and was annoyed. He said I had enough suffering with my children, with nursing them, and with my illnesses. . . . My confessor forbade me, for three years, to impose penances on myself. I did what he told me (Aut. 1, 129–130).[47]

See how the Lord used Pancho to aid his wife's spirituality. It is very helpful to have a spouse's healthy perspective on things. We each have blind spots that sometimes need to be pointed out.

Conchita was frequently ill, and Pancho was the one to watch over her day and night. He didn't want anyone else to do so.

Conchita made certain edifying resolutions about her husband:

I will be naturally affectionate without exaggeration or extremes: a holy middle ground, serving him in all his needs, watching over his

---

46 A Mother's Spiritual Diary, 12.
47 A Mother's Spiritual Diary, 19.

desires so that nothing may be lacking in his use or comforts—always keeping my whole heart for Jesus.

I will take special care of his soul. I will wisely look for occasions to incline him to God without his feeling it, to speak to him about Him, letting words fall into his heart that like seeds will produce their effect.

I will act in such a way that he will find in me, consolation, holiness, sweetness and total abnegation.... Never in any way will I speak ill of his family.[48]

For his part, Pancho was faithful to his promise that his wife would receive the Eucharist daily. Conchita recalled:

From the day after we were married until he died, he let me go to Communion every day; when I got married, I made this condition which he fulfilled. He took care of the children while I was coming back from church, and when I was sad or worried, he would say to me: "Go to Communion."[49]

A Mother of Nine Children

Conchita gave birth to nine children: Francesco, Carlos, Manuel, Concepción, Ignacio, Pablo, Salvador, Guadalupe, and Pedro.

When Fr. Philipon was researching Conchita's family, he wrote:

When, at the end of my first sojourn in Mexico, in 1954, after questioning them down to the most minute details, I stated to her children: "Your mama was a great saint and a great mystic," they straightaway replied, "Saint or mystic,

---

[48] *A Mother's Spiritual Diary*, 34.
[49] Maria Guadalupe Labarthe, R.C.S.C.J., "He Was a Good Man" handout.

we don't know, but she was the greatest mother that ever lived!"[50]

Conchita made these retreat resolutions in regard to her motherhood:

I will be very concerned and vigilant about [my children].... I will recommend that they should be charitable to the poor, and suggest they deprive themselves of what they have for personal use.... I will not weary them by overloading them with prayers and make piety tedious. On the contrary, I will make every effort to make it agreeable to them and they will practice it, especially in the forms of ejaculations.... I will study each one's character and will encourage them in so far as it is proper. As a rule, I will never yield and, without swerving, I will not change my decisions and resolves. I will learn how to gain their confidence.... I will make men out of my sons, teaching them to control themselves in the least things, without ever offending God. May He deign to grant me it. Rather, death, a thousand times, than sin. I ask this of the Lord with all my heart."[51]

I must form the hearts of my eight children [one had died], fight against eight temperaments, keep them out of harm, introduce them to good and to make progress in it. A great deal of patience, great prudence and a great deal of virtue are necessary for carrying out this mission of mother in a holy way. In all my prayers, the first cry from my heart is to ask graces for my husband and my children. It is obvious I expect everything from above, from this infinitely bountiful God and from Mary, the Mother of us all, to whom I have entrusted and commended them in a very special way.... A

---

[50] A Mother's Spiritual Diary, 38.
[51] A Mother's Spiritual Diary, 35.

*loving devotion to Her will save them from all the dangers of this
wretched world, so full of perils.*[52]

Conchita breaks into prayer for her children in this beautiful
petition to the Blessed Mother:

*Oh Mother, help us, clothe us all with Your mantle of purity,
never abandon us until our eternal happiness has been assured.
O Mary, encompass Your purity around my children! May they
never stain their soul, so much loved! May they ever be devoted
to God! May He alone be their very breath and life, Oh Virgin,
watch over, safeguard them! They are Yours before they are mine*
(*Diary*, Aug. 16, 1899).[53]

The Death of Four Children

"*I believe the union of suffering is stronger, more indestructible than that of
love, the one producing the other. . . . The love of suffering is the love of Jesus,
solid and authentic. May no one deprive me of this quite hidden treasure
which is mine. . . . My Jesus, I am ready to drink my chalice down to the
last drop.*"[54] Conchita embodied these beliefs in her motherhood.

Conchita and Pancho suffered unspeakable pain when their
second child, Carlos, died at six years of age due to typhoid fever.
As she wrote in her *Diary*:

*In 1887, on March 28, on a Monday at midnight, my son Carlos
was born. I was able to nurse him. He was a very lively child,
intelligent and precocious. He lived only six years and died of
typhoid fever on March 10, 1893. In the midst of his suffering,
he said: "May Thy will be done on earth as is it in Heaven." He*

---

[52] *A Mother's Spiritual Diary*, 35.
[53] *A Mother's Spiritual Diary*, 35.
[54] *A Mother's Spiritual Diary*, 30.

suffered a great deal and died without being confirmed. My sorrow has never left me. His death was breathtaking for me, I felt such pain as I had never felt before. I could not tear myself away from him, but the voice of obedience speaks and immediately I made the sacrifice of leaving him behind.[55]

Conchita notes how this agonizing loss affected her spiritual life:

After Carlos' death my soul felt strong desires for perfection. Scruples tormented me. My conscience reproached me for having told him the medicines he took were pleasant to the taste when they were not. I only wanted him to take them. I did not know how to overcome these scruples. Finally, as a last remembrance I kept one of his garments. I felt my heart was attached to it. One day the Lord gave me the inspiration to make the sacrifice of giving it up and gave me the grace to do so. Only a mother could understand my feelings. I called a poor child to come in and I dressed him in Carlos' garment. On doing so I felt such sorrow as if my child had been taken away from me again (Aut., 1, 131–132).[56]

See the ups and downs of Conchita's sentiments. This is an authentic, human response. In our humanity, we fluctuate between letting go, accepting God's will, and holding on, trying to cling to something that soothes our pain. Note that God allowed Conchita to keep Carlos's little garment for the time when she needed it most. Then Jesus gently urged her to part with it, giving her the grace to let go again. In the process of letting go, there is healing. Grief is profoundly real and heart-wrenching. Mourning is like a dance of emotions. When we turn to Jesus, He cuts in and leads

---

[55] *A Mother's Spiritual Diary*, 18.
[56] *A Mother's Spiritual Diary*, 18.

the dance and calms the emotions. In His eyes we begin to perceive a new horizon of hope and healing. He will give us joy again. He will dry our tears as He did Conchita's.

God ministers to those who mourn. In the words of Scripture:

> The spirit of the Lord GOD is upon me
> because the LORD has anointed me ...
> to bind up the brokenhearted ...
> to comfort all who mourn ...
> to give them a garland instead of ashes,
> the oil of gladness instead of mourning,
> the mantle of praise instead of a faint spirit;
> that they may be oaks of righteousness,
> the planting of the LORD, that he may be glorified.
> (Isa. 61:1–3)

The Blessed Mother, too, understands the heart-piercing pain of accompanying a child in suffering and death. Conchita drew closer to Mary at the foot of the Cross. Mothers who have suffered the loss of a child, consider Blessed Conchita your prayer partner. Sixteen years after Carlos's death, when Conchita was a widow, she suffered the tragic death of her youngest child, Pedro. She was inconsolable:

Tuesday ... April seventh, a heart-breaking day for me: During Mass I was uneasy, interiorly urged, without knowing why, to go home. After a few household tasks were done, I started to sew. While I was sewing, suddenly I heard a voice which said to me: "Pedrito is in the pool in the garden." I thought he was calling me and automatically, I repeated the same words: "Pedrito is in the pool in the garden." I ran, flew. and the children who heard me, cried out to me: "Yes, mama, he is here!" I did not see anything, for several instants I did not know what was happening to me. I took him in my arms, soaking wet, stiff . . . a corpse.

A few minutes before, he had been at my side. The other children told me that on leaving the room, he told them that he was going to fetch some water for pigeons. There were three servants near the pool, but no one saw him fall in. . . . I almost went out of my mind, trying as much as I could to resuscitate him, but in vain. His heart had stopped beating, and there was no pulse, His eyes had their pupils dilated and they were lifeless. My God! I felt my soul torn and, my son in my arms, I offered him to the Lord, in sorrow, bitterness, remorse, believing it was due to my negligence that he was now dead. And I remembered how, at the moment of death, his father had left him in my care.

Police officers came to make out an official report. Also, a doctor and his assistant came, but all their efforts were in vain. I wrote my mother and Father Felix about what had happened, but the Lord willed I remain alone. My mother could come only five hours later, and Father Felix arrived at night.

I placed myself at the foot of my large Crucifix and there, bathing His feet in tears, prostrate, I offered Him the sacrifice of my son, asking Him that there be fulfilled in me His divine will. I spent the night watching over the corpse of my son. At midnight I laid him in his little coffin. As I held him in my arms, I felt frozen. It was a terrible feeling (Diary, April 7, 1903).[57]

Imagine the horror of this tragedy, and her agonizing temptation that this was *possibly* preventable. Conchita's heart was paralyzed in pain. She must have longed for her husband's arms to enfold her and their son. Her mother's heart would break during

---

[57] *A Mother's Spiritual Diary*, 79.

the prayer vigil over the lifeless body of her youngest child. That haunting night must have felt as if it would never end, her agony rising from earth to Heaven.

Perhaps the Blessed Mother came to kneel beside Conchita to keep the night watch over the corpse of so holy a little child. Could a mother ever be the same? Only Jesus can heal the crater in the heart of a mother who loses a child.

"I felt frozen." Parents who have lost children, and even those who have come close to losing one, know that paralysis of the heart when pain is so deep that we cease to feel. Perhaps then Jesus and Mary do the feeling for us.

Years later, Conchita's son Pablo died in her arms at the age of eighteen—another complete and painful sacrifice. Conchita was especially close to Pablo, as he was exceptionally pure. He suffered heroically, guided by his good mother.

June 21, on the feast of St. Aloysius Gonzaga: Today Pablo received his last sacraments. This morning he wanted Father Pedro Jimenez to be called, to whom he made quite willingly a general confession. When he had finished, his confessor told me: "Do not ask that Pablo become well. Let him go to heaven. He is a child, for in a few minutes he finished his general confession."

At half past three in the afternoon he received holy Communion, Viaticum, and with fervor answering all the prayers. So as not to tire him, I had him make an act of thanksgiving somewhat later, he had a terrible headache, the result, it seemed, of typhoid fever.

June 22. Today, Sunday, I had him removed from his room. He has a terrible fever. I was suffering very much but he was calm and resigned.

Two or three days before he fell ill, after supper, he said to me: "My little mama, very soon, you are going to see a dead man here." I don't know what I felt then, but very early in the morning I got up to see whether he was dead. These days I frequently had a presentiment he would die and spoke to him while he was resting in bed, to see if he was alive. My God! Is it possible? Let this chalice pass from me! None the less Thy will be done not mine!

June 25. He no longer recognized me. I stayed close to him. He cried out: "I want my mama! Call my mama!" I don't know what I felt. I began to cry. His whole desire is to go and I sense death is coming. He never closed his beautiful blue eyes. For a few moments he fixed them on me. That look I keep in my heart.

June 26. With great effort, which was not my own, I helped him die a good death. I saw him agonize and expire, then right after I kissed his forehead, I began to pray. As soon as he died, I put in his hands the crucifix I always wear over my heart. I took it away after I had laid him in the coffin. I opened his eyes, the color of the sky. I kissed his forehead and bade him farewell. Now his is no longer mine (Diary, June 30, 1913).[58]

A mother is never prepared to lose a child. This was the third time that Conchita would bury a son. The pain must have deepened with each loss. But this mother was exceptional in her love and faith. She knew that Jesus had a perfect plan, and she wouldn't question the divine will. She surrendered to God. Again, she said to Jesus, "Let me cry," as she wept rivers of tears over the dead body of her child. "I ... bade him farewell. Now he is no longer mine."

---

[58] *A Mother's Spiritual Diary*, 80, 81.

Beautiful Holiness

"Let me cry" in no way indicates resistance to God's will. Rather, we are asking God to give us a moment to grieve, because in choosing His will, it comes at the cost of dying to ours. Perhaps Conchita's tears bear some resemblance to the Lord's sweating of blood in Gethsemane.

The only comfort for Conchita was that her son now belonged solely to his Creator. Conchita knew that God is trustworthy. The final gaze of love between Conchita and Pablo was imprinted upon her heart and memory. Once again, Conchita let go.

Manuel, the Jesuit Priest

When Conchita's son Manuel decided to pursue the priesthood and enter the Society of Jesus, his mother became one of his formators in the spiritual life. In a letter to her son, written while he was still a seminarian, she advised him:

> Give yourself up to the Lord, truly with all your heart and soul, and never give up. Forget creatures, above all forget yourself. Live only for Jesus. May He reign in your soul. I cannot conceive of a religious who is not holy. We are not to give ourselves to God half-heartedly. Be generous toward Him. Life is too short not to sacrifice ourselves to Him out of love.
>
> It is evident that my maternal heart is afflicted, but I am happy to be able to offer to the Lord this sacrifice on behalf of your soul, a thousand times more loved than your body. Pray, ever pray for me.... I have told the whole family about your decision. They will pray for you.... I have wrapped you up in the mantle of Mary since your childhood. She will be your mother, love Her most dearly (Dec. 9, 1906).[59]

---

[59] A Mother's Spiritual Diary, 82.

Upon entering the Jesuits, Manuel went to Spain for a long period of formation. In 1919, Conchita learned that part of a finger on Manuel's right hand had been amputated. She wondered if he would be ordained. She admired how her son suffered with courage. He became a priest, and in a heroic act of sacrifice, he asked to be sent to the missions. Therefore, he was unable to return to Mexico to be near his family again.

Years later, Conchita went to Spain following her pilgrimage to Rome and Jerusalem. Manuel had become quite learned and mature in the spiritual life. Conchita wrote about their visit, "*We talked, laughed and cried, and thanked God.*" Later, she commented, "*When we had to say good-bye I suffered a great deal, for perhaps we had seen each other for the last time. He also wept. Finally, we parted. I was greatly pained and renewed my offer to God out of love for Him*" (February 2, 1914).[60] Conchita surrendered, but undoubtedly her maternal heart was pierced. The sacrificial offering of the mother and son likely moved the tender Heart of Jesus.

Concha, the Nun Who Died

Conchita's daughter Concha was born after three boys. Her parents adored their little daughter. Conchita and Concha enjoyed a unique union of soul. The spirituality of the mother permeated the daughter. Concha entered the convent and became Sr. Teresa de Maria Inmaculada. The correspondence between Sr. Teresa and Conchita numbers more than three hundred letters. Their visitations were very numerous also. They enjoyed the same love for Christ and zeal to save souls. Conchita prayed ardently for her daughter to become a religious of the Cross.

---

[60] *A Mother's Spiritual Diary*, 83.

Beautiful Holiness

Later, Conchita wrote, "*I'm enchanted [by] Concha's virtue, Concha who is now Sister Teresa de Maria Inmaculada. I blushed with shame on seeing myself now so old and without virtue while she made such giant steps forward (Diary, Jan.17, 1915).*"[61]

Concha pronounced her perpetual vows on October 23, 1916, and Conchita wrote in her *Diary*, "*It is a day of unforgettable happiness! Teresa de Maria Immaculada, my daughter Concha, has become forever the Lord's spouse!*"[62]

> *Sister Teresa made her entrance into the chapel, a lighted candle in her hand, pure, modest, trembling with emotion, radiant with joy. She pronounced her vows, in a placid and strong voice. Her mother, marveling, contemplated Sister Teresa de Maria Inmaculada. She is an angel.... She will be a great saint (Diary, Oct. 1916).*[63]

Sister Teresa was a faithful nun appreciated by her sisters in Puebla and in Monterrey. She settled into the daily routine of prayer in the contemplative branch of the Sisters of the Cross of the Sacred Heart of Jesus.

Soon, she was overcome with illness in the hot climate of Monterrey and began to spit blood. After many difficult hours of physical suffering, she became so ill that she was transferred back to Mexico City. The superior and the archbishop permitted Conchita to stay near Sr. Teresa while she was ill. Conchita wrote these details in her *Diary*:

> *On the national feast of Our Lady of Guadalupe, December 12, they had her hold a blessed rose, brought from the Basilica, supplicating the Most Holy Virgin that Teresa would be able to*

---

[61] A Mother's Spiritual Diary, 83.
[62] A Mother's Spiritual Diary, 83.
[63] A Mother's Spiritual Diary, 91.

receive Viaticum. She regained the use of her reason, and the last sacraments were administered to her. She was conscious of everything. I do not know how to thank God.... She recognized me and said to me, "My dear little mama!" Poor child! My soul burst, my heart was shattered on seeing her suffer so much! She repeated to Jesus: "Behold my body ..." "Behold my blood." I looked at her and I wept, offering her to the eternal Father, begging Him to take her if that was His will (*Diary*, Dec. 12, 1925).

Then Conchita wrote, "*Yesterday, December 19, at one forty-five in the afternoon, Teresa died! God of my heart, be a thousand times blessed! After twenty-nine days of illness and sharp pain in her whole body, the daughter of my life died. She was an angel, a victim, a saint* (*Diary*, Dec. 20, 1925)."[64]

Conchita bade farewell to her daughter and buried her fourth child. Imagine the vulnerability of Conchita's heart. In her communion with Jesus and Mary, she was stripped of the most precious loves of her life—her husband and four of her nine children. God's plan for Conchita continued to unfold through many trials and tribulations. She grew in virtue, becoming more the image of Christ crucified.

Her Surviving Children

Having lost her husband, three sons, and a daughter, Conchita cherished her surviving children even more, and they eventually gave her twelve grandchildren. Consuelo, one of her granddaughters, is a religious sister.

Three boys, Francisco, Ignacio, Salvador, and Conchita's daughter Guadalupe (Lupe) survived their mother.

---

[64] *A Mother's Spiritual Diary*, 92.

Beautiful Holiness

About Francesco (called Pancho, like his father), Fr. Philipon writes:

> Pancho is a handsome man, ... a businessman, but above all a man of honor and a fine Christian. His brothers and sisters, who owe him a great deal, love him as a second father. When his papa died, he was seventeen and courageously went to work to help his mother raise her seven other orphans. He went through many hours of difficulty, not hesitating to make long business trips in Europe and North and South America. Conchita had utmost confidence in him and relied very much on him for the education of her other children.[65]

About Ignacio, Fr. Philipon writes:

> Ignacio, after having raised a very fine Christian family, with his wife Chabela, dearly loved by Conchita, died surrounded by the affection of his family in the house where his mother died, at San Angel. He prayed in memory of his mother who loved him so much and who said of him: "Of all my children, he is the one most like his father."

About Salvador, Father writes:

> Salvador was the last born boy. His mother watched over him with the greatest tenderness, imploring God to have him find a wife who would make him happy. After his marriage, Conchita writes in her *Diary*: "All is over for me.... But a mother always rejoices in the happiness of her children" (*Diary*, Sept. 24, 1929).

---

[65] *A Mother's Spiritual Diary*, 92.

Family Life: School of Sacrificial Love

About Guadalupe (Lupe), Father reports:

> Lupe was a very proper and charming daughter. Salvador and she were the two *enfants terribles* of the family, each having a big heart.... Conchita loved all her children and followed each one in his or her own life. I have never found on their lips the slightest reproach directed against their mother. She herself gave them the most beautiful testimonial when she said: "*I am not worthy of the children God has given me.*"[66]

No one is worthy of one of God's greatest gifts—children. God entrusts to parents the grace of procreation. What could be more important than forming children's souls for eternal life?

Conchita's union with Jesus made her the excellent formator of her children, the dutiful wife who prepared her husband for Heaven, the sorrowful mother who assisted her children in death, and the mother of two vocations to the religious life.

Conchita's family was incorporated into the fabric of her being. Here's a sample of how she prayed precisely for each child's needs.

> Lord, preserve Pancho's righteousness, his blessed judgements with which You have endowed him. Lord, Ignacio worries me. Keep him in purity of conscience. Lord, may Pablo be all Yours. Lord, may Salvador use his viciousness for his good and Your glory. Lord, as to Manuel and Concha, those two souls so pure and so crucified for You, grant them perseverance. Lord, my two angels who are in heaven, Carlos and Pedro, may they ever attend You on Your throne.

---

[66] *A Mother's Spiritual Diary*, 93.

Beautiful Holiness

Oh Mary, Mother of my soul, protectress of orphans, make Poncho's devotion to you grow. May it grow too in all my children. I give them to You as Your own. Cover them with Your mantle, keep them ever pure, keep them in Your Son's heart, grant them good inclinations and love of the Cross. You know, I do not know how to educate them, I do not know how to be a mother. You know, Oh Mary. Shelter them in Your bosom, keep them pure for Jesus. Oh Mary, for Him alone (Diary, Oct. 30, 1908).[67]

---

[67] *A Mother's Spiritual Diary,* 78.

INDIVIDUAL OR GROUP REFLECTION

Ponder

"Can a woman forget her nursing child, or show no compassion for the child of her womb? Even these may forget, yet I will not forget you" (Isa. 49:15, NRSVCE).

Engage

1. How does your family resemble Conchita's?
2. How is God calling you to better serve your loved one(s)?
3. Which member of Conchita's family do you relate to most?

Pray

O Yes, my Life, speak to this heart which belongs wholly to You, speak to it in the solitude of Your cloister, in the atmosphere of Your Cross. From all eternity, by Your grace, You have made me come out of nothingness. From my tenderest childhood You have drawn me to suffering. You have shown me the folly of love, but love of the Cross; You have transformed me into it (Diary, March 21, 1906).[68]

4

Prayer Life: Divine Intimacy

Then you will call on me and come and
pray to me, and I will listen to you.

—Jeremiah 29:12

For Blessed Conchita, prayer was always an encounter of love, a heart-to-heart dialogue with the triune Lord. We'll discover in this chapter how Conchita was formed in prayer by her parents initially and then by Christ Jesus, Mary, and the Holy Spirit over her lifetime.

The most noble utterance of man is prayer, the elevation of the soul to God. We are made for prayer, for conversing with the Persons of the Holy Trinity. Simple and sublime, prayer spiritually places us in the arms of God. In prayer, Jesus leads us to a deeper union with Himself. The exercise of prayer becomes an exercise of love.

Prayer is gift and necessity, an ever-new experience of divine love, a joy that refreshes us. The world disorients us; daily prayer orients us to God and to what is proper to love. Jesus teaches us to pray, and it becomes a joy to spend time with the Lord in communion of heart.

I think that Conchita was always a student of prayer, learning from Jesus and Mary, from saints, and from spiritual directors and reading good spiritual books. And like her, I will always be a student of prayer because there is always more to learn about the transforming art of prayer.

Conchita reached the highest heights of mystical prayer, being fully animated by the Holy Spirit. She wrote many books that can inspire us to live a life of prayer, including *Holy Hours*, *Roses and Thorns*, *I Am*, and *Eucharistic Meditations on the Gospel*. Her writings provide a school of prayer, a syllabus of mysticism.

The *Catechism* explains the term *mystical* in this way: "Spiritual progress tends towards ever more intimate union with Christ. This union is called 'mystical' because it participates in the mystery of Christ through the sacraments—'the holy mysteries'—and, in him, in the mystery of the Holy Trinity" (CCC 2014). Likewise, St. Louis de Montfort writes:

> The term "mysticism" becomes another manner of express-ing the contemplation of divine mysteries. In the power of the Holy Spirit, contemplation admires the divine truths and is called "mystical" because, on the one hand, these truths are totally penetrated with mystery and, on the other, they are not able to be grasped by human intelligence or be manipulated by it. The milieu of mystical contemplation is sacramental union, mystical union of the creature with God in Jesus Christ. Thus, mystical contemplation has as its goal unity with God in the encounter with Jesus Christ.[69]

The Lord is the architect of our prayer life. The same Holy Spirit who led Jesus and Mary to pray will also lead us to pray if we yield our heart to God's will.

---

[69] St. Louis de Montfort, "Mystic," in *Handbook of the Spirituality of St. Louis De Montfort*, EWTN, https://www.ewtn.com/catholicism/library/mystic-12838.

The Art of Prayer

Conchita learned the art of prayer from a young age growing up in a pious family. As a child, she felt as though Jesus had stolen her heart.

> *From my tenderest childhood, I felt in my soul a strong inclination toward prayer, penance, and, above all, purity. Penance was always a joy as far back as I could remember* (Aut., 15–16).
>
> *While riding about the countryside with my father and my sister Clara, I spend hours reflecting on how I could manage to live in a mountain cave all by myself, far from everyone, giving myself up to penance and prayer whenever the spirit moved me. I was delighted at the thought and pondered it in my heart.*[70]

Conchita was already thinking in terms of solitude, silence, penance, prayer, and how the spirit moves her. Her young soul experienced the delights of God and understood what it is to ponder Him in her heart. Prayer and penance were coupled for Conchita.

In her teens, both her parents and Jesus encouraged Conchita to attend the dances in her hometown together with other teenagers. Conchita learned valuable lessons at the dances:

> *At the heart of this ocean of vanities and festivals, I felt within my soul a burning desire to learn how to pray. I inquired, I read, I kept myself as much as I could in God's presence. This was enough to begin seeing a great light shed on the nothingness of worldly things, on the vanity of existence, on the beauty of God. I felt a great love for the Holy Spirit.*[71]

---

[70] *A Mother's Spiritual Diary*, 6, 7.
[71] *A Mother's Spiritual Diary*, 10.

Beautiful Holiness

Conchita already knew how to keep herself in the presence of God.

We meet mystics in Scripture. Jesus Christ, Mary, and Joseph are all mystics. In the Gospels we find Jesus praying the prayers of blessing and healing, prayers of thanksgiving to His Father, the prayer of meditation, contemplation, the prayer of tears, the prayer of agony on the Cross, the prayer of surrender at the end of His life. It isn't surprising that Jesus desires His disciples to become mystics.

Saints paint a portrait of prayer as lofty as the heavens and as practical as picking up our cross daily. Consider the "nada" of St. John of the Cross; the "mansions" of Teresa of Ávila, the "confessions" of St. Augustine, the "devout life" of St. Francis de Sales, the "little way" of St. Thérèse of Lisieux, the "dialogue" of St. Catherine of Siena, the "poverty" of St. Francis of Assisi, the "exercises" of St. Ignatius of Loyola, the "consecration" of St. Louis de Montfort, the "trust" of St. Faustina, the "mercy" of St. John Paul II, and Conchita's "Love Crucified." Saints have left us schools of prayer. Blessed Conchita deposited into the Church's treasury a legacy of prayer.

Conchita's Prayer

Prayer formed and informed Conchita's abiding communion with Christ Jesus. She didn't compartmentalize prayer, works, sacrifices, the duties of her vocation, and apostolates. All that Conchita was and did was clothed in prayer and crowned with love of God. For us, she is a spiritual mother who teaches us to pray with great confidence based on God's goodness—with lively trust in the promises of Jesus.

What promises about prayer did Our Lord make? Here are just three:

1. "Ask, and it will be given you; seek, and you will find; knock, and it will be opened to you. For every one who asks receives, and he who seeks finds, and to him who knocks it will be opened." (Matt 7:7–8).
2. "The LORD is far from the wicked, but he hears the prayer of the righteous" (Prov. 15:29).
3. "If you abide in me, and my words abide in you, ask whatever you will, and it shall be done for you" (John 15:7).

For Conchita, prayer was like breathing. It was the organic extension of her soul resting in God, loving Him, talking to Him, enjoying His friendship, walking with Him daily on a journey Heavenward. Daily Eucharist was foundational. I don't think it's a stretch to say that Conchita's life was a continuous act of loving God, but that's not to say that she didn't have a prayer regimen.

Conchita's *Diary* and her biographers paint a rich picture of her prayer life. Some spiritual practices included attending daily Mass, daily vocal and mental prayer, hidden hours of nocturnal prayer vigils, annual retreats, Ignatian Spiritual Exercises, and meditation on Scripture and on the lives of the saints. Her ascetical practices include sleeping on the hard floor, wearing a hair shirt for reparation, and fasting often on toast and coffee. These were always done with the permission of her spiritual director. She desired to be one with Jesus in every way, discovering Him in people and in history.

Conchita explained that, when we are in the state of grace, our prayers have great efficacy:

A soul in the state of grace always reflects God. Every created soul, as by a divine instinct, and without realizing it, bears within itself the reflection of the Trinity and traces of its unity. But the soul who has simplified itself by the exercise of the virtues, the soul who has allowed itself to be formed by the Holy Spirit, without resisting Him, the soul who because of the degree of transformation along which it has advanced, has torn aside the veils that hid God from its view and has traveled the road of thorns which separated it from Him, who has focused itself upon the Divinity unifying itself, becomes like a mirror which, before the image of the Divinity, copies, reads, understands, and can transmit to the world the echoes of heaven.[72]

A person of abiding prayer can "transmit to the world the echoes of heaven." The world cries out for some echoes of Heaven. Prayer is meant to be a transformative experience, so we become authentic heralds of the living Christ. We need not be a master catechist, apologist, or theologian to transmit to the world echoes of Heaven, but we are called to be authentic witnesses infused with prayer.

Absent prayer, we lose touch with our heart and with reality. We lose sight of God. We lose our spiritual compass. If we don't fill our minds with prayer, our thoughts will become filled with anxiety, resentments, and lies. Prayer is an elixir of truth that orders the soul to God.

Conchita does not address prayer like a theologian. Hers is the voice of experiential knowledge—an authentic mysticism rooted in Jesus' school of prayer. Conchita became *imbued with prayer through the indwelt Holy Spirit.* Jesus ordained Conchita's prayer life to be suited to her prophetic mission in the Church. Her prayer, led by the Holy Spirit, was Trinitarian, Marian, Eucharistic, missionary for

[72] Concepción Cabrera de Armida, *Prayer* (Modesto, CA: Sisters of the Cross of the Sacred Heart of Jesus), 3.

the Church, rooted in the Cross. Her prayer life was the flowering
of her baptismal priesthood.

The Cross was Conchita's standard by God's design and her
ardent will to be united with Jesus in every way. Her prayers center
on the perfect sacrifice of the pierced Heart of Jesus. The sword
that pierced the Heart of Jesus on the Cross opened Heaven. Jesus
prayed on the altar of the Cross; His victory sprang forth from its
crossbeams. Conchita believed what Paul taught, "For the word
of the cross is folly to those who are perishing, but to us who are
being saved it is the power of God" (1 Cor. 1:18). Jesus taught
Conchita about the dynamism of divine love at work on the Cross.
She understood that Love crucified is the bridge to resurrected life.

Jesus' Words to Conchita on Prayer

Through the generosity of Fr. Domenico, I received several pages
of a prayer workshop containing the words of Jesus to Conchita.
These are from her *Account of Conscience*, or *Diary*, dated in May
and June of 1900.[73] Conchita was thirty-eight years old when she
received these lessons on prayer.

Following is a sample of the reflections Jesus entrusted to Conchita. Although abridged here for our purposes, these reflections
provide ample insights on prayer. The excerpts from Conchita's
Diary are in italics and are followed by my commentary.

Prayer Power

*Today, after my communion, full of fire, Jesus said to me: Oh, my
beloved daughter, I want to speak to you about prayer.... Prayer
is the anticipated union of the soul with God. Heaven is continuous prayer; the clear contemplation of the Divinity and its total*

---

[73] CC. vol. 13, (263-328), May 1–June 6, 1900.

possession and the prelude to such possession. Prayer is the mysterious ladder that leads the soul to this mansion of ineffable delights. Prayer is the cry of the soul which God always gladly hears. Prayer inclines the Heart of God, calms His wrath, takes the sword out of His hands, makes Him smile, and turns the scourges of His justice into a shower of graces. Oh, and what power prayer has on the throne of God, but the prayer that comes from a pure and crucified heart ...!

Jesus motivates us to pray. Prayer that moves God must come from "a pure and crucified heart," like that of the repentant tax collector in Luke's Gospel (see 18:9-14). For simplicity, I think a person in the state of grace, living his or her life and vocation ordered to God's law of love, striving for virtue, overcoming vice, and frequenting the sacraments, especially the Eucharist and Reconciliation, will likely be considered a person with a pure and crucified heart—one who is dying to self and embracing his or her crosses daily with love. When we put love into our prayer, Jesus smiles. Parents know how the love of their children moves the heart. We can tug on God's heart with prayers of pure love, fearless petitions, and gratitude.

Prayer Has Many Stairs

"Look," He continued. "Prayer has many double parts ... many stairs. There, in that divine chamber where the purified soul penetrates, there are infinite extensions; beauties and heavenly enchantments ... precious gardens and crystalline fountains ... divine sounds and harmonies ... but also, beasts that tear apart ... furnaces that purify ... very intense crucibles ... seas of bitterness ... very dark darkness ... terrible tempests ... black clouds.... However, in the midst of all this there is a divine Sun ... a Jesus,

*a Father who cares, a Little Dove that you know. Isn't it true,
little daughter, that you have gone through all this for my goodness?*

*"But you still have a long way to go, great surprises and great
Crosses. Prayer and the Cross are the two levers that sustain the
life of the spirit. There are many kinds of prayers and infinite
degrees to which to ascend. Go on, my daughter; do not faint; go
on until the end, I accompany you even if sometimes you do not
touch me or feel me."*

Prayer is both an experience of sublime beauty and, frequently,
a spiritual battle. The three enemies of prayer are the spirit of the
world, the flesh (concupiscence), and the devil. Mostly we battle
ourselves due to interior disquiet, disordered affections or vice,
lack of self-discipline, or duplicitous motivation. The development
of a prayer life requires discipline, a rule or regimen so the holy
habit of prayer is acquired.

Jesus gives this vital advice: "Go on ... do not faint, go until the
end." We might fall back, but the call to prayer persists. Be brave in
responding to the call. Jesus teaches Conchita that prayer and the
Cross are the two levers that sustain life of the spirit. The Sanctifier purifies prayer through crosses, trials, and tests. A religious
sister told me that when I'm tempted to get off the Cross, I should
ask Jesus to nail me tightly to it. In a long season of suffering that
nailed me to the Cross, I learned to pray from a pierced heart.
The season and the pain passed, but the foundations of love and
prayer remain.

At thirty-five years of age, I had my first spiritual-direction ap-
pointment with a priest who directed me for fifteen years. Father
was a Trappist monk with a great love for the teachings of St.
Thomas Aquinas. This learned, prayerful priest knew well the workings of the interior life. I approached him for spiritual direction

after experiencing a life-changing conversion and becoming a daily communicant. Basically, I had fallen in love with Jesus and wanted to grow in virtue. Father spoke plainly, which is what I needed. His advice: Let the Church's liturgy form your spiritual life. The Church is a good spiritual mother, so pray liturgically with her. Come hell or high water, make a daily holy hour; schedule time for silence and solitude before the tabernacle. Persevere to pray daily until your last breath. The devil will tempt you to stop. Never stop. If you feel nothing but distain for prayer, pray anyway. Each year of your life, you should grow in virtue and in union with Jesus.

In the early years after my conversion, I was working and raising two little boys. I had to be intentional in developing a daily prayer life. Thirty years later, I've never ceased to follow Father's advice, which has served me very well.

The Need for Meditation

Meditation is necessary for every man who lives on earth, and for the spiritual life it is indispensable.... The world is lost because it does not meditate. Meditation is the door that leads to holiness, and the stairway to prayer. The man who meditates is saved, because meditation is the lightning rod of sin, and the man who does not sin is Mine, and I will reward him as such. The whole life of man should be constituted in meditation, because from meditation is born or springs praise, and man, in his passage on earth, should do nothing else but praise Me.

... No man can meditate without his lips, and his heart moved by it, spontaneously bursting forth with praises to Me, whether of gratitude, admiration, or deep loving reverence. I am, daughter, the only One worthy of the praise and love of all hearts, and whoever departs from this unique Object, which is Me, errs and becomes disordered.

*Meditation drags man to the practice of a Christian, upright,
and ordered life. Meditation does not prevent work, but prepares
it, fortifies it, and makes the soul supernaturalize it. How many
incalculable evils would be avoided by the holy practice of meditation! In it is the source of the divine teachings! It is the door that
leads to divine favors, and prayer is the key to that door of gold and
precious stones; Satan abhors meditation, because it is the great
weapon with which the soul defends itself from his snares and wiles.*

The word *meditation* derives from the Latin *meditatio*, which
means "a thinking over." The Church defines *meditation* as "reflec-
tive prayer. It is that form of mental prayer in which the mind,
in God's presence, thinks about God and divine things."[74] The
intellect and imagination are engaged to prompt our interior conversation with the Lord.

Jesus beseeches us to meditate so He can share with us the
mysteries of His life, His Heart, His mind, and His plan. Conchita
wrote that Jesus sometimes has so much to say! Other times, He's
silent. I've learned that the silence of God can speak volumes to
the soul. I think the language of love is one of silent communion,
of pure presence and good company wherein two heartbeats unite
in one rhythm of love. Meditation helps us to discover the Kingdom of God within.

It's beautiful to meditate on Scripture: Christ's hidden childhood, Mary's divine pregnancy, St. Joseph's dreams, Elizabeth's
miracle, John the Baptist's leap for joy, the Samaritan woman's
awakening at the well, Magdalene's liberation, Peter's testament
of love, Paul's conversion, Bartimaeus's healing, John's fidelity at

---

[74] Fr. John Hardon, *Modern Catholic Dictionary*, s.v. "meditation,"
Catholic Culture, https://www.catholicculture.org/culture/li-
brary/dictionary/index.cfm?id=34827.

the Cross. Jesus told Conchita that meditation is a lightning rod of sin; that is, protection from sin. When we stop running, recollect, and meditate, we are likely to encounter the presence of God. In the light of His presence, we see ourselves in truth, where sin and love are incompatible. Meditation can move us to prefer God over self and over sin. There are countless fruits of meditation.

Prayer of Meditation

Meditation, daughter, is a magnifying glass with which the divine secrets are discovered with astonishing clarity to the gaze of the spirit.... The door that leads to the purification of the soul and the cleansing of the heart is this meditation.

It is a mistake to believe that the spiritual path can be undertaken without the anticipated purification of the soul, and for this reason there is so much falsehood in such a matter. The true path of the spirit can only be crossed by clean and sacrificed souls; why? because it carries in itself many thorns, and many passions, and both things demand the purity of a sacrificed, loving, and self-sacrificing heart.

Meditation contains many degrees and steps; they are of an astonishing variety and bear in their physiognomy (features) different colors. It has the property, like prayer, of molding itself to all understandings and hearts, always producing, in disposed souls, abundant fruits for their sanctification.

The world is lost, little daughter, I repeat, because it does not stop to consider its ruin ...! Cold dissipation envelops it; pride obfuscates its mind, flattery lulls it to sleep, and cowardice and human respect precipitate it into hesitation, doubt, and the darkness of a thousand passions that plunge it into the dreadful mire of all vices. Souls are lost because meditation and the sacrifice that goes with it, without ever being separated from it, are lacking!

Prayer Life: Divine Intimacy

Extreme busyness of life, mediocrity, lethargy, and duplicity are some adversaries of meditation. It is prudent and necessary to prioritize prayer and schedule time for meditation.

A homeschooling mother of eight children shared with me that she arises at five o'clock each morning, one hour before everyone else in the home, to meditate for an hour. She told her husband and children that, in order to be a good wife and mother, she must spend the first hour of the day with Jesus. In Conchita's life, too, prayer was a priority. Her children unanimously testified to this during their interviews with Vatican investigators.

How to Meditate

Meditation on the Mysteries and on My Most Holy Life is very fruitful for souls; but that of My Passion should be man's daily bread. This meditation on My Passion and My sorrows has, or carries within itself, the virtue of kindling souls in the fire of My love and in the fire of sacrifice. The souls who frequently meditate on My Passion, do not take long, if they are clean, to burn in the divine fire. There is no fuel on earth more suitable for kindling hearts in holy love than the continuous meditation on My sorrows for man. The meditation that reaches My internal pains, borders on prayer, because of the divine and copious fruits that it brings to souls. Happy are the souls who manage to penetrate through the wound in My Side to the depths of My divine Heart ...! There, in that Fountain of pain and love, is where all self-love drowns and dies, and the soul then begins to live of Christ alone....

Meditation and prayer are not virtues, but mysterious and divine stairways that lead to heaven by means of the virtues, facilitating them for the intrepid souls who climb them.

The enemies of meditation, daughter, are the whole squadrons of Satan, multiplied, who, by every means within their reach, prevent the soul from carrying it out. The war that these evil spirits wage against the soul that wants to ascend this ladder of meditation is terrible. In order to defeat them, the Warrior Virtues of Firmness, Determination, Constancy and Overcoming are needed. Correspondence [with Jesus] and Fidelity are also indispensable to overthrow these fierce and untiring enemies.

One thing, above all, the soul that undertakes the laborious ascent of meditation needs, a beautiful and indispensable virtue on which this ladder needs to rest so that it does not fall down; do you know, my daughter, what is this virtue, the foundation of meditation, and of prayer above all? That of humility, that of humility, and that of humility, and the deeper this foundation is, the firmer and higher this ladder will be. Any meditation or ladder, which is not fixed upon such a foundation of deep humility, will more or less fall to the ground sooner or later.

St. Augustine wrote that the way to Christ is first, humility; second, humility; and third, humility. St. Thomas Aquinas said that humility is seeing ourselves as God does, acknowledging that every good we have is from God as gift.[75] Pride hides itself in so many ways it is necessary to pray daily for the grace of humility which is truth.

Note the *warrior virtues* that Jesus speaks of—each is necessary to battle against enemies of prayer. The devil never rests, so we should be vigilant to discern the spirits. Consider which spirit is operating in and around you: your human spirit, the Holy Spirit, or an evil spirit? Invoke the Holy Spirit. Rebuke the evil spirits. Do not let an evil spirit rob you of meditative prayer. Eyes on Christ, heart engaged, the devil crushed underfoot, persevere in prayer.

[75] St. Thomas Aquinas, *Summa Theologica*, II-II q. 161.

The Prayer of Quiet

*The Prayer of Prayer ... Quiet ... Calm and Restful, it borders
on Contemplation, more than on prayer. It consists of a very lively
Presence of God, which leaves it suspended and raptured without being able to do anything else but love, love, and only love;
without memory and understanding intervening, and without the
senses producing the least distraction. It seems that the soul is
sleeping in the arms of the Beloved, but it is not so; because, far
from sleeping, its heart beats and does not cease to love that one
unique Object, which has it absorbed within itself.... It seems
that she does not move, and yet, with a quiet and calm flight, she
crosses the eternal spaces, I will say, growing, without her feeling
it, the heights to which she ascends.... She does not realize what
she has climbed, until she descends and occupies herself with
things of the earth....*

*Then she notices that she breathes another air less pure, that
she has descended from her Center, that her eyes see other sad
and faded colors, that she is cold ... because she lacks that divine
color where she had been without realizing the great fire that
produced it....*

*This prayer leaves in the soul a great detachment from the
things of the earth, and a constant tendency to those of heaven....
The soul sighs lovingly for the infinite Center of its rest, which it
seems to have scarcely tasted, and all its longing consists in working
to make itself worthy of this lofty favor. However, this prayer, as
almost all are, is gratuitous.*

The prayer of quiet borders on contemplation, according
the Lord's message. This would be infused prayer—a gratuitous
gift of God that is given to pure, generous souls. Christ is never
outdone in generosity. When He sees that we're making real

effort, praying with constancy, not for our sakes but out of pure love for Him, He desires to feed us more of the delights of the higher echelon of prayer. Try as we may, we can't cause ourselves to ascend to new heights. It is the Holy Spirit's prerogative to grant the prayer of quiet to souls whom He sees as pure and generous with Him.

Blessed Conchita, like the widow who gave her all to God and kept back nothing for herself, was lifted to the heights of prayer, but her ascent was made on the ladder of the Cross.

Conchita's School of Prayer

Between August 1922 and November 1923, Conchita wrote a book for priests, titled *Be Perfect*. The texts below are drawn from that book[76] and represent different periods of her life. Conchita's plan of prayer bore great fruit in her soul, in her family, and in her apostolates.

Conchita teaches that prayer can infuse our daily lives. At Mass, we liturgically worship, petition, and thank Jesus as His Church. In adoration of the Blessed Sacrament, we personally commune with Jesus in mental prayer, meditation, and silence. But we can make all the moments of life prayerful by simply lifting up our hearts: "I love you, Jesus." I may see a child at the grocery store and pray to Jesus, "Lord, thank You for children!" When we love the Lord, He is always on our mind. We ponder Him and the divine mysteries. In prayer, we consider the many facets of His Person and behold the very face of God.

---

[76] Specifically, they are taken from the booklet *Prayer* (Modesto, CA: Sisters of the Cross of the Sacred Heart of Jesus, 2016), a translation of chapter 26 of *Be Perfect*.

Prayer Life

Through prayer man rises from earth to heaven, he comes into contact with God, and he embraces Him intimately with that purest emanation of the soul by means of which he penetrates the divine secrets.[77]

How many souls chosen to receive the divine confidences of the Heart of Jesus separate themselves from Him because they don't persevere in prayer, because they do not "live on in His love."[78]

All the infidelities that are noted in vocations, spring from leaving prayer, and on the other hand, a soul who prays however imperfect, and sinful it might be, can achieve sanctity.[79]

Conchita doesn't pray from the surface, but from the depths. Her prayer is her gift of love. Jesus told Conchita that many souls who would receive His divine confidences cannot because they separate themselves from Him when they cease to pray.

Vocal and Mental Prayer

Vocal prayer is the favorite of the Church. It is as it were the body; and mental prayer is the soul, letting itself go, losing itself inflamed in love, into the grandeurs and splendors of God. What is it they do in Heaven: pray.[80]

Vocal prayer is essential to the Christian life. Jesus taught the Our Father. Jesus prayed liturgical prayers in the synagogue, and He offered personal prayers to the Father on many occasions. Vocal

---

[77] *Prayer*, 9.
[78] *Prayer*, 10.
[79] *Prayer*, 11.
[80] *Prayer*, 12.

and mental prayer are the first stages of prayer. We can think of vocal prayer as a monologue and mental prayer as a two-way action between us and Jesus. "Mental prayer is above all a quest" (CCC 2705). Meditating on Scripture or the Mysteries of the Rosary helps us to silently ponder and then dialogue with Jesus about His life and ours.

Prayer Ejaculations

Life can be seeded with ardent ejaculations, which are as arrows, which the soul casts at God's Heart. They are as the signs of longing from the place of exile for the fatherland; and these ejaculations are habitual in the saints. They united everything to God, in this way making the divine Presence within their hearts continuous.

St. Joan of Chantal would say 60 times daily: I adore You, Will of God, take possession of all my being.

St. Francis of Assisi would say: My God and my all.

St. Gertrude repeated 200 hundred times: I adore, praise, and bless the Most Holy Trinity.

St. Vincent would say in all things: God be blessed.

And Jesus worked under the eye of His Heavenly Father entirely united to the Holy Spirit.[81]

Prayer ejaculations are beautiful and practical for staying in the presence of Jesus. One may pray throughout the day, "Jesus, I love You," or "Jesus, I'm sorry," or "Jesus, be glorified," or "Jesus, help!" These phrases can arise spontaneously from our hearts throughout each day, so we may remain in His presence.

---

[81] *Prayer*, 13.

The Prayer of Pain and Suffering

There is another form of prayer, which is the prayer of suffering, the prayer of pain. Who can deny that the person who suffers with patience prays, becoming a holocaust, drawing down precious graces upon him/herself and upon other souls?

The suffering that has been offered in communion with that of Jesus acquires a supernatural power and thus transformed, it would break that heaven of bronze, opening a path right to the throne of God.[82]

Pain and suffering touch us all. We might shed many tears in the silence of the night, mystified by pain that breaks our hearts or our bodies. Sometimes we endure seasons of suffering that wear us down. When we unite our suffering to the Lord's Passion, pray, and persevere in hope, we please God and gain grace for others. Suffering of itself is evil, but united to Christ's Passion, human suffering becomes an offering of love. When our hearts are pierced with mental, physical, or spiritual suffering, we have the Crucified Jesus and the Mother of Sorrows to hold on to. They will refresh our soul with their love and grace. "Prayer is the life of the new heart" (CCC 2697).

Battles in Prayer

The soul then passes through paths where both spirits, the good and the evil, do battle within it. It feels thrust upward toward God, with lively, even sensible touches of the Holy Spirit, when suddenly a black cloud seems to envelope it, freezing it and making it feel ennui, desperation, and horrible sadness. The soul travels between two opposing steams and two opposing winds

---

[82] *Prayer*, 13.

with its heart torn to shreds. It feels itself drawn to prayer and frozen in it.

Vivid lights from heaven come suddenly to its understanding, very lofty points of union followed by a painful counteraction with rejection, inner tremors, impatience and even falls, that it might be humbled. It navigates amid a sea of bitterness, on a dark horizon, to the sudden attack of the two spirits, and only love, humility and self-contempt can sustain it.[83]

Prayer is a spiritual battle. In prayer, we experience grace and spiritual accompaniment from the Holy Spirit, Mary, our guardian angels, and our saint helpers. Also, we meet the devil trying to thwart our prayer time. He presents various temptations to distract or stop our prayer. We should be prepared for the spiritual battle. St. Paul teaches, "Put on the armor of God" (Eph. 6:11). Know that "in all these things we are more than conquerors through him who loved us" (Rom. 8:37).

In the battle of prayer, the Holy Rosary is a very powerful weapon against demonic temptations. Keep a Bible or a good spiritual book near you in prayer, as St. Teresa of Ávila suggested. If the spiritual attack worsens, it is prudent to pray personal prayers of liberation from evil. Pope Leo XIII's prayer to St. Michael the Archangel is very effective! Conchita's spiritual formation was likely influenced by the Spiritual Exercises of St. Ignatius of Loyola, with its teaching on the discernment of spirits. Conchita knew that prayer is a battle that is won by love and constancy.

Contemplation

The contemplative ardor has no limit in the soul and love continues to increase, purifying it. Only God knows to their depths the

---

[83] *Prayer*, 18.

riches which are encompassed in contemplation, as well as their multiple dangers. And do you know where the Holy Spirit placed the very high grace of contemplation, where He puts these lavish favors? Only with the deepest humility, in the concealment and obscurity of a very pure and very sacrificed soul. Without these indispensable conditions, the Holy Spirit does not descend with special grace. Any contemplation that does not bear within itself these divine characteristics, is false, and what is worse, of incalculable dangers for the soul.

To free oneself from thousands of artificial tricks of the demon, one needs a wise and holy director who knows through experience, if possible, what these difficult and dangerous paths are, their pitfalls and obstacles, as well as a simplicity and complete clarity on the part of the soul. This path of contemplation should never be undertaken without a holy guide.[84]

Contemplative prayer is a gift of God. We cannot confer this gift upon ourselves. We can only dispose ourselves to it by seeking the Lord in silence and solitude. The Lord is generous in conferring the gift of contemplative prayer upon whom He wills.

As Jesus told Conchita, at this level of prayer, a good spiritual director, a priest, monk, religious sister, or a spiritually mature layperson who has formation in spiritual direction is necessary for discernment, protection, and growth. Conchita is an excellent model, who consults her priest director each step of her journey.

It can be challenging to find a spiritual director, so I recommend the apostolate SpiritualDirection.com. A virtuous prayer partner may be helpful in the absence of a spiritual director.

---

[84] *Prayer*, 22–23.

Beautiful Holiness

Prayer of Union

Union has an infinite number of degrees of sublime intimacies with the Father, with the Divine Word, and with the Holy Spirit Himself; bonds which we can only believe because God is charity.

There are three types of union within a single union: One with the Divine Word, another with the Holy Spirit, and another with the Father, all of them holy and most perfect.[85]

It's a beautiful gift to pray with each of the Three Persons of the Holy Trinity. Before the Father, I pray as a daughter. Before the Lord, I pray as a disciple. Before the Holy Spirit, I pray as a Marian vessel. Conchita's spirituality was Trinitarian. She received exquisite locutions and visions on the life of the Holy Trinity with lofty theological insights.

Union with the Divine Word

Union with the Divine Word made flesh is the first, more exterior union, even though it is internal or mystical, for all that rubs more directly against the creature, in that semi-exterior order, always concerns the Divine Word, because of His union with the most Holy Humanity and because of His thirst for debasement.

With untiring patience, He endures it, He lifts it up, sustains, animates, teaches, and cleanses it, placing it on the paths of perfection. In this stage, Jesus illumines the soul with the radiations of His Divinity, afterwards casting it into seas of battles, desolations, darkness, and rejections, which always begin and develop in the field of prayer.[86]

[85] *Prayer*, 23, 24.
[86] *Prayer*, 24, 25.

Conchita always emphasized the Incarnation, falling in love with the holy humanity of Jesus, the God-Man who has a heart of flesh. This was a central theme of her spirituality and prayer: divine love incarnated in Jesus making it possible for us to be saved and to be united with Him in a bond of love. "I led them with cords of compassion, with the bands of love, and I became to them as one who eases the yoke on their jaws, and I bent down to them and fed them" (Hos. 11:4). If we pray, even in a sea of distractions, or with coldness of heart, Jesus observes our motivation and intention and blesses us.

Union with the Holy Spirit

And the happy day comes when the Divine Word Himself gives the Holy Spirit to that soul, and then as another order of graces begins for it, this Holy Spirit begins to clarify for it the holy mystery of the Trinity, causing it to fall much deeper in love with the second Divine Person and with the sublime mystery of the Incarnation. He adorns the souls with its graces, charisms, and gifts to make with it the spiritual mystical marriage, which excels in virginal purity and fruitfulness.... And what does the soul do then, having been enveloped in such incomparable favors? It remains awed, amazed, annihilated in the arms of the Holy Spirit.[87]

Prayer is the work of the Holy Spirit. St. Paul tells us, "No one can say 'Jesus is Lord' except by the Holy Spirit" (1 Cor. 12:3). Prayer is a school of the Holy Spirit. He makes prayer life dynamic. To be in the arms of the Holy Spirit is to be loved. One of the most efficacious prayers to say throughout the day is "*Veni, Creator Spiritus*: Come, Creator Spirit. Invade my heart. Possess me. Direct

---

[87] *Prayer*, 26.

my path. Teach me to love. Be my joy. Sanctify me." Holiness is the work of the Sanctifier. The Holy Spirit, with His gifts and charisms, anoints, equips, transforms, and sends forth. The Holy Spirit will never cease to amaze us!

Union with the Father

After this, one day the Father comes to lay His gaze upon the soul, because the Divine Word dwells there. That Divine Word attracts Him, and He envelops that throne of the creature's heart in which the Divine Word dwells, with paternal tenderness, and through the action of the Divine Word, the Father is given to the soul who already belongs to the most Holy Trinity in an awesome manner. The Father finds pleasure in the fact that, in imitation of Himself, and through a special and immense love, derived the love He Himself has for the Word, the soul sacrifices Christ in holocaust to Him with the same aims of charity.[88]

Mystical union with the Father is love so pure and perfect that it inebriates the soul. The Father's blessing is the experience of paternal tenderness, which informs the soul of its dignity in the Father's love. How can we please Abba, Father? By letting Jesus reign in us. Let Him imprint Himself upon our souls, so that when the Father looks at us, He sees His Son. We need the Father's blessing because we are His children. Christ Himself received the Father's blessing.

Authenticity in Prayer

To pray is to come to Jesus as you are. In prayer before the Eucharistic Host, we can be small like Jesus in the Eucharist. In prayer

---

[88] *Prayer*, 26, 27.

before a crucifix, we can be vulnerable like Jesus on the Cross. In speaking with God, there is no need of masks, walls, or games. Our Lord sees us as we are. He knows our wounds better than we do. And He loves us.

Prayer is a sacred duty, a privilege of believers, a school of love that heals, restores, and endows. Fear not to pray about the most daring of your hopes. The Holy Spirit likely planted those seeds of hope within you. In prayer, release control except that of uniting your will to God. In letting God be God, we discover the relief that comes when God takes over. His plan for us is far more glorious than we can imagine. And when or if we fail to pray, let us bravely confront the reason we stopped praying and then begin again.

Prayer holds exquisite possibilities before the eyes of your soul. Be brave about acting upon inspirations you receive in prayer. Never give up. You'll see evidence of the fruit of your prayers by growth in virtue. Are you more patient and loving in your vocation? Jesus calls you to prayer because He loves you and wants to be with you. Yes, Christ Jesus desires your company! Conchita will help you to receive, listen, hear, and act in prayer.

Individual or Group Reflection

Ponder

"Have no anxiety about anything, but in everything by prayer and supplication with thanksgiving let your requests be made known to God. And the peace of God, which passes all understanding, will keep your hearts and your minds in Christ Jesus" (Phil. 4:6–7).

Engage

1. What has Conchita taught you about prayer?
2. Do you have a favorite prayer or type of prayer?
3. What are your obstacles to prayer, and how can you overcome them?

Pray

"Let anyone who thirsts come to Me and drink" (cf. Jn 7:37). Oh Jesus, in the world of souls, we are dying of thirst because we have strayed away from You, Who are the fountain of life! "Give us that water," we say today with the Samaritan woman. Give us to drink from that Heart, which is a divine wellspring of life that will flow without ceasing, even to eternal life. O Jesus, why do we not meditate daily upon Your Divine Words, where You throb with all the tenderness of Your Infinite Love? O Jesus, Your gospel is very life among us! You Who came to earth that we might have life and "life in abundance" (Jn 10:10).

Your doctrine is my breath, my drink, and the light that brings joy to my eyes. Your words are my strength in struggles. My rest, my peace, my best companions, and my reward. This is because You are there. My Doctor Who knows me and Who curses my every ailment. The Shepherd Who guides me as His beloved sheep. The King Whom I serve. The Friend from Whom I hold nothing back. The Husband Whom I worship. He Who has the remedy for every disorder. The Divine Word Himself. Amen.[89]

[89] Concepción Cabrera de Armida, *What Jesus Is Like* (Staten Island, NY: Alba House, 2008), 36–37.

5

Vision of the Cross:
Communion of Suffering

But rejoice in so far as you share Christ's sufferings, that you
may also rejoice and be glad when his glory is revealed.

—1 Peter 4:13

In Corinth, St. Paul zealously proclaimed, "For Christ did not send me to baptize but to preach the gospel, and not with eloquent wisdom, lest the cross of Christ be emptied of its power. For the word of the cross is folly to those who are perishing, but to us who are being saved it is the power of God" (1 Cor. 1:17–18).

Reflect a moment, *the word of the cross*: this word that St. Paul preaches is the Father's word that He spoke. It is His definitive expression of infinite love and mercy for mankind. Therefore, it is the power of God. It is powerful because it is a living Word, Christ's perfect sacrifice, the realization of salvation for humanity. It speaks life and love over death and darkness. This Cross that is folly in human terms is victory in Christ's terms. The Cross divides because it depicts suffering—the worst, most horrific pain. But look deeper and see beyond the beaten, raw, bleeding flesh of the God-Man hanging on the Cross. Look with the eyes of your soul into the eyes of Christ on the Cross. See in His eyes the tenderness, the love, the peace, the gift of self that Jesus is pouring out to you and me—every last drop of His precious blood.

We are the recipients of His loving victory on the Cross. Receive the gift. This gift of Jesus on the Cross caused the temple veil to be torn in two, the earth to quake, the sky to darken, the demons to be defeated, sins to be forgiven, man to be redeemed, and Heaven to be opened. This is the Cross that Paul heralded wherever he preached. It's a glorious mystery revealed by the Word and has eternal fruitfulness.

In the world's view, the Cross is madness, its message absurd, its power nil. God made provision for our time and culture, which rejects the word of the Cross of Jesus. A married laywoman, a mother, would arise to sound a trumpet and herald the power of the Cross like St. Paul. This power *cannot* be stripped away by all the sin and evil in the world. As Paul teaches, "Where sin increased, grace abounded all the more" (Rom. 5:20). God chose Conchita to echo the word of the Cross.

> Her message is not her own, not a message proceeding from her, but one that she has received to communicate it and to give it, because Conchita is foremost and above all a word of God for today's world. What is this word? It is Jesus and Jesus crucified. The doctrine of Conchita and her work in the Church is the Doctrine of the Cross; it is the Work of the Cross.[90]

Conchita's Message Is the Word of the Cross

Kairos is a Greek word meaning the right time or opportune moment. God's action in history comes at the precise time when

---

[90] *The Message of the Cross*, 5.

humanity needs the grace, message, or sign. Today, Conchita gives us a living word that calls us to love and to suffer for love of Jesus and souls. As she wrote in her book *Message of the Cross*:

> *The message of the Cross is of a vibrating* actuality *not because the world is willing to listen to it, but because it has a great need of it. The Cross is the symbol of redemption. It is a sign of the only salvation for the world, a perceptible and synthesized figure of our faith, a mysterious and distinctive sign of the Church which we use upon ourselves in the name of the Father, of the Son and of the Holy Spirit. It is of vital urgency to have a clear awareness of what the Cross of Christ means, of what it accomplishes in the mystery of the person. But in this world in which "God has died," the Cross of Christ has become unintelligible, absurd, without meaning.*[91]

Today, we live in a world in which "God has died" in the minds of many. Christ looks to His friends like Conchita to lift up the Cross with its living Word. Jesus looks to you and me to bear witness to the word of the Cross that is life, not death. Let us embrace Christ's covenant of love formed in the shape of His Cross.

Many people recoil at the idea of identifying with Christ Crucified. I suspect that you will be able to relate to what I will share now. In a long season of suffering, the weight of my cross was so heavy that I thought I'd literally die from the pain. The only solace I ever found was in uniting my suffering to Jesus on the Cross. When I placed my pain next to Christ's Passion, I gained perspective and purpose. One day in Adoration, while gazing on the crucifix above the altar, I realized clearly that Christ's Cross tells a breathtaking love story. We feel pain because we love and become vulnerable. We have given our heart to someone who has

---

[91] *The Message of the Cross*, 6.

wounded it. Well, Christ did the same. And by His wounds, ours are healed. No sadder human condition exists than not to love because it demands sacrifice or includes suffering.

When we experience our crosses, Jesus is with us mystically, holding us. We begin to look more like Jesus. Blessed Conchita helps us to understand that *this glorious cross* is a living blessing.

Suffering for the sake of suffering is evil (see 1 Cor. 13:3). Suffering has meaning and value only when united to Jesus' Cross. The Cross is the bridge to Resurrection and must be viewed in the light of Easter. If suffering is separated from love, it is not of God. Much of the pain that envelops the world today has nothing to do with God or love but only with sin and evil. Only Jesus, who is Love, redeems the world of pain and suffering. Jesus called Conchita to join in His act of redeeming love for the salvation of souls. Is He inviting us to do the same?

Jesus Assigns a New Name: *Cross of Jesus*

God gave Conchita a new name that denotes the meaning of her predestination, of her life. You will be called "Cross of Jesus" because that is the source of all the graces that you have received (*Account of Conscience*, 24, 85).[92]

Conchita's new name, *Cross of Jesus*, denoted her mission, message, and new identity. It's meaningful that Jesus gave a new name to Conchita. This is consistent with what God does when He enters into a covenant with a person. Abram was given the name *Abraham*. Jesus called Simon *Cephas*; Saul became *Paul*. What new name might the Lord assign me? Has God assigned a new name to you? This is something to ponder.

---

[92] *The Message of the Cross*, 6.

Vision of the Cross: Communion of Suffering

According to St. Augustine, the Virgin *conceived in her heart before she conceived in her womb.*[93] In a similar manner, at the revelation of her new name, Conchita conceived in her heart a new identity: Cross of Jesus. She prayerfully pondered what her new name meant, and the mystery would unfold over time.

Theologian Fr. Roberto de la Rosa, M.Sp.S., gave a talk to explain how God spoke to Conchita through a vision of the Cross.

How did God talk to Conchita? The *spiritual experience* of the contact with a living God is ineffable; it is useless to try to reduce it to concepts, to diagrams that necessarily fragment reality. That is why God talks to people through "symbols," concrete means of communication that cover the whole person because they appeal to the imagination, to the feelings, to the dreams, to the senses.

It suffices to remember the great moments of Revelation: the vision of Isaiah: "I saw the Lord seated on a high and lofty throne; his train filled the sanctuary. Above him stood seraphs ... and they were shouting these words to each other: 'Holy, holy, holy is Yahweh Sabaoth'" (Is. 6:2–3). The vision of Ezekiel: "I looked ... a great cloud with flashing and brilliant light around it, and in the middle, in the heart of the fire, a brilliance like that of amber, and in the middle, what seemed to be four living creatures.... The sight was like the glory of Yahweh" (Ez. 1:4, 28).

Conchita also had a vision. Its importance is decisive not for its charismatic nature but because it is a direct intervention, language, and communication from God.[94]

---

[93] See *Discourses* 215, 4.

[94] *The Message of the Cross,* 9.

Beautiful Holiness

Spiritual Betrothal

For Conchita, the year 1894 was vital and fruitful. She was thirty-one years of age and was caring for her husband, who was ill. She had given birth to three children: Francisco, Carlos, and Concha.

On January 23, 1894, she made a Total Surrender to Our Lord. She herself formulated the surrender and it was approved by her spiritual director. In response, Jesus gave her the grace of spiritual betrothal. It is a grace of mystical order, the kind that St. John of the Cross and St. Teresa of Ávila, in the sixth mansion, spoke about. It consists of an extraordinary union between the Word made flesh and a soul, and it is preparation for an even greater grace that the mystics call *spiritual marriage* or *transforming union*.[95]

Conchita writes in her *Diary*:

I was submerged in deep contemplation, very still, understanding many things in great depths, listening to the words of Jesus. He was doing it all. He put his hand on my head; his gaze seemed to bathe me completely. And I, all I could do was weep unceasingly. What could I tell you since I could think of nothing else to do but annihilate myself?

Jesus told me: "Now you are truly my spouse, and in my eyes, you are beautiful, with a veil of innocence and dress of penitence: I love you very much, and now I ask you to call me Spouse."

"Not that Jesus, for I am embarrassed."

"Ask me anything you want; today I cannot deny you anything."

"I ask that I may always do your will and save many souls."[96]

---

[95] Levy, *Priestly People*, 21.
[96] Levy, *Priestly People*, 22.

Then on February 4, 1894—which she considered one of the happiest days of her life—Conchita made perpetual vows of poverty, chastity (according to her married state), and obedience to God. Her vows also included obedience to her husband, her mother, her spiritual director, and her bishop. These vows preceded a defining grace in Conchita's spiritual itinerary. In imitation of Jesus, who made His perfect self-offering on the Cross, Conchita would learn the glory of the Cross.

The Vision of the Cross

That same month, February 1894, Conchita received a defining grace, the vision of the Cross. She was praying at a church in San Luis Potosí, the Iglesia de la Compañía. Later, she wrote:

I saw a great fire, like rays of light, almost white, very clear and brilliant, even more brilliant than electricity. In the center of this light was a very white dove with its wings extended and below it, in the depths of the immense light, was a large cross, very large, with a heart at its center. The heart had very sharp thorns that surrounded it and seemed to be pressing against it very tightly and even penetrating it. It hurt just to look at these thorns. There was a lance whose tip pierced the heart and made the blood pour out upon the cross.

The heart was alive, not just painted. It was a pulsating human heart, made of flesh, and yet, at the same time, glorified. It was as though surrounded by a moving fire-like material, as if inside a fire pit, and on top sprouting from its interior, another type of flame, like tongues of fire of greater intensity, distinct from the fire that surrounded the cross. These flames leapt about violently, like eruptions from a volcano, covering and then uncovering a smaller cross that was planted on the heart or maybe coming out from it.

Beautiful Holiness

Without my willing it or expecting it, I began to experience visions of this cross multiple times. This lasted two months or more, to the point that it was not only during times of prayer, but other times as well; during the day, at night, whenever, even in the middle of my daily tasks, that cross would appear to me.

"What is this?" I would ask myself. "What does the Lord want?"[97]

Conchita's inquiry, "What does the Lord want?" is very relatable for us. It's an important question to ask of Jesus along our journey. The Lord wants to direct our path. He reveals His plan for us in various signs along our way. Like Conchita, we must anticipate that Jesus will take hold of our hand and lead us on the path He chooses.

Later Jesus told Conchita:

The world is buried in sensuality, no longer is sacrifice loved and no longer is its sweetness known. I wish the Cross to reign. Today, it is presented to the world with my Heart, so that it may bring souls to make sacrifices. No true love is without sacrifices. It is only in My crucified heart that the ineffable sweetness of My Heart can be tasted. Seen from the outside, the Cross is bitter and harsh, but as soon as tasted, penetrating, and savoring it, there is no greater pleasure. Therein is the repose of the soul, the soul inebriated by love, therein delights, in its life.[98]

May I suggest that we take a moment to reflect on this message from Jesus? He beckons us specifically to make sacrifices of love for the salvation of souls. It is breathtaking that we can taste

---

[97] Levy, *Priestly People*, 23.
[98] *A Mother's Spiritual Diary*, 32.

the sweetness of His Heart only by the way of crucified love. He "wishes the Cross to reign." This reign begins within you and me. When Jesus says that sacrifice is no longer loved, it is a personal call to conversion of heart.

Conchita's vision of the Cross developed into a new, profound school of spirituality that continues to thrive. It became clear that Jesus desired to establish this new spirituality of the Cross by means of five apostolates founded by Conchita and called "Works of the Cross": (1) the Apostleship of the Cross, (2) the Sisters of the Cross of the Sacred Heart of Jesus, (3) the Covenant of Love Communities, (4) the Fraternity of Christ the Priest, and (5) the Missionaries of the Holy Spirit Priests. Conchita is the mother of these movements in the Church.

About a month after the vision, Conchita's sister Clara sketched the mysterious cross. Later, a painter from San Luis Potosí, Margarito Vela, created an oil painting of the cross in the vision. Conchita commented that the painting, though very good, portrayed only a slight idea of the vision because it couldn't capture the size of the big cross.

This image, known as the Cross of the Apostolate, is universally spread in drawings, sculptures, medals, and prints to be venerated by the five Works of the Cross. The Cross of the Apostolate graces the cover of this book.

The Symbolism of the Cross

The Lord told Conchita that the Cross represents His Gospel and that everything about the Cross is centered on love. The vision relates to Conchita's mission to remind the world of the power of love immolating itself in the Crucified One.

The rich symbolism of the Cross of the Apostolate has been studied by theologians. There's a consensus that, at the core, the spirituality of the Cross is based on the priesthood of Christ. Fr. Ricardo Zimbrón Levy, M.Sp.S., offers an explanation:[99]

1. The large cross represents the external passion of Jesus; it is the altar upon which Christ the priest offered the holocaust of his body and blood to the Father. It is also the cross that we must carry if we want to be disciples of Jesus. "If a man wishes to come after me, he must deny his very self, take up his cross and follow me" (Mt 16:24). It is our "daily cross" (cf. Lk 9:23), united with the Cross of Christ, which participates in its redemptive value and allows us to reach a very special intimacy with him.

2. But suffering of itself has no value: "If I hand over my body to be burned, but have not love, I gain nothing" (1 Cor. 13:3). For that reason, the symbol of the Holy Spirit hovers over the Cross, the Spirit that filled the heart of Christ, the Spirit that enkindled in Christ his immense love for the Father and all mankind, and that moved him to offer himself as a victim to God to remove our sins: "Moved by the Holy Spirit, he offered himself as a spotless offering to God" (Heb. 9:14). The Holy Spirit is also the one who reveals the value of the Cross of Christ to us and leads us to embrace it. Without the light of the Holy Spirit, the Cross of Christ can only be considered as a "scandal and madness." Only with the grace of the Holy Spirit can we understand that "what seems to be a mark of weakness in God is stronger than all the strength of men and what seems to

---

[99] Levy, *Priestly People*, 24.

be the foolishness of God, is wiser than all the wisdom of men" (1 Cor. 1:25).

3. The heart in the center of the Cross, embraced by flames, encircled by thorns, and pierced by a lance, signifies the immense love of Christ for his Father and for us, which reached its maximum expression in his painful surrender "unto death, death on the Cross" (Phil 2:8).

4. The small cross "planted upon the heart," symbolizes the interior sufferings of Christ, his pain over the lamentable situation of humankind who, because of sin, does not live in love. It symbolizes his sadness over the ingratitude and lack of comprehension of many souls, as well as his sorrow for being abandoned by his friends and for the infidelities of those who were associated most intimately with his work of salvation.

5. The light and clouds symbolize the loving presence of the Father, whose love is the beginning and origin of the salvation of man, and who is pleased by the perfect surrender of the Son, who out of obedience gives his life as a ransom for all mankind.[100]

Archbishop Luis M. Martinez offered a succinct explanation.

In the Cross of the Apostolate, one can find all the treasures that Jesus bequeathed to us. The Cross expresses Jesus' priesthood in a graphic manner. Therefore, to understand it and to comprehend our spirituality, we need to understand Jesus' priesthood.

Jesus' priesthood has one beginning: LOVE;

Jesus' priesthood has one essence: IMMOLATION;

---

[100] Levy, *Priestly People*, 25.

Jesus' priesthood has one end: THE GLORY OF GOD
AND THE SALVATION OF MEN.[101]

Archbishop Martinez developed the spirituality of the Cross
as it relates to priesthood in the Church:

> The priesthood of the Lord is the center of the Church,
> instituted to perpetuate his sacrifice and to distribute
> his fruits. It is the center of the new life, it is the center
> of history, and it is the center of the universe—because
> the only thing that satisfies the Father is the love of the
> Son, which manifests itself in his "obedience even unto
> death on the Cross." And all the joys that the Father
> encounters in his creatures, or the glory that he receives
> from them, are bound to the priesthood and the sacrifice
> of Christ.[102]

The Vision Bears Fruit:
The Apostolate of the Cross

The Apostolate of the Cross is "an association of Christians in the
Church who, moved by the Holy Spirit, follow Jesus Christ priest
and victim, contemplative and solidary, and who, in communion
with Jesus, collaborate with His salvific mission. The Apostolate
is open to all People of God: lay persons, religious, and ordained
ministers." ... The symbol of the Cross of the Apostolate and the
intercessory cry of Conchita, "*Jesus, Savior of all the people, save
them!*" embodies their lifelong mission.[103]

---

[101] Levy, *Priestly People*, 25.

[102] Levy, *Priestly People*, 25.

[103] Statutes and Regulation of the Apostleship of the Cross, June
2020, http://www.apcross.org/Statutes&Regulations-AC-ENG-
LISH-JUNE-2020.pdf.

Conchita wrote about the beginning of the apostolate:

In February, my spiritual director wrote to me and stated, "You will save many souls, but through the apostolate of the cross." He was referring to the fact that I, through my sacrifices, united with those of Our Lord, would save many souls. But upon reading the document, when I reached the part where it states "apostolate of the cross," ... I felt a world of light that made me see that not only could I be an apostle of the cross, but that thousands of souls could join me in being that, too. This was the origin of the Apostolate of the Cross.[104]

Remember, Conchita was only thirty-one years old, a wife and mother with many duties. The year 1894 proved to be a pivotal time when her mystical union with Jesus grew deeper. Conchita found a way to order her life according to her manifold duties. She was able to do this because, for her, everything is an exercise of incarnational love. With the vision of the Cross, Conchita's spiritual life accelerated.

The statutes of the Apostolate of the Cross encourage a spirituality of self-offering love, an invitation to union with Christ Crucified, Priest and Victim. The statutes require a commitment of the members consistent with canonical associations in the Church and so may also serve as a basic rule of life for all laity. They are as follows:

1. To do the will of the Father with love
2. To be docile to the inspirations of Holy Spirit
3. To lovingly embrace our daily cross, and, inspired by the Gospel, fulfill our duties according to our state of life

[104] Levy, *Priestly People*, 26.

4. To offer Jesus to the Father and offer ourselves in union with Him in all realities of life

5. To offer Mass and Communion for ordained ministers and vocations

6. To give witness to the faith and proclaim the Gospel

7. To commit ourselves to building a more just and dignified world

8. Thereby to extend the reign of the Holy Spirit through the formation of a priestly people, in union with the Virgin Mary and following her example[105]

Conchita's vision of the Cross and its developing spirituality is as lofty as it is practical. It can enliven all vocations: priests, nuns, parents, and children alike. Each vocation experiences the intersection of love with suffering. A priest is a victim of divine love and personally participates in Christ's perfect sacrifice. A religious sister is a bride of Christ whose spiritual marriage is intimately lived with Christ crucified and risen. Spouses and children who sometimes suffer sicknesses, strife, deaths, and temporal worries identify with the pierced heart of Jesus. Love suffers because love cares. And the more we love and care, the more we resemble and radiate Christ.

Conchita's Participation

While Conchita inspired and promoted the Works of the Cross, she participated in them only as she was able to without compromising her marriage and children and without conceding her daily spiritual itinerary of prayer. Fr. Levy explains how Conchita maintained her family and her apostolates.

---

[105] Statutes and Regulations of the Apostleship of the Cross.

Conchita was not someone who could have committed to very many meetings or activities. Her time was taken up with her pregnancies and the births of her nine children, amidst baby bottles and sleepless nights and as she put it, "amid sewing clothes, problems with servants, economic difficulties, and family parties." ...

Therefore, she is the perfect secular model. She represents those who have much to do in this world. But just because they are busy does not mean that they are not invited to holiness. It is precisely by the offering up of their daily work, which is many times painful and full of suffering, that they progress in holiness.[106]

We can appreciate Father's words that being busy does not mean we are not invited to holiness. It seems that God keeps busy His closest friends, the saints, and while they work and pray, He sanctifies them. But the Lord commanded that we rest also, especially on Sundays! Conchita selflessly served both the domestic and the universal Church. The Holy Spirit magnified her gift to both. Conchita's vision of the Cross initiated a season wherein she would produce more fruit for the Church.

A Religious Community for Women

In 1894, the same year Conchita saw the vision of the Cross, she received the first promptings to start a religious community of women to live the spirituality of Jesus, Priest and Victim. "I suddenly received an internal vision," Conchita recalls in her *Diary*, "of an immense procession of religious women with a large red cross on their backs":

---

[106] Levy, *Priestly People*, 30.

They were processing side by side and took a long time to pass me by. I was astonished and did not understand what this meant, so I remained silent. Suddenly, I heard the voice of my Jesus, who told me:

"There shall be a congregation which shall be called the Oasis because there is where my heart shall rest. And thus, shall the religious women be who will form it."

He told me that after the Congregation of the Sisters of the Cross was approved, there would follow a congregation of religious men, his brothers, and they, too, would be approved by the Church. Both congregations would give him much glory.

On Holy Thursday in 1894, after I received Communion, he told me: "Within a few years you will adore me at the Oasis on this memorable day, amidst many living crosses.... You will be the foundation of this congregation, a foundation that is not seen, but that nonetheless carries the entire weight of the building."[107]

Often saintly people like Conchita are not visible in apostolates. Nonetheless, they bear the weight of God's work. Remember, those who remain hidden in their sacrificial spiritual works are building up the Church. In God's eyes, they are necessary for the work of redemption. Those who help bear the weight of the Church are sometimes hidden in monasteries and cloisters but also in family homes where parents pray and labor in love raising children in the Faith.

Two years following this message, in 1895, Conchita's family moved from San Luis Potosí to Mexico City because of her husband's employment. In 1896, Jesus told Conchita that the Oasis

---

[107] Levy, *Priestly People*, 32.

would be established the following year. Her many prayers would finally be answered.

The Sisters of the Cross of the Sacred Heart of Jesus

At the start of 1897, Conchita and Fr. Alberto Mir, S.J., discerned that it was an opportune time to begin searching for vocations for the founding of the Sisters of the Cross. The Apostleship of the Cross had begun, and there were many lay associates in that community. Fr. Mir searched for signs of vocations among those in the ranks who were outstanding in their commitment to the Apostleship. Eventually, he discovered three young women who were agreeable to establishing the first convent. With the help of Conchita's older brother Don Octaviano Cabrera they rented a house and furnished it. The first "Oasis" was founded in simplicity and poverty on May 3, 1897, at 24 Calle de Popotla. Conchita was present and attended the Mass and celebration. "*Thank you, my God, thank you a thousand times!*"

Of course, Conchita returned to her home to care for her husband and children with the same abundance of love. We can imagine her joy in seeing the fulfillment of her hope and the fidelity of God's promise. She was probably relieved that she wasn't imagining the things that God spoke to her.

The order grew rapidly; by July there were seven postulants. Bishop Ramón Ibarra invested them in the habit of novices, and Fr. Mir gave them daily instruction. They started their life of community with much fervor and grace. A central charism of the order is to pray for priests — or, as Conchita put it,

The holy duty to supplicate to God that priests be his glory, configured each time more perfectly with the Supreme and

Eternal Priest, and that through them, the world of today will receive the grace of God. The motto of this institution and the program of its life are the words of Christ, "For them I was consecrated."[108]

Here, Conchita's charism of intercession for the holiness of priests developed into an ecclesial apostolate. The Lord would continue to root this charism in the Church since He told Conchita that He desired priests to shine with the light of holiness.

This Beautiful Cross: Jesus, Save Them!

Five years prior to the vision of the Cross, Jesus told Conchita that her mission was that of saving souls. She didn't fully understand the weight of the mission or how it would be realized in her life with her family. The 1894 vision clarified what Jesus had told her in 1889. Fr. Philipon wrote about how Conchita internalized the vision:

From then on, Conchita tried very hard to live out her own symbol, in hidden and quiet sacrifice, always within the framework of her family life as a wife and a mother. For her, once seen, that Vision began to draw back the veil that was hiding the plans of God. Now, the word of the Lord, which had been like a barely audible melody during her first spiritual exercises in 1889 — *Your mission is that of saving souls* — returned to resonate now in its full orchestration, as the principal theme of a concert: *Jesus, Savior of all mankind! Save them! Save them!*[109]

---

[108] Levy, *Priestly People*, 35.
[109] *A Mother's Spiritual Diary*, 34.

Continue the Work of St. Margaret Mary: His Heart and His Cross

At the time that Conchita lived (1862–1937), Margaret Mary Alacoque (1647–1690) was a "Blessed." In her *Diary*, Conchita wrote what Jesus told her about Blessed Margaret Mary.

St. Margaret Mary was chosen to reveal the burning love of the Sacred Heart to a world that needed the confirmation of divine mercy—just as Blessed Conchita reveals the interior sufferings of the Heart of Jesus on the Cross to a world that has forsaken sacrificial love. Conchita's vision and doctrine present hope to a languishing world in need of the Heart and the Cross of Jesus.

Fr. Philipon writes about Conchita's connection to St. Margaret Mary:

> The Lord reveals to Conchita that she will have to continue in the Church the work of Margaret Mary. Conchita is deeply embarrassed by the idea, but she tells her spiritual director in obedience,
>
> *"Father, I hesitate to tell you this, but it was Jesus Himself who evoked the memory of Margaret Mary. He told me that He had chosen both of us, one for one thing, the other for another, that is, one to reveal His Love and the other to reveal His suffering.... Do you understand me?"* (*Diary*, May 1894).[110]

In a letter to Fr. José Alzola, a Jesuit provincial, Conchita shares what Jesus told her:

> *The Apostolate of the Cross is the work which continues and completes that of My Heart, and which was revealed to Blessed Margaret Mary. I tell you that this does not mean only My*

---

[110] *A Mother's Spiritual Diary*, 33.

external Cross as a divine instrument of Redemption. This Cross is presented to the world to bring souls toward My Heart, pierced on the Cross. The essence of this Work consists in making known the Interior Sufferings of My Heart which are ignored, and which constitute for Me a more painful Passion than that which My Body underwent on Calvary, on account of its intensity and its duration, mystically perpetuated in the Eucharist.

I tell you, up to this day, the world has known the love of My Heart manifested in Margaret Mary, but it was reserved for present times to make known its suffering, the symbols of which I had shown simply and in an external way. I say again, there must be a penetration into the Interior of this boundless ocean of bitterness and an extension of knowledge of it throughout the world for bringing about the union of the suffering of the faithful with the immensity of the sufferings of My Heart, for their suffering is mostly wasted. I wish them to profit from it by way of the Apostleship of the Cross for the benefit of souls and for consolation of My Heart.

I was delighted to discover the connection between Blessed Conchita and St. Margaret Mary. Thanks to my mother, I have a lifelong devotion to the Sacred Heart; and twice I visited and prayed at the tomb of St. Margaret Mary. Her incorrupt body rests on the altar in the chapel at Paray-le-Monial in France.

Jesus wants the world to profit by uniting its vast suffering to the immensity of His suffering on the Cross. He wants to prevent us from wasting suffering. This message is rejected today. Jesus searches for men and women of all vocations to be brave in their witness to the power of the Cross. How often do we consider the interior sufferings of Jesus and offer consolation or reparation?

To be clear, we should pray for the alleviation of suffering and healing. God is a miracle-worker, and we started this book with a miracle of healing. But whatever suffering remains, if the healing doesn't come, then the offering of suffering in union with the Cross is a powerful act of love.

Speaking of devotion to the Sacred Heart, St. Margaret Mary said, "I do not know of any other exercise in the spiritual life that is more calculated to raise a soul in a short amount of time to the height of perfection and to make it taste the true sweetness to be found in the service of Jesus Christ."[111]

Almost two hundred years later, Jesus told Conchita, *"This Cross is presented to the world to bring souls toward My Heart, pierced on the Cross. The essence of this Work consists in making known the Interior Sufferings of My Heart which are ignored."*[112]

---

[111] Quoted in "The 12 Promises of the Sacred Heart of Jesus to St. Margaret Mary Alacoque," Welcome His Heart, https://welcome-hisheart.com/12-promises.

[112] *A Mother's Spiritual Diary*, 33.

Individual or Group Reflection

Ponder

"If any man would come after me, let him deny himself and take up his cross daily and follow me" (Luke 9:23).

Engage

1. How has Conchita's vision of the Cross touched you?
2. How has suffering impacted your life?
3. How is the power of the Cross active in your life?

Pray

Although we do not deserve it, we open our arms and our whole soul with holy enthusiasm so that this Heart of Love can empty out its bitter sufferings into them, because we experience our greatest happiness when consoling Him. At your side and with your help, Mary, what can we fear? I know that you are ever at the foot of Calvary. This being the case, let all the crucifixions come, because in the shadow of our blessed Mother nothing will be too hard for us, for we can do all things in him who comforts us. Amen.[113]

---

[113] *What Jesus Is Like*, 95.

6

The Mystical Incarnation: Highest Grace

Christ . . . lives in me.

—Galatians 2:20

Conchita didn't have a Pauline Damascus moment of radical conversion. She experienced a transformative central grace, however, called the "mystical incarnation." Jesus said, "If any man loves me . . . my Father will love him: and we will come to him and will make our home with him" (John 14:23). This great promise of Jesus is realized dynamically in Conchita's highest grace.

The spiritual life is transformation, inhabitation, and union with God. Our longing for a Savior who reconciles us with God is fulfilled in Christ's coming. The gift of the Incarnation is the realization of God's union with man. The essence of love is incarnational.

In his Letter to the Ephesians, Paul taught that Christianity is gift and experience: "that Christ may live in your hearts through faith . . . rooted and grounded in love" (3:17). Faith gives us roots, and divine love give us wings. Christ in you is life. Love is mutual possession.

To the Galatians, Paul further described the Christian life: "I have been crucified with Christ; it is no longer I who live, but

Christ who lives in me; and the life I now live in the flesh I live by faith in the Son of God, who loved me and gave himself for me" (2:20). Paul boldly testifies to transformation in Christ; it is the heart of discipleship. Jesus gave Paul a new identity and a heart like His own.

Paul referred to the Church as Christ's Body and spoke of Christ's spousal love for the Church. The spousal language of the Eternal Word reveals God's desire for divine intimacy with His people. Divine love creates, unites, and is fruitful and dynamic. Paul experienced Jesus not only on the road to Damascus but every moment afterward.

The many theologians, clergy, and religious sisters who have written about the mystical incarnation agree that this grace is not easily captured in words. Sr. Laura Linares Romero, R.C.S.C.J., writes in her dissertation, "We are going to enter into Conchita's experience of God and this a privilege that we must do with 'bare feet' ... because it is to enter into her intimacy with God. What a great gift!"[114] Humbly, we will approach this subject, hoping that Jesus and Conchita will help us benefit from it.

Sr. Linares's dissertation and the book *Mystical Incarnation* by Dom Bernardo Oliver, O.C.S.O., provide the most updated writings on the mystical incarnation. Conchita's *Diary* is the central original source of all that has been written about this defining grace.

The mystical incarnation is not reserved for Conchita. Fr. Domenico states, "While the members of the Family of the Cross

---

[114] Sr. Laura Linares Romano, R.C.S.C.J., *The Mystical Incarnation and Its Dynamism in Concepción Cabrera De Armida* 3rd ed. (Ediciones Religiosas del Sagrado Corazón de Jesús, 2018), 4. Fr. Domenico and Sr. Linares, a priest and a religious sister in the orders initiated by Conchita, have generously provided an English translation of the third edition of her dissertation, written originally in Spanish.

inherit this call to the mystical incarnation, according with each one's grace, the grace is opened to all Christians because of the grace of their baptism. I think it's important to underline the perspective that is it open to all."[115]

A Baptismal Grace

It is breathtaking to consider the degree of transformation in Christ available to the baptized. Have you ever thanked your parents for taking you to the baptismal font? Baptism is a dynamic sacrament that animates our entire life to the degree that we cooperate with grace. Baptismal grace incorporates us into Christ and His Church and makes us anointed participants in the divine life of the Trinity. Imagine!

Explaining the mystical incarnation, Jesus tells Conchita, "*Look, My daughter, the mystical incarnation is a transforming grace in the sense of assimilating the creature with its Model, which is Me. It is a transformative, unifying grace.*"[116] Jesus would unfold this very profound transformation of soul incrementally for Conchita.

Dom Bernardo Olivera writes of the universal call to transformation in Christ, "The Church is Christ's Body and each one is a member of Her and of Him. This is to say that the whole of Christian life can be summarized into the double inhabitation, both unifying and transformative."[117] Further he explains,

> Tradition is also rich in images. It is sufficient to recall the "divinization," the "pneumatization," the "Christification," the "betrothal," the "filiation," and the "transforming union" in reference to the Christian experience, in whole

[115] Fr. Domenico Di Raimondo, M.Sp.S., e-mail, July 22, 2022.
[116] *The Mystical Incarnation and Its Dynamism*, 6.
[117] *The Mystical Incarnation and Its Dynamism*, 11.

or in part. Obviously, each one of these representations offer various stages and steps, which prepare a gradual and progressive itinerary.[118]

Each of these words contain a world of meaning about transformation in Christ Jesus. And this is our calling facilitated by the Holy Spirit. Jesus pursues you and me on our spiritual journey through hills and valleys, on our series of Good Fridays and Easter Sundays. Striving for transformation in Christ, we fall backward and leap forward, in seasons of shadows and periods of illumination. Have you ever tried to hide from Jesus? He finds you! Christ pursues us, makes known His indwelt presence, gives gifts, and leads us into surprising depths of loving relationship and friendship. The richness of this mutual love is mysterious but real. Saints give their life for it. Throughout millennia, Christians give witness to transformation in Christ.

Conchita's *central grace* deepened her communion with Jesus. This grace was for God's glory and for the enrichment of souls. The Lord chose a simple laywoman to initiate an important mystical development.[119] With this intriguing background, we ask the Holy Spirit to help us understand the mystical incarnation as a grace for the baptized. Let us approach it with simplicity and depth, savoring Conchita's experience of the Lord.

---

[118] Dom Bernardo Olivera, O.C.S.O., *Mystical Incarnation in Concepción Cabrera de Armida* (Modesto, CA: Sisters of the Cross of the Sacred Heart of Jesus, 2009), 10-11.

[119] During the study of Conchita's writings in the process of canonization, the Holy See wanted to have more clarity about this grace. Fr. Domenico advised that the Holy See request an ample theological study to clarify the experience of Conchita, its theological implications, her mystical life, her frequent recourse to dialogues and conversations with Jesus, and so forth.

Our Christian Life

Because Christianity is *a life*, a Christian life cannot easily be defined according to specific formulas. In the lives of the saints, there are various personal articulations of the one New Testament. The dynamism of divine love flowers in new ways. Seemingly within each soul is a distinct ray of divine life that is that soul's, but it also belongs to Christ and to the Church.

Dom Bernardo outlines five points belonging to Christian life:

1. Entrance into the Kingdom of God (synoptic Gospels)
2. Entrance into eternal life (Gospel of John)
3. Life in Christ or life in the Spirit (Letters of St. Paul)
4. Pilgrimage toward the heavenly Sanctuary (Letter to the Hebrews)
5. Life in faith with works (Letter of St. James)[120]

These points summarize one call that is ours: to be wholly transformed in Jesus Christ. "Abide in me as I abide in you. Just as the branch cannot bear fruit by itself unless it abides in the vine, neither can you unless you abide in me. I am the vine, you are the branches. Those who abide in me and I in them bear much fruit, because apart from me you can do nothing" (John 15:4–5). Clearly, whatever good I may do, it is Christ in me at work. On our own, we have no life.

Providence and the Mystical Incarnation

We frame the experience of the mystical incarnation as part of the Christian life, Dom Bernardo explains:

> The grace that Conchita received on March 25, 1906 (Feast of the Annunciation), may be primarily considered in this

---

[120] Olivera, *Mystical Incarnation*, 10.

way: an explosion or outburst of her feminine and motherly experience of the inhabitation and transformation in Christ which had been operating within her for a long time and now was definitely irreversible. It would expand itself throughout her future life.[121]

Or, as Our Lord put it to Conchita,

> When I put the seal of the Holy Spirit upon your soul on the day of your Baptism, I gifted you with the mystical incarnation, and this grace kept on developing itself without your realizing it, until it achieved its goal, sharing the journey of My life in you and clarifying for you the ideal that I had in your soul, transforming it into Myself and deifying it (A.C. Vol 48: pp 149-150, May 31, 1927).[122]

Providence had been at work in Conchita from her conception in the mind of the Holy Trinity. This is also true for us; our lives are not accidents. Little did Conchita realize as a child or a teenager or a newlywed what hidden gifts rested within her soul. I think God's mysterious work within us is altogether fascinating. We are full of potentiality! Our part is to remain in the state of grace so that what God seeded in us will come to fruition.

Conchita was so very diligent in the care of her soul and her spiritual life during her long journey. She was well prepared by Jesus to receive the grace of the mystical incarnation.

Dom Bernardo presents a timeline of mystical graces that Conchita received. Note how Providence carefully constructed Conchita's foundation:

---

[121] Olivera, *Mystical Incarnation*, 12.
[122] Olivera, *Mystical Incarnation*, 12.

- First spiritual exercises: "Your mission is that of saving souls" (August 1889)
- "My Father has His gaze on you" (1892 or 1891)
- Branding of the monogram "JHS" (January 14, 1894)
- "Betrothal": the union of wills in complete surrender to her crucified Spouse (January 23, 1894)
- Vision of the Cross of the Apostolate (February 1894)
- Purification of the human substance: purity and humility (November 16, 1895)
- "Ray of warmth and light" between God and the soul (August 31, 1896)
- Grace of "betrothal" with the Word, in the Spirit, before the Father (February 9, 1897)
- Contact with the purity of the Holy Spirit (June 17, 1899)
- Piercing of the heart (July 25, 1906)
- Mystical incarnation: mutual possession as in a single substance (March 25, 1906)
- "You are My host" (1906)
- "This is My Body, this is My Blood" (February 22, 1909)
- "You do not belong to yourself, you belong to the Church" (February 2, 1911)
- New awareness: "This is My Body …" (1915–1916)
- Assimilation to Mary, Mother (June 10, 1917)
- "To love with the Holy Spirit" (1927)
- The "*third love*" (1931–1932)
- "As if I dripped of purity and divinity" (August 11, 1934)
- "I abandon myself to the God that abandons me" (October 6, 1936)

This timeline of grace is sublimely rich. We begin to grasp the extravagant generosity of Jesus, who builds grace upon grace to effect transforming union with His creature. We see the foreshadowing and then the imprint of the grace of the mystical incarnation upon Conchita.

And although we are amazed by this list of graces, we might be surprised if we were to list all the graces of our lifetime. They would tell God's love story for you and me also.

Let us continue to unfold the glories of the mystical incarnation.

"In summary," says Dom Bernardo, "the central grace of Conchita's life, the mystical incarnation, enlightens and revitalizes everything that precedes and everything that will follow. This grace plunges its roots in baptism and will never end, not even in death (A.C. Vol 61: p.133, April 19, 1933)."[123] After receiving this capital grace, Conchita lived it in these terms: "uniting, transforming, maternal, foundational, Marian, Christological, ecclesial, priestly, Eucharistic, redemptive, Trinitarian, paternal, pneumatic. ... "[124]

Preparation: The Promised Grace

Conchita was thirty-five years old in 1897 and was raising seven children. In preparation for the mystical incarnation, she received a preeminent grace on February 9, 1897. Some scholars and some saints have called this "the grace of transforming union," or "spiritual marriage."[125] On February 14, five days after this grace, the Lord announced:

> Prepare yourself for the day on which the Church celebrates the incarnation of the divine Word. On that day, I came down to unite Myself with Mary, taking flesh in her most pure womb, to save the world. On that day, I want to unite Myself spiritually with your soul and bestow a new life upon you, a divine and immortal life,

---

[123] Olivera, *Mystical Incarnation*, 14.
[124] Olivera, *Mystical Incarnation*, 14.
[125] Olivera, *Mystical Incarnation*, 16.

in time and in eternity.... Prepare yourself, purify yourself, cleanse yourself, because the gift that is being prepared for you is very great, very great (A.C. Vol. 9: pp. 33–34, February 14, 1897).[126]

Conchita diligently tried to prepare herself, believing that the foretold grace was imminent. Over the years, Conchita continued to prepare, but at times, she simply forgot about it. Nine years passed before the promised grace was bestowed upon her. I'm reminded of the Scripture passage "For still the vision awaits its time; it hastens to the end—it will not lie. If it seems slow, wait for it; it will surely come, it will not delay" (Hab. 2:3). If the Lord promises something, wait for it, because He is always faithful to His word. And the process of waiting holds its own treasures.

In Conchita's Words

Best of all, though, is to hear Blessed Conchita describe the mystical incarnation in her own words. Here is her *Diary* entry for March 25, 1906:

Before Mass, prostrate before the tabernacle, I humbled myself as much as I could. I asked Him for pardon. I renewed my vows to Him. I offered to not fill my heart with dirt, with earthly things as up to now. Thus emptied, I received Him in Holy Communion. I had wished to tell Him a thousand things in the "Incarnatus" and I did not even know at what time it took place.

Then, in the first mementos of the Mass, I suddenly experienced the presence of my Jesus near me, hearing His divine voice say to me (Oh my God, can this be true? But how not, if I experience You, if I touch You, if I am loving You here, as if I had just received Holy Communion, Jesus of my soul!): "Here I am; I desire

---

[126] Olivera, *Mystical Incarnation*, 16.

to become *mystically incarnate in your heart. I accomplish what I offer—I have been preparing you in a thousand ways, and the time has come to fulfill My promise. Receive Me."*

Then I experienced a joy with inexpressible shame. I thought that I had already received Him in Holy Communion but as if He had guessed my thoughts, He continued: *"No, it is not that way. Today you have received Me in another, different way. I am taking possession of your heart. I incarnate Myself in your heart, never to be separated again. Only sin can move you away from Me and I warn you that every creature that also occupies it will diminish my Real Presence—that is, in its effects, because I cannot be diminished.... This is a very lofty grace that My kindness has been preparing for you. Humble yourself and be thankful for it."*

"But, Lord, may I be bold enough to ask You, what it was that You had offered me, that which You had asked of me? Was it not a betrothal?"

"It has already been fulfilled: this grace is infinitely greater."

"My Jesus, is it spiritual marriage?"

"It is more, because marriage is a type of union that is more external, but to be incarnate, to live and grow in your soul, without ever leaving it, to possess you and for you to possess Me in one substance, not only giving Me your life without reservation, but also Myself to your soul, is a compenetration that you are not able to understand. This is the grace of graces" (A.C. Vol. 22: pp 170-173).[127]

We have glimpsed into the soul of Blessed Conchita—her experience of Christ. Her dialogue with Jesus shows her simplicity and purity. There is much for us to ponder here.

---

[127] Olivera, *Mystical Incarnation*, 17-19.

The Mystical Incarnation: Highest Grace

Dom Bernardo connects Conchita's grace with the Mass:

The experience took place in a liturgical context: the Eucharistic celebration of the day of the feast of the Incarnation. After the Creed (Conchita refers to this point as the "Incarnatus"), when the Roman Canon had already begun, coming to the first "memento" something happened: she received the grace of the mystical incarnation.[128]

Sr. Linares asks, "Why the Incarnation?" Then she connects it to Conchita's spiritual exercises of 1889, when Conchita heard, "Your mission is to save souls":

Yes, my Adored Jesus: now I see that to fulfill my mission of saving souls I will succeed only by having You, only by offering You. Now yes, my thirst to save souls will be quenched, at least I will be certain that with that price graces are indeed bought for them. Now yes, I am happy in my own misery, because it is not I who buys, who works, who lives, but Jesus in Me, the Word in me, God doing everything in His poor creature, blessed a thousand times! (CC 22, 408–416: 21 July 1906).[129]

Jesus responds: "You would be nothing alone, or your merit would be greatly diminished, but in union with the Word, you are like the key to heaven, which is the cross, and with it, you can open the eternal treasures for the salvation of the world. You have Me, Treasure of treasures, and with Me, you can profit with the heavenly Father, whatever you want. Do you see the greatness of the mystical incarnation in your soul?" (V. 8, pp. 171–172).[130]

---

[128] Olivera, *Mystical Incarnation*, 19.
[129] *The Mystical Incarnation*, 18.
[130] *The Mystical Incarnation*, 18.

Two Days Later: The Chain of Love

Having bestowed this noble grace upon His faithful daughter, Jesus provided a way for Conchita to live their mystical union moment to moment. On March 27, 1906, two days after the mystical incarnation, Jesus spoke:

> You see, you are going to make a chain. Every hour of your life shall be a golden link of this chain. I want this chain to remain unbroken until your death. I shall choose many other souls that will, without interruption, continue to add more links to this chain that I want you to start.[131]

Jesus repeatedly told Conchita to "fill each hour of her life loving God and loving others. He said her love would be a source of all the virtues. That is why this practice became known as the "Chain of Love."[132] This practice consists of an hourly offering of Jesus to the Father and, in union with Jesus, the offer of her life. Conchita told Jesus that she didn't mean to disappoint Him but she would forget to make the offering.

Jesus told Conchita that He understands the limitation that exists in His creature and that it is possible to offer Him to the Father without words, as they are not necessary. Rather, the Lord asks for a simple interior look, pure and unworldly, with a plea of tenderness and charity. It was a perpetual thought of love that Jesus was asking from Conchita. This is pleasing to Jesus and is the essence of offering the Chain of Love.

This practice of offering the Chain of Love can become a lifestyle, a way of practicing the virtues, especially love. Sometimes Jesus would ask Conchita, "What are you doing?" and she'd say,

[131] Levy, *Priestly People*, 187.
[132] Levy, *Priestly People*, 187.

"I'm cooking." Jesus would say, "Don't forget about Me." He was teaching Conchita how to incorporate the mystical incarnation into her daily duties, growing in the virtues of Christian life.

Later, Conchita wrote:

> *I have begun to offer Jesus to the Eternal Father, just as Jesus told me to do; I do this frequently for the salvation of the world. And how content and empowered I feel having this celestial treasure I can use for the good of others! Now my thirst for saving souls shall be quenched because I am certain that with this treasure, I can obtain the graces that others need.*[133]

On April 2, 1906, Conchita received from Jesus a set of fourteen rules—a spiritual program for the Chain of Love. Its main objective is for souls who practice it to advance on the journey of transformation in Christ.

1. Practice true humility.
2. Be pure of mind and body.
3. Be a person of prayer.
4. Practice self-effacement and modesty.
5. Live the poverty of Christ.
6. Forget oneself so as to think only of Jesus.
7. Practice detachment from all earthly affections.
8. Love the Mother of Jesus and imitate her example.
9. Do everything with purity of intention.
10. Be totally honorable and righteous.
11. Accept suffering with love.
12. Love Christ selflessly and with complete surrender.
13. Respond faithfully to the grace of God.
14. Live in Christ and only for Him.

---

[133] Levy, *Priestly People*, 188–189.

Beautiful Holiness

Development of the Mystical Incarnation in Conchita

The development of the mystical incarnation in Conchita took place over the course of many years, as seen in the timeline below. Transformation in Christ is a graced process led by the Holy Spirit through seasons of the soul.

- 1907-1908. The Offering. "Jesus told Conchita, '*You have with you the sacrosanct Victim of Calvary and of the Eucharist, which you can constantly offer to the Eternal Father for the salvation of the world. This is the most precious fruit of the great favor that I have worked in you by becoming incarnate in your heart.... My Father will ask you to give an account of this sublime co-redeeming act that he has placed in your hands; you are rich with the treasure of heaven, and you must constantly profit from it, in favor of sinners, of your present and future children.*' (CC 28, 63-64: 19 Oct. 1907)."

- 1909. Transforming Union: This is My Body, My Blood. "Jesus said, '*Look, since the mystical incarnation, your body is like My Body, and your blood is like My Blood, because I have the property of transforming.... Souls are sinking, daughter, and it is necessary to save them. Ask for their salvation, repeat to the Eternal Father to save them, and tell Him with Me, "This is My Body, this is My Blood." May your children repeat these same words. I promise you that heaven will open upon hearing them from pure and loving hearts.*' (CC 32, 119-126: 22 February 1909)."

- 1917. Together with the Heart of Mary for Priests. Jesus explains, "*I want you to repeat, and in union with these words make yourself responsible for what they say: 'This is My Body, this is My Blood.' And thus, offer yourself to the Eternal Father in My union, by the most intimate members of the church, My priests,*

> but in union with Mary. *She, the creature most transformed in*
> *Me, as I have told you, repeated this same thing in her great*
> *and growing union, which made the Eternal Father smile, and*
> *pour Himself out in graces* (CC 41, 340–341 (8-7-1917)."[134]

According to Dom Bernardo, the three stages of the mystical incarnation are these:

1. Priestly Stage: He offers the Word … and you in union with Him.
2. Eucharistic Stage: This is my Body.
3. Marian Stage: Do everything in union with Mary.[135]

The three stages correspond with the above timeline in which Conchita matured spiritually to carry the weight of this grace. Admittedly, she was not perfectly faithful to all of Christ's expectations, but she persevered.

Conchita's Maternal Priesthood and Spiritual Motherhood

When I inquired of Fr. Domenico if the grace of the mystical incarnation was similar to St. Teresa of Ávila's transverberation, or mystical marriage, he replied that Conchita's grace is much more closely connected to the Blessed Mother in the Incarnation of the Word. Beautiful!

Conchita's mystical maternal priesthood was the development of baptismal grace enlivened by the mystical incarnation. She would identify profoundly with the Blessed Mother.

She asked Jesus that her heart would beat in unison with His; that what He loves, she might love; that what He suffered, she might suffer. "Jesus tells her, 'By receiving Me in the mystical incarnation

---

[134] Linares Romero, *The Mystical Incarnation*, 10, 11, 12.
[135] Olivera, *Mystical Incarnation*, 7.

in your soul, you receive Me and in Me the Church with all her priests' (CC 53, 33-40: 29 Nov. 1928)."[136] Sr. Linares elaborates: "Jesus will explain to her that when Conchita received the grace of the Mystical Incarnation, Jesus did not enter alone, *but with all His Mystical Body*, which is the Church. She must carry in her maternal heart the Church, especially priests, and give herself unconditionally in their favor."[137] Or, as Our Lord tells Conchita, *"By the reflection of Mary, in the mystical incarnation, your heart will be like a storehouse of these graces for the good of all priests"* (CC 54, 160-161: 25 Nov. 1929).[138]

"You must love priests as I love them," says Jesus; *"the good and the not good, with My same heart, tenderness, and charity, as He who gave blood and life for their illustrious vocations and for their sanctification"* (CC 54, 29: 20 Nov. 1929).[139] Conchita offered her life and her heart for the sanctity priests, being devoted to their interior renewal. Her love for the Eternal High Priest extended to all His priests. This is a very Marian characteristic also.

The Effects within Conchita

After the grace of the mystical incarnation, Conchita was aware of the immediate effects. She wrote:

> *This immense favor has filled me with holy joy, peace, and indescribable wellbeing, but it has left my body exhausted, worn out. I do not know how to express it.... Even now when I am writing, the Living Presence of Jesus has not left me. It is as if I had just received Holy Communion, feeling its effects in my soul: a yearning*

---

[136] Olivera, *Mystical Incarnation*, 26.

[137] Olivera, *Mystical Incarnation*, 26.

[138] Olivera, *Mystical Incarnation*, 30.

[139] Olivera, *Mystical Incarnation*, 29.

for solitude, and for approaching the tabernacle. I do feel that Living and Real Presence in my soul as a sharp break in the face of anything that is less perfect. I have experienced a deeper concern, and inconceivable tenderness (March 25, 1906).[140]

Conchita was a simple laywoman who was filled with the weight of divine love—the indwelling of the Word. Now forty-fours years old, she had a new impulse to be purer and more pleasing to Jesus. Naturally, Conchita turned to Mary. Our Lady helped Conchita to see more vividly the essence of the divine within and without. Mary deeply enriches our union with her Son, Jesus.

At the end of her spiritual exercises on March 30, 1906, Conchita wrote:

My soul seems to awaken from a dream. It seems to me that on penetrating into my soul, my Word has brought me in a new measure, more secret and hidden, more intimate and luminous, where the Beloved dwells.

Now I am going to go home to carry out my duties there and meet again creatures which deprive me of some time to spend with You and to maintain a certain indispensable contact with the world. Since that is what You wish, I wish it too.... I came alone, and I leave with Him. He will live and grow in my soul if I set no hinderance. I'd rather die than commit such a betrayal. He has told me that He would not leave my soul. He would possess me, and I would possess Him.[141]

Conchita is a diligent mother, a humble mystic who returns to the duties of her vocation, and a widow with sole care of her seven

---

[140] Olivera, *Mystical Incarnation*, 29.
[141] Olivera, *Mystical Incarnation*, 31.

children. Dom Bernardo, Conchita's director, explains about how this grace was lived: "Conchita was a woman and mother. It is not surprising, then, the unitive, compenetrative and transformative grace into Christ was received by her in a maternal manner. She received the gift according to her own ability and natural manner of reception. Divine grace adapts and incarnates itself according to its human recipient."[142]

Later, Conchita told Dom Bernardo this about her family:

> It is a point about which I do not speak, namely about my children, when actually my concern to raise them occupies the greatest part of my life. I bear them constantly in my heart, and more so their souls than their bodies. Here is pretty much the same prayer I make for each one of them, many times a day.[143]

The vocation to which God calls us is precisely the manner and circumstance where we can be sanctified. When we make retreats or pilgrimages or have graced prayer experiences, we would like to suspend time so we can soak in the graces. We would like to linger longer in the good company of Jesus. We do not want to lose the experience of Jesus that enkindled our hearts. Re-enter we must, carrying more of Jesus within. Retreat graces planted in us will rightfully bloom where we live our vocation.

The Lord is a God of order, and we should order our lives according to our vocation. For Conchita, the mystical incarnation did not fade or change. Jesus had promised that it was permanent, and it lasted throughout her lifetime.

---

[142] Olivera, *Mystical Incarnation*, 32.
[143] *A Mother's Spiritual Diary*, 77–78.

1935 Crowning of the Mystical Incarnation

The spiritual itinerary of the mystical incarnation was crowned in 1935, two years before Conchita's death. Jesus told her:

> *And now, without taking one iota away from the graces, you must direct everything to the glory of my beloved Father. May everything in you, in your body, and in your soul, have this holy end: the glory of My Father. Simplify these acts into a single love in performing them, with a single desire, so that, without ceasing to do them, they will converge to unity in their substance: the glory of My Father* (October 29, 1935).[144]

Blessed Conchita had matured; her soul was full; her life was a love offering refined in the crucible of suffering. She was transformed into Christ Crucified at the time of her death. She embraced the glorious Cross that she saw in the Vision. She identified completely with Love Crucified. Imagine how many souls she carried to the Heart of Jesus.

Can We Live the Mystical Incarnation?

Can we live the mystical incarnation? Sr. Linares asks and answers this question. "Yes, of course we can live this grace in varying degrees." It is rooted in Baptism, articulated in St. Paul's letters, and lived by the Blessed Mother throughout her life.

Our Lord told Conchita:

1. *The Eucharist is the perpetual incarnation in souls, another kind of incarnation that concludes when the sacramental species conclude, leaving only their effects, but in the end incarnation none the less* (July 24, 1906).[145]

---

[144] A Mother's Spiritual Diary, 17.
[145] Linares, The Mystical Incarnation, 33.

2. *In every sacrament, this incarnation is mystically renewed in
    every soul, especially in the Eucharist. Every Mass is a kind of
    mystical incarnation in which the Word descends and unites
    Himself with man; and in every Communion this very thing is
    reproduced, raising human nature, divinizing it. God perpetu-
    ated the mystery of the Incarnation of the Word through grace
    in His Church, and through her in every Christian heart, in
    the sacraments.*[146]

How We Can Live the Mystical Incarnation

We each have a unique vocation, a calling and a spiritual itinerary. Sr. Linares reveals how we can live our form of the mystical
incarnation:

1. "Live more consciously the grace of our baptism: Jesus
    dwells in me, He remains in me, this changes all my
    attitudes towards others. It is no longer just me. He has
    life in me. He communicates life to me; He transforms
    me; He makes me like Him, so that I look, listen and
    act like Him. May I be able to say with Conchita: "Not
    what I do, but what You do" and surrender my will,
    the control of my time, and of my life."

2. "Go out to meet the other because Jesus is in me and
    He is also my brother, we are one Body, therefore I am
    interested in the other, in his well-being."

3. "Let us say that Conchita receives the mystical incarna-
    tion, in an extraordinary way; with special intensity.
    But we are also called to live this presence of God in
    our interior, in different degrees, that involves us in its

---

[146] Linares, *The Mystical Incarnation*, 33.

dynamism of offering all to the Father; and going out to build communion."[147]

This grace belongs to the Lord, who initiates. It belongs to us to respond with docility, faith, and courage. I suspect that within us there is something greater to which we are called; something that we have not yet discovered or lived. Jesus beckons us to the greatness of soul that enlivened saints.

The Mystical Incarnation and the Chaplet of Divine Mercy

This is my personal observation. Conchita received the grace of the mystical incarnation in 1906, and then followed the Chain of Love and, in 1909, the mystical priesthood. Conchita died in 1937.

In 1931 in Poland, Jesus appeared to a simple nun named Helen Kowalska, known as Sr. Faustina. In a vision, Jesus entrusted to Sr. Faustina a message of Divine Mercy. He dictated to her the Chaplet of Divine Mercy. On rosary beads, we pray, "Eternal Father, I offer you the Body and Blood, Soul and Divinity of Your dearly beloved Son, Our Lord Jesus Christ, in atonement for our sins and for those of the whole world."

Through the mysticism of Blessed Conchita, a simple laywoman, and the mysticism of St. Faustina, a simple nun, we learn how to offer Jesus' Body and Blood mystically to the Father for the salvation of souls. We can think of St. Faustina and Blessed Conchita together as spiritual mothers interceding for the salvation of souls as we pray the Divine Mercy Chaplet.

If we live our form of the mystical incarnation, our baptismal priesthood will be fruitful. Through this grace, God calls us to the highest union. This the desire of the Heart of Jesus.

---

[147] Linares, *The Mystical Incarnation*, 34.

Individual or Group Reflection

Ponder

"Do you love me?" (John 21:15).

Engage

1. How is your transformation in Christ being realized, or hindered?
2. Ask Jesus how you can live your personal mystical incarnation grace.
3. How does Jesus reveal His love for you, His beloved?

Pray

Oh, my beloved, adorable and charming Jesus! Overcome by such tenderness from Your filial Heart, I come to tell You that I accept, before heaven, earth, and the seas; before the Father and You, my Lord, and before the Holy Spirit, the spiritual and mystical motherhood, in every form, toward You, my beloved Jesus, and for the thousands of children You desire to give me. Be they priests, men, and women, whatever You wish. Only what You wish. Because Your pleasure will be my pleasure and Your will shall be my own will. I will give You up to death by sacrificing You mystically on the altar of my heart, my beloved Son, day, and night, in every breath and beat of my heart up until the last one of my life!... I will love you in a motherly way with all the tenderness of love, with all the fidelity of love, with all the generosity and self-denial of a tender, ardent, unselfish, and pure love. Only You and Mary! Only Your consolation, Your desire, and Your glory (A.C. Vol. 48: pp 382–384, September 27, 1927).[148]

---

[148] Olivera, *Mystical Incarnation*, 52.

7

Union with Mary: The Virgin of Guadalupe, the Virgin of the Cross, the Virgin of Solitude

Let it be done unto me according to your word.

—See Luke 1:38

In the eyes of his mother, a child perceives that he or she is lovable, cherished, welcomed. Mary's loving maternal gaze tells us that we are lovable. We have seen how a biological mother stares at her infant with so much love. Imagine the look of love in our Heavenly Mother's eyes. Mary is the Mother we need for many reasons. Our spiritual poverty is very real.

In this chapter, we'll explore Conchita's Marian character and calling. Conchita's Marian spirituality can form us as better instruments of Mary. Throughout the life of Blessed Conchita, Our Lady played a prominent role. Jesus called Conchita to imitate Mary's mission, maternity, sorrows, and solitude.

Mary's role in salvation history is to physically birth Jesus Christ into the world. Until the end of time, Mary has the maternal mission of spiritually birthing Christ in souls. She and the Holy Spirit are the only two artisans who can birth Jesus in souls.

Beautiful Holiness

There are three Marian titles that identify Conchita's Marian character: the Virgin of Guadalupe, the Virgin of the Cross, and the Virgin of Solitude. Each title has characteristics related to a particular mission.

The Virgin of Guadalupe appeared as the Mother pregnant with Jesus to deliver His people from the Aztecs' satanic practices and false religion. Mary appeared on Tepeyac Hill as a Mother who has authority. She called the people to conversion and wanted to establish a sanctuary of hope and healing. The tilma is her enduring love letter to the Americas. Conchita's entire life was touched by Our Lady of Guadalupe.

The Virgin of the Cross is a school of suffering love. All Marian virtues engaged on Calvary. Mary's fiat was magnified; her sorrow, complete. She offered her Son to the Father as Victim and Priest. She suffered the interior agonies of the Passion. In the mutual gift of the Son and the Mother on Calvary, redemptive love opened Heaven. Conchita assumed union with the Virgin of the Cross during the middle of her life, especially following her vision of the Cross and the mystical incarnation.

The Virgin of Solitude embodies a school of contemplative prayer, silence, sacrifice, and supplication. Mary remained after the Ascension to aid the apostles and to birth the Church through the offering of interior suffering. In solitude, Mary relived her Son's life mystically. Conchita was called to live Marian solitude in her later years.

Conchita's Marian Foundation

In studying Conchita's Marian horizon, we learn the beauty of Marian mysticism. We can go beyond devotion to imitation of Our Lady.

Cardinal Raniero Cantalamessa writes:

Union with Mary

To say that Mary is the mirror of the Church means in practical terms that after having first considered a word, an attitude, or an event in the Madonna's life, we then ask ourselves what this means for the Church and each one of us. What should we do to practice what the Holy Spirit wished to communicate to us through Mary? The best answer we can give is *not devotion to Mary, but imitation of Mary.*[149]

In practice, how do we move from devotion to imitation of Mary? Devotion includes our prayers, consecration, affection, and gratitude for Mary—all very important. Imitation includes surrender to God's will and initiatives. Imitation means that we enflesh the Marian virtues, and that requires discipline and asceticism (sacrifices). Imitation means that we participate in Mary's mission of birthing Jesus in the world. Imitation means that our hearts will experience the seven-times-pierced heart of Mary. Imitation of Mary is the harder path than devotion, but with greater fruit. Ideally, we practice devotion to *and* imitation of Mary.

The little girl who loved Our Lady matured into a woman who embodied Mary's life—her joyful, sorrowful, and glorious mysteries. Jesus told Conchita:

Her Heart is presented with roses, but underneath is found thorns. The roses signify graces for her children, acquired with almost infinite sorrows, with tears and with martyrdoms the weight of which I alone was capable of measuring. It is quite natural for a mother, and so much the more Mary, to keep for herself the thorns and the

---

[149] Fr. Raniero Cantalamessa, O.F.M. Cap., "Mary, Mirror of the Church," in *Redemptoris Mater: Study Guide to John Paul II's Encyclical Mother of the Redeemer* (Denver: Endow, 2007), 83.

sorrows: it is the roses and the tenderness that she presents to her children, not the sacrifices (*Diary*, June 30, 1917).[150]

The Virgin Mary has spiritual authority from God to move in His power to do whatever Jesus asks. Our Lady moves in power to bring souls to Christ and to protect her children from the enemies of salvation. With Mary, Conchita is able to fulfill her arduous mission to be Love Crucified.

Her Mother's Example

Conchita was schooled in Marian devotion by her good mother, Clara:

Still, at my mother's knees I learned that Mary was also my mother; she taught me to invoke her, to love her with all my heart; very early in my life she planted the seed of devotion to her in my soul (V. 1, 56).[151]

The seeds that Clara sowed took root in the rich soil of her little girl's soul. Conchita described her mother as a saint. Clara trained her little girl to love Mary. All you mothers and fathers who sowed seeds of faith in your little ones are God's sowers. Keep watering the seeds you sowed with faith-filled, hopeful prayers—more so, if your children have fallen away from the Faith.

Fr. Carlos Francisco Vera Soto writes in his study of Blessed Conchita:

The love Conchita had for Mary was taught very early. The rosaries, the altars raised around her loving image, the

[150] *A Mother's Spiritual Diary*, 175.
[151] Cantalamessa, "Mary, Mirror of the Church," in *Redemptoris Mater*, 83.

prayers, the exclamations, the trusting prayers, the possibility of appealing to Mary in her adversities.[152]

Growing up with Marian devotions like these provides rich spiritual food for children, and their hearts become attuned to Our Lady's love and protection.

For Conchita, Mary was very accessible, not only for spiritual needs but also for temporal necessities. Conchita's *Diary* reveals an incident in which the Blessed Mother saved her.

Conchita went to visit a priest, and when it was time to go home, to her surprise, the carriage wasn't there as planned. As time passed, Conchita got very upset and decided to walk home. She didn't know the way home by foot, so she went into a shop to seek directions. Suddenly, a man came out who frightened her. He wanted to guide her home. The man got very close to Conchita and smelled like wine. She couldn't avoid the man, so they walked a short way together. Conchita became increasingly aware of the risk at hand, so she ran. She prayed to the Blessed Mother. It was nighttime. She knew that her husband was serving dinner to a friend. Far from home, she was overcome by acute anxiety. Then Our Lady intervened. As Conchita and the drunkard turned the corner, a trolley was approaching. Conchita had to break away from the man's embrace as he tried to stop her from jumping onto the trolley. Conchita knew that the Blessed Mother saved her as the trolley proceeded, leaving the man behind.

Mary is accessible for all our needs. I suspect we each have stories of Mary's intervention in our lives. She intervened in mine in a dramatic way in Lourdes to bring me back to Christ and the

152 Fr. Carlos Francisco Vera Soto, *The Flower of Mexico: The Spiritual Itinerary of Concepción Cabrera de Armida*, trans. Lucia Carrington (PDF, Mexico City, 2015), 12.

Church. Well before I realized it, the Blessed Mother knew that my life needed to change trajectory. She took care of this at her shrine in Lourdes.

The Virgin of Guadalupe

Conchita is a daughter of Mexico, and her spirituality was greatly influenced by the apparitions of Guadalupe. The Hill of Tepeyac is considered holy, a miraculous place where pilgrims arrive from all over the world. The Mexican people, with their tribulations, take consolation in the words of Mary to Juan Diego: "Am I not here, I who am your Mother? Are you not under my protection?"

The Shrine

From childhood, Conchita and her family were frequent pilgrims to the Shrine of Guadalupe. It is a place of miracles, conversions, and healing. Our Lady's presence there is tangible, and her essence remains in torrents of grace long after her initial apparition. The miraculous tilma of St. Juan Diego is considered a living icon of Our Lady. It is stunning to see, life-changing to encounter. The heart knows that the Blessed Mother is there. I know from personal experience.

In September 2014, two priest friends from the Archdiocese of Washington, D.C., invited me to join their pilgrimage to Guadalupe. I was in the vestibule of the shrine, absorbing all the beauty therein, when I received a phone call from my brother, a medical doctor. Our mother had suffered a heart attack and had been hospitalized, and he was at her bedside with her. Stunned by this news, I ardently desired only to be with my mother. I told my brother that I'd fly home as soon possible. My brother replied, "You know that Mom would want you to stay and pray to Our Lady of Guadalupe for her recovery. Mom's receiving treatment and not in imminent danger of death. I'll keep you informed and let Mom know where you are." We hung up.

I fell to my knees to pray. Through tearful eyes, I gazed at the radiant tilma hung high above the altar. I implored Mary: "My mother! Please go to her—help her—save her please. I don't want to lose my mother. I'm far from her. But you can be close to her. Please." I kept pleading to Mary from my anxious heart. Suddenly, peace overcame me. I was where Jesus wanted me to be, in the gaze of the Virgin of the miraculous tilma. I spiritually carried my sick mom to Our Lady of Guadalupe, a place of healing. Suddenly, I knew that Mom would be all right; and indeed, she recovered.

Guadalupe and Conchita's mission

Jesus connects Conchita's life and apostolates to the Virgin of Guadalupe who appeared in 1531, more than three hundred years before Conchita's time. To the people of South America, Mary is a universal mother—but, thanks to her apparition at Guadalupe, she is also "one of them"! And she is so beautiful, pure, and holy. You feel as if you have an audience with the living Mary when you gaze at the tilma.

Conchita often visited the shrine. Her *Diary* reveals that she went there to "*to empty her heart as a child with its mother*" (*Diary*, March 24, 1894).[153] If we assume the posture of a child, we will empty our hearts to our Mother. Mary helps us to sort out the movements of our hearts. She reaches to help us, who are muddied from life's messes. Mary becomes our maternal course corrector and spiritual compass.

Conchita's apostolates were birthed under the banner of the Virgin of Guadalupe:

[153] Vera Soto, *The Flower of Mexico*, 166.

Beautiful Holiness

The Works of the Cross came to light under the maternal protection of Our Lady of Guadalupe. Her name was found in the poor chapel of the first Oasis of the Contemplatives of the Cross. The Missionaries of the Holy Spirit were founded in the Chapel of Roses, the site of the last apparition of the Mother of God. And the very day of the Pontifical coronation of Our Lady of Guadalupe, the symbol of the Works of the Cross, the Cross of the Apostolate, arose on the summit of Tepeyac, dominating from that moment on, the whole city of Mexico.

Conchita's whole spiritual life is enveloped in her love for the Mother of God. In her *Diary* she writes, "The Lord granted me feelings full of tenderness toward the Holy Virgin."[154]

Jesus tied Conchita's mission to the Virgin of Guadalupe. There, through the instrumentality of Mary, Jesus planted a victory flag, having abolished the Aztecs' human sacrifice. Jesus touched the hearts of the people with a Mother so beautiful that she was exceedingly more desirable than their false religion; her message in the tilma was more attractive than the horrors of human sacrifice. Conchita's mission echoes a similar message—namely, through the instrumentality of Mary and the Holy Spirit, liberation from evil and a revolution of love would be realized to renew humanity.

Mary: Teacher of the Spiritual Life

For Conchita, Our Lady was also a great spiritual master. She recalled these words spoken to her by Jesus: "*The holiest and most perfect creature that ever existed was Mary. Do you know why? Because*

---

[154] Vera Soto, *The Flower of Mexico*, 166.

from the first instant of her being, she corresponded with all the inspirations of the Holy Spirit. Mary is the best teacher of the spiritual life" (*Diary*, September 22, 1895).[155]

"Because she corresponded with all the inspirations of the Holy Spirit."

What would we be if we corresponded with all the inspirations of the Holy Spirit? Mary models the spiritual life by her perfect example of life in the Spirit.

Conchita's journey of Marian transformation was not one smooth process. Occasionally, she was discouraged because of her human weaknesses. Once she prayed:

> My Mother, I cannot do anything by myself, but with you; as you take my hand, you who know my inconsistency and weakness, I can reach the end doing what Jesus asks of me, out of pure gratitude and love.[156]

Later, Conchita had the idea of writing her own obituary: "burial of her 'Self.'" Here is her charming obituary:

> "Today, at 7:30 in the morning, the 'Self' of Concepción Cabrera de Armida passed on to a better place. Jesus and Mary ask for your participation in lifting her up in prayer so that she may not rise from the dead and return to her old ways." – I hope this happens this way, my God![157]

I need to write a similar personal obituary as well! It may be a fruitful spiritual exercise to remind us that death to self is a call to arise in Christ.

---

[155] Vera Soto, *The Flower of Mexico*, 166.

[156] Levy, *Priestly People*, 126.

[157] Levy, *Priestly People*, 126.

Beautiful Holiness

Conchita: Mary and Martha, Contemplative and Active

There is a Mary-Martha pattern in Conchita's life in which she was first in a posture of prayer, like Mary, and then in a posture of action, like Martha. For example:

> I love you, my Mother, and I ask you through the sorrows of solitude in which you remember these marvels, to teach me true humility that does not consist of disregarding the favors of heaven, but in attributing them to God, penetrated with our nothingness and misery. Amen.[158]

Afterward Conchita wrote:

> Today I will visit a hospital or some sick person, in honor of Mary, speaking of her with much fervor and causing as many hearts as I can to love her.[159]

Another instance of prayer and action:

> My Mother, with what shall I pay you for your interest in my eternal salvation? Only with gratitude, carrying out your precious lessons in the actions of my life. Everything passes away except to have love, to have known how to dry the tears of Jesus, and your own.
>
> Jesus wept over Jerusalem—and that moves my heart to its depths. He wept for the inconstancy of the human heart which would change its love into hatred, its praises into demanding His death on the cross. He wept thinking of me, because I would betray Him so many times; because I would receive Communion

---

[158] Concepción Cabrera de Armida, *Roses and Thorns* (Staten Island, NY: Society of St. Paul/Alba House, 2007), 26.

[159] *Roses and Thorns*, 26.

in the morning, loving Him, and would give Him over to death in the nights of dancing and entertainment which would destroy the innocence of my soul.[160]

Afterward Conchita noted:

Today I will feed a poor person, remembering the scorn which Jesus received. I will ask Mary to obtain pardon for me.[161]

As an aside, Conchita was not the only mystic to realize the importance of integrating the complementary roles of Mary and Martha. On Mary and Martha, Servant of God Fulton Sheen writes:

Christianity does not ask the modern woman to be exclusively a Martha or a Mary; the choice is not between a professional career and contemplation, for the Church reads the Gospel of Martha and Mary ... to symbolize that she combines both the speculative and the practical, the serving of the Lord and the sitting at His feet.[162]

The lives of the saints teach us how to balance prayer and the demands of charitable work. When Conchita was sixty-four years of age, she had the aches and pains of an aging woman. But since Jesus asked her to be faithful to her duties as a mother, a mother-in-law, and a grandmother, she was diligent in serving her family. She wrote:

I would like to be like Mary (the sister of Lazarus who sat at Jesus' feet to listen to him), but instead, I live the life of Martha (the

---

[160] *Roses and Thorns*, 104–105.
[161] *Roses and Thorns*, 104–105.
[162] Fulton Sheen, *The World's First Love: Mary, Mother of God* (San Francisco: Ignatius Press, 2010), 181.

other sister, who tended to the needs of the Lord). This is what YOU want, my Jesus, and so this is what I want also, although I long to be before the Tabernacle.[163]

On another day, Conchita wrote:

Jesus is still making a "Martha" of me, especially with Chabela, who lives nearby. First, I go to the British Hospital near Chapulte-pec. Then I go to Lupe's house in the Roma neighborhood. I have to take two trolleys and then walk the rest of the way. I am abso-lutely exhausted by the time I eat supper. I offer my stair climbing, which causes me such pain, to the point of tears, to Jesus. I offer my tiredness to him and his absences from my life. But I behave badly toward him. I arrive so very tired with aches and pains in my legs and feet, and therefore, I spend but a few moments with him, and then I have to lie down, and from my bed, I express my love for him.[164]

Blessed Conchita interweaved the contemplative and active lives. For men, St. Joseph is the father who threads contemplation and work together. No vocation—be it motherhood, fatherhood, priesthood, or religious life—has legs without the pillar of prayer. Vocations thrive if prayer thrives. Works thrive if they're conceived in prayer.

The Virgin of the Cross

Jesus told Conchita, "*Mary was the first to continue My passion.*"[165] Mary's interior life is a world that we wish to learn about. I often meditate on Mary at Bethlehem, in her home in Nazareth, at Cana,

---

[163] *A Mother's Spiritual Diary*, 122.
[164] *A Mother's Spiritual Diary*, 122.
[165] *A Mother's Spiritual Diary*, 167.

at the Cross, and her experience of Christ's Passion. Conchita will teach us about how Mary continued the Passion of Jesus and how we can imitate Our Lady.

Following the vision of the Cross and the grace of the mystical incarnation, Conchita gradually became more cruciform for the glory of God. Throughout her life, she suffered physical illnesses and thought she was on the brink of death a few times; but she recovered and carried on. Conchita's greatest sufferings, besides the deaths of her husband and her children, were her interior sufferings. Jesus conformed Conchita to the Virgin of the Cross. Conchita contemplated the mystery of Mary, who was the first host to incarnate Jesus in herself. Conchita was to *study the attributes of that pure and sacrificed host and imitate them* (SD 41, 102; February 27, 1917)."[166]

Jesus taught Conchita, "*I want you to offer yourself as did Mary, with her very virtues and qualities. Imitate her and model your own heart on this so beautiful an image.*"[167]

The word *victim* is often found in Conchita's writings. It is important to understand what this term means. Sr. Elzbieta Sadowski, R.C.S.C.J., explains how the word *victim* applies to Conchita.

The expression "victim," "victim souls" in Conchita's usage, does not carry that doleful sense which was a typical understanding of the mystery of the Cross in her era, and which could lead to a certain masochism. The doctrine of the Cross is solidly founded on a spirituality of self-giving which leads to a total going forth from self, an imitation

[166] Concepción Cabrera de Armida, *You Belong to the Church* (Rome: Libreria Editrice Vaticana, 1999), 21.
[167] *You Belong to the Church*, 21.

of and conformity with Christ who came to give his life as a ransom for the many (Mt 20, 28).[168]

Think of the words of St. Paul: "I appeal to you therefore, brethren, by the mercies of God, to present your bodies as a living sacrifice, holy and acceptable to God, which is your spiritual worship" (Rom. 12:1). I suspect that many of us can relate to the experience of offering ourselves and our sufferings for the salvation of souls.

The Virgin Mary is a victim of divine love. God possessed her body and soul to do with as He willed. She was not her own but was all the Lord's. Saints have written about Mary's mystical, unbloody passion, in which she was intimately united to her Son's sacrifice. How can this be? It's the paradox of the Cross, the mystery of crucified love, union with the pure Lamb of God in one act of unified love. God incorporated Mary into Christ's joys and sorrows, His sacrifices and works. Jesus chose Conchita to extend the life of Mary mystically on earth. Conchita would do whatever Jesus asked.

Saints uniquely venerate and imitate Mary, as Sr. Elzbieta tells us:

With all the saints, closeness to Mary takes on the character and form of their personal grace. Thérèse of Lisieux will say of Mary: "She is more a mother than a Queen." Bernadette will venerate in her the Immaculate Conception. Conchita will contemplate Mary, according to her characteristic viewpoint, in the mystery of her inmost association to the Cross of her Son for the glory of the Father for the salvation of the world. For Conchita, the Virgin Mary is above all the "Virgin of the Cross."[169]

---

[168] *You Belong to the Church*, 20.
[169] *You Belong to the Church*, 20.

Union with Mary

Conchita's Marian itinerary essentially followed a scriptural, dogmatic path. She contemplated the Blessed Mother in her role in God's plan of salvation and in her joyful, sorrowful, and glorious mysteries. Conchita pondered the mystery of the Crucifixion, Jesus on the Cross, and Mary's role at Calvary. Jesus revealed to Conchita:

> It was there, at the foot of the Cross, that Mary saw My Church born, that she accepted in her heart in the person of St. John all the priests in place of Me, and further, to be the Mother of all mankind (*Diary*, April 28, 1928).[170]

Then Conchita understood:

> I have better understood the inexpressible pains felt in the purest Heart of Mary, the sole creature who read and understood the interior sorrows, the sufferings of Her Divine Son, just as she was the only one to be able to measure His pains, to grasp His purity and His innocence, to bear too the infinite weight of human ingratitude which crushed Him. Without being culpable, she lived an existence of suffering in union with her most holy Jesus and obtained graces for culpable sinners. Once Mary had consented to the Incarnation of the Word, never was the divine plan erased from her spirit. Her mother's heart, broken, contemplated the Innocent and Divine Martyr.
>
> The life of this Virgin-Mother was, after that of Jesus, the most crucified. Her constant meditation of the future ever kept her soul torn while in her little home in Nazareth. Who could have dreamed on seeing these two pure beings living the very same kind of life, that actually they bore within them for the cruelest

---

[170] *A Mother's Spiritual Diary*, 167.

martyrdom for the sake of mankind! Yes, Mary held an immense place in the Redemption of mankind! How great Mary is and how much we owe her (Diary, Sept. 1, 1898).[171]

We can see how much Conchita loved Our Lady and how she had grown to appreciate Mary's interiority. For instance, Conchita's favorite Marian mystery was the Presentation of Jesus in the Temple:

She recognized in this privileged mystery the fundamental attitude of the mystical incarnation and the offering of love, the quintessence of the teachings of the Cross: the oblation of the Word to His Father and the total offering of self out of love in union with Christ, but through Mary's hands.[172]

Conchita beautifully articulated the deeper meaning of this scriptural mystery. Now, when I pray the Joyful Mysteries of the Rosary, I will personalize the offering of Jesus to the Eternal Father.

In February 1907, on the feast of the Presentation, Our Lord told Conchita,

The mystery that is being celebrated today concretizes your mission: the constant offering in your heart of the Victim that is to be immolated on behalf of the world. The sorrow that comes about is a holy sorrow, sublime, chosen and most pure, since the creature does not undergo it seeking itself, but suffers solely on account of My suffering. Here you have the perfection of sorrow and of love.[173]

---

[171] *A Mother's Spiritual Diary,* 168.
[172] *A Mother's Spiritual Diary,* 171.
[173] *A Mother's Spiritual Diary,* 171.

We can be part of Conchita's family and lovingly present Jesus to the Father in imitation of Mary. May The Holy Spirit and the Virgin of the Cross teach us the perfection of sorrow and of love.

The Virgin of Solitude

During the last part of Conchita's life, she was mystically (and sometimes physically) conformed to the Virgin of Solitude. One of Conchita's most profound revelations, recorded in her *Diary*, speaks of Mary's solitude as a martyrdom of love:

> *For these last years, destined for the reign of the Holy Spirit and the final triumph of the Church, was reserved the veneration of the martyrdom of Mary's solitude, His most beloved Spouse. During this martyrdom, only the might and force of this Spirit of God could keep her alive. Mary lived, it might be said, miraculously and solely to merit the graces requisite for her maternity on behalf of mankind. She lived to give her testimony about Me in my humanity, as the Holy Spirit testified about My Divinity. She lived to be in some way the visible instrument of the Holy Spirit in the nascent Church, while the Holy Spirit acted on the divine and wholly spiritual plane. She lived to provide its first nourishment for this unique and true Church, and to merit in heaven the titles of Consoler, Advocate, Refuge of her children.*
>
> *This phase of Mary's life, constituting for her Heart, a source of bitterness, the quintessence of martyrdom, the purification of her love at the same time an inexhaustible source of grace and mercy of the world, has remained unknown.*
>
> *At the foot of the Cross all her children were born. My death gave them life in the heart of My Mother. But before her death she had to manifest this maternity on earth, gaining, by the sufferings of My absence, an infinitude of graces present, and future*

for her children. Her title Mother of mankind, Mary won by the martyrdom of her solitude after My death. Has the world been aware of this?

The time has come when the children should show they are real children, showing their veneration for this heart broken by this subtle and most painful martyrdom, lived through for the sake of their own happiness. There, Mary gained graces for each and every man. It is time for her to be thanked (Diary, June 30, 1917).[174]

We are being schooled on the depth of Mary's sacrifice—how this Mother relived the martyrdom of her Son by remembrance. Heaven would wait for Mary as she labored on earth.

Let us ponder these sentiments of Jesus' heart for Mary. Let us take to heart the part about thanking Our Lady for her complete sacrifice of solitude and her patient longing to be reunited with Jesus in Heaven. The Lord invites us to be "real children" of Mary in imitating her actions. We cannot fathom the graces that Mary procures for us and for the world. Let us honor Mary's solitude, sacrifice, suffering, and supplication. The solitude that Mary experienced was related to asceticism, which is the conscious withdrawal from creatures to be alone with God. Our Lady spent her solitude in loving contemplation of her Son.

Jesus told Conchita how she would be assimilated to His Mother:

I have granted certain souls to be assimilated to Me through the external stigmata of my wounds, lashes, etc., but to my Mother I gave my perfect likeness in her interior, after My Passion, with all my Heart underwent. It is in this aspect that you will imitate

---

[174] *A Mother's Spiritual Diary*, 175–176.

her. *My image will be imprinted on your soul, but a sorrowful one. You will taste the bitterness of Mary ... experiencing in your heart the echo of her sorrows. In union with Mary who in all truth cried out to heaven in unison with me: "This is my Body; this is my Blood" offering Me on behalf of the world and of my nascent Church. And do not think that this manifestation of Mary in her solitude, in her martyrdoms of absence, will bring sadness to men: her sorrows will be celebrated, in the fruit of multiplied graces and mercy for mankind.*[175]

The fruit of suffering is cause for celebration. Mary's suffering draws the multiplication of graces and mercy for humanity. We cry out for mercy and grace.

Then there is Mary's solitude, about which Jesus spoke to Conchita so beautifully:

Each time that Mary, my most Holy Mother, felt the pain of my absence in whatever form (which was continually), she immediately offered it to the Father for the salvation of the world and of the newborn Church. This apostolate of suffering (which is that of the Cross) in Mary, during this period of solitude, was the most fertile and caused heaven to pour itself out in graces.[176]

The Lord calls Mary's solitude her "apostolate of suffering." The physical separation from her Son was agonizing. Conchita received the grace to live Mary's solitude. *"God wants me to be alone. For this moment, it is the hour of solitude: to be in Mary's company, to imitate Mary in her solitude during the last days of her life."*[177]

---

[175] *A Mother's Spiritual Diary*, 175–176.
[176] *You Belong to the Church*, 22.
[177] *You Belong to the Church*, 22.

Beautiful Holiness

If you are alone, prayerfully unite your solitude with Mary's and offer a sacrifice of love with her. Your offering will mean very much in the divine economy.

Regarding souls who love Mary, Jesus says:

In My spiritual life ... in souls, My mother was never separated from Me, that is, the imitation of both of our lives must be simultaneous on earth. The souls who love her most and who are most like her, are the souls who are most perfectly like Me. You must imitate her in the practice of the virtues. Observe the virtues she practices in her solitude, in the last stage of her life, her outlook, and her soul wholly turned toward heaven, and her self-effacement glorifying Me on earth. Through her passionate love, aspiring for paradise, she merited graces from heaven for the newborn Church (SD 41, 63; February 18, 1917).[178]

This is a little catechism on the imitation of Christ. To be transfigured in Jesus, we must imitate Our Lady — her virtues, her outlook, and her self-effacement. Our Lady schools us in the science of the Cross in the mystery of solitude.

There is an interior martyrdom ordained for each person. The Divine Architect works with precision in purifying, forming, and sanctifying you and me. When God asks something of us, He provides all necessary grace for it. Silence, solitude, suffering, and sacrifice: these are hallmarks of incarnational love. We feel the interior sufferings of Jesus and Mary in our union with them. It's as if they share with us a most precious part of themselves — a little drop of their suffering.

On Conchita's union with the Virgin of Solitude, Fr. Carlos Francisco Vera Soto writes:

---

[178] *You Belong to the Church*, 22.

It is interesting that in the last stage of her spiritual itinerary, when Conchita has already received manifold graces of transformation into Christ, she is now impelled to live this aspect of the life of Mary. Thinking of the Virgin we may realize that she lived like any other creature the birth of the Church, the privations of the physical presence of her Son and she submerged, like anyone else, in this abyss of contemplative silence and solitude, which, on the other hand, was so dynamic and fertile that it pushed the development of the Church through all the known world.

Conchita will receive that kind of "instruction" about the journey of the life of Mary, perfect Christian, model of continuation of Jesus, marvel of docility to the Holy Spirit. This stage with Mary was a stage of profound contemplation. This woman that since the beginning "kept all those things in her heart" must have covered with the internal sense, one by one, the steps that her Son lived; remembered his words, his gestures, his voice, his figure. Nobody has been so similar to God as Mary, and no one has ever assimilated God so much as she did. Conchita will then start to follow that spiritual path in the hands of Mary.[179]

The wonders of Mary fill us with awe. No one is deserving of so glorious a Mother except Jesus. Engaging Mary in the spiritual life is the quickest path to the Heart of Jesus. Our Lady counseled and encouraged the first apostles of the Church. How great their love for and reliance on Mary was! We need her maternal presence and grace so that we can grow into the stature of true disciples—humble, obedient children of God.

---

[179] Vera Soto, *The Flower of Mexico*, 70.

Beautiful Holiness

Jesus told Conchita:

I want to unify you to Mary, consolation of the grieving, and with her you shall fly over the paths that are waiting for you, if you are her true daughter. She is the Mother of holy hope; exercise this theological virtue as she did, the virtue of hope, which is the virtue of solitude and of pain, the virtue that looks to the sky and makes the heart expand (CC: 41, 210-211).[180]

The Virgin of Solitude was Conchita's Mother of hope when all seemed dark at the end of her life. Ponder Our Lady as the "Mother of holy hope." This title given by Jesus speaks volumes about our need to have hope. Jesus refers to the virtue of hope as "the virtue of solitude and pain" but also the virtue that looks heavenward and expands the heart. There is too much hopelessness in the world today. Let us imitate the Mother of holy hope—the restorer of the hope of Christians.

The last twenty years of Conchita's life were "an unusual period of literary fecundity"[181] in which she wrote, published, and distributed many mystical works on topics including the solitude of Mary, the Holy Spirit, St. Joseph, the Heart of Jesus, the virtues, and Christ the King.

After Conchita's beloved spiritual director Archbishop Ramón Ibarra died in 1917, Msgr. Emeterio Valverde guided her for the next eight years, and then Archbishop Luis Martinez became her director for the last twelve years of her life. Msgr. Valverde "made his best efforts to accompany Conchita in the painful and heartbreaking process of living this mystery of solitude."[182] Arch-

---

[180] Vera Soto, *The Flower of Mexico*, 72-73.

[181] Vera Soto, *The Flower of Mexico*, 72-73.

[182] Vera Soto, *The Flower of Mexico*, 72-73.

bishop Martinez greatly illumined Conchita's extended time of lived Marian solitude. The Virgin of Guadalupe, the Virgin of the Cross, and the Virgin of Solitude beautifully coalesced in the life of Conchita.

Our Lady leads us to the rarefied atmosphere of the holy. As our Heavenly Mother, Mary sees in you and me something of the holy that we cannot perceive of ourselves. She sees how Jesus and the Eternal Father love us. She sees the Sanctifier residing in you and me, who are His temples. She sees our weakness, sin, and wounds. She is God's provision for our spiritual health and welfare. Mary forms each of us to be the best version of a child of God.

Individual or Group Reflection

Ponder

"My soul magnifies the Lord, and my spirit rejoices in God my Savior" (Luke 1:46-47).

Engage

1. What has Conchita taught you about Mary?
2. How are you imitating Mary in your life and vocation?
3. What is Mary's role in your life and in your family's life?

Pray

O most loving and beloved Mother!... Tell Jesus what I need, holy Virgin, so that I may acquire what I lack to resemble His family! And how great it is! You see that I am not humble, not patient, not mortified; that I look for my self-interest in things large and small, and live clinging to earth with my heart full of degrading inclinations.

Tell Him that when I draw near the wedding of the Lamb in Communion, I lack love, the beautiful wine of charity. O my beloved Mother, obtain this for me from our Jesus, Grant me this favor, most holy Mother, so that those around me may believe in Him as in Cana, seeing my vices changed into virtues. Amen.[183]

---

[183] Vera Soto, *The Flower of Mexico,* 58.

8

Eucharistic Life:
Communion of Love

Did not our hearts burn within us?

—Luke 24:32

On her tenth birthday, December 8, 1872, the solemnity of the Immaculate Conception, Conchita made her First Holy Communion. She believed that she was tepid and thoughtless because all she recalls about receiving the Eucharist for the first time was the immense interior delight of her soul and the great joy of wearing the beautiful white dress. From that day forward, however, she developed a profound love for the Blessed Sacrament. "*When I was around fifteen or sixteen,*" she recalled, "*I was permitted to receive four or five times a week, and soon after, every day. I was happy, so happy when I could receive! It is an absolute necessity of my life.*"[184]

Remember, Conchita lived prior to the Vatican II liturgical reform. Eucharistic adoration and devotions such as holy hours and Eucharistic processions played a major role in the normal life of the Christian. In Conchita's time, sometimes Communion was offered outside of Mass as an ordinary practice. And frequently,

---

[184] *A Mother's Spiritual Diary*, 7.

after the Latin Mass (the norm prior to Vatican II), people would enjoy Eucharistic adoration as a private devotion.

We learn of Conchita's Eucharistic life through her *Diary* and several books that she wrote from prayer encounters with Jesus, such as *Before the Altar, Holy Hours, I Am: Eucharistic Meditations on the Gospel,* and *Irresistibly Drawn to the Eucharist.* Conchita had a special charism to communicate the love of Jesus in a powerful way.

Being a mystic, Conchita was in the world but not of the world. She was engaged in family life, society, and the Church; she was a shepherdess of souls and a wise counselor. Frequently, it was before the Blessed Sacrament that she could be alone with her Beloved Jesus. Conchita was drawn to the Sacrament of the Altar because she perceived, tasted, and loved God in such an extraordinary way. Many refer to Conchita as an apostle, or mystic, of the Eucharist. We will learn why she is very deserving of this reputation and how we can become more committed to the Eucharistic life.

Conchita speaks to Jesus in the Eucharist

Conchita's paternal grandmother was known to be exceedingly devoted to the Blessed Sacrament. In their hometown of San Luis Potosí, she founded the apostolate the Perpetual Vigil of the Holy Sacrament. Conchita's mother also had a deep devotion to the Eucharist and to Mary. In her *Diary*, Conchita noted that whenever possible, her mother took her and her siblings to visit the Blessed Sacrament. Thus, Conchita's lifelong love for the Eucharist was seeded in her family, cultivated by Jesus, and watered by prayer.

Conchita's experience with her mother reminds me of my own mother, who took me to visit Jesus in the Eucharist. I always felt at home while gazing at the tabernacle and praying. My practice of daily adoration has continued for more than thirty years. I can relate to how very important this would be to Conchita. It's beautiful to observe parents bringing their young children to visit Jesus in the Blessed Sacrament.

Our reflection in this chapter will center on Conchita's love for the Eucharist and on lessons that Jesus taught her during holy hours. Let us begin by considering the words of Conchita herself:

> *Holy Eucharist: sacred and immaculate Host that holds the Godhead itself, I cannot speak of you, yet the irresistible attraction of my whole being makes me break out sobbing, as only the tears of the soul can tell you what I feel. I see you in a transparent Host as material substance, but faith takes away the veil with which you cover yourself, love shaking the foundations of my heart makes me feel your presence, and the joy you cause it to feel lifts it up to the sublime hope of possessing you, overcoming all the obstacles that separate us. Oh Lord! I will pass away, generations will come and go, and only you, you, will never pass away. When you end your mission of charity on earth, you will keep on giving yourself forever in heaven to the hearts that belong to you.... Let me be one of them, Lord, please* (T. 75).[185]

Conchita's ardor for the Eucharist is a lived reality. Ponder her words: "Faith takes away the veil with which you cover yourself." We may be tempted to think that mystics such as Conchita possess special graces that we do not. To some degree, that may be true. But Conchita rightly acknowledges that *faith takes away the*

---

[185] Juan Gutiérrez Gonzales, M.Sp.S, *Irresistibly Drawn to the Eucharist* (Staten Island, NY: St. Paul's, 2002), 2.

veil. She is walking in faith, as we do. Faith has eyes to see, ears to hear, a heart to love. Through the eyes of faith, we see Jesus in the Eucharist. The hidden God revealed Himself in time and history in the Person of Jesus Christ. In faith we know Him. In the Eucharist we have communion with Him.

The Eucharist and Spiritual Desolation

In her *Diary*, Conchita expresses the superficial coldness of heart that occurs in times of desolation and simultaneously the knowledge—even confidence—that below the tumultuous surface, in the depths of the soul, there exists the inextinguishable fire of divine love:

> *December 4th, 1895, my soul is suffering great sadness and desolation, But I do not want to fall or faint in the fight even if it lasts until I die. Furthermore, in spite of the desolation which overcomes me, in the depths of me I feel a constant force that draws me to cling to the Eucharist; everywhere, at night, during the day, I feel this divine attraction in the very depth of my soul. I am frozen in the upper part of my spirit, and yet inside an everlasting fire is burning, a fire that never goes out. I have suffered a sadness whose weight has made me shed abundant tears; I have not been able to control myself especially in front of my most adorable Eucharist* (T. 561).[186]

The soul anchored in God—such as Conchita—remains enkindled at its core. That Conchita "has not been able to control [herself] especially in front of [her] most adorable Eucharist" reveals her ardor for Jesus. Conchita releases her entire heart in the presence

---

[186] Gutiérrez Gonzales, *Irresistibly Drawn to the Eucharist*, 7.

of Jesus; her soul spills into the Eucharist. Our hearts, too, can spill into the Eucharist. We can simply *be* with God. Conchita is brokenhearted before the Blessed Sacrament. She feels undone, and weeps uncontrollably. Jesus is there, receiving her. The tender Heart of Jesus that wept at the death of His friend Lazarus also weeps with us who are His friends. In the Eucharist, Jesus and Conchita come together as one heart—bathed in sorrows or joys—incorporated in love.

In times of desolation, it is even more important to present ourselves to the Blessed Sacrament. The source of spiritual desolation may be our own negligence in prayer or a test from God or a demonic attack. Conchita likely experienced each of these at times. Whatever the case may have been, she ran to the Eucharist, to her Jesus, for everything. She has a healthy distrust of herself and heroic trust in Christ.

I Offer Him Everything

Conchita was irresistibly drawn to the Eucharist, where she offered to Jesus herself and her sorrows, losses, disappointments, and family problems. Initially, her mother-in-law didn't like her and told her so.[187] She suffered painful humiliations from her sisters-in-law.[188] Her husband had quite a temper until, with Conchita's help, he changed so radically that his sisters were astounded—or as Conchita wrote, "he sweetened."[189] Throughout the many trials of her life—preparing her parents for death, burying her husband and four children, and facing the financial burdens she incurred as a widow, to name a few—Conchita presented everything to the

---

[187] *A Mother's Spiritual Diary*, 22.

[188] *A Mother's Spiritual Diary*, 21.

[189] *A Mother's Spiritual Diary*, 21.

Beautiful Holiness

Blessed Sacrament. The offering that Jesus desired most was every cell of Conchita's being. As she herself put it:

> Sorrows, setbacks, disappointments, much misery to lament over creatures who make life bitter ... let it all be for God, and may he support us and all our works. I clearly see the all-powerful hand of God and his cooperation in everything, in all that happens, and it is admirable.... I feel very sensibly, a loving confidence in Jesus. The Holy Eucharist draws me irresistibly.[190]

Jesus wants our offering to be complete, with nothing held back. On the Cross, Christ's oblation was total; nothing was withheld. Every atom of His Being; every sentiment of His Heart was offered to the Father to save souls. In *The Imitation of Christ*, Jesus says:

> Look, I offered myself wholly to the Father for you; I also gave my whole body and blood for you for food, that I might be wholly yours, and you should remain mine. But if you stand upon yourself and do not offer yourself freely to my will, the offering is not fully made, nor will union between us be complete.[191]

When we receive the Eucharist, do we surrender every atom of our being to Jesus? There's a little prayer that I offer when I receive the Eucharist. "Your Body in my body. Your Blood in my blood. Your Soul in my soul. Your Divinity in my humanity. Transfigure me, Lord." I imagine that I disappear into Jesus, and He makes me a new creation. I pray, "No more Kathleen, only Jesus." This is my

---

[190] A Mother's Spiritual Diary, 21.

[191] The Imitation of Christ 4, 8; see also Raniero Cantalamessa, The Eucharist: Our Sanctification (Collegeville, MN: Liturgical Press, 1993), 25.

ardent prayer. The Eucharist puts us into contact with the flesh of Jesus, the God-Man. We touch Jesus, and He touches us. How can we remain unchanged? We see how Conchita was changed by her experience of God. It should be like that for us.

My Heart's Only Happiness

Conchita always sought more of God, less of herself, and nothing of the world that passes. "The Eucharist is really the burning bush where God reveals himself as Yahweh, that is as the one 'who is there, who is present,' close at hand for his people (cf. Ex 3:14)."[192] God told Moses to take off his shoes when he was standing on holy ground. We must show reverence, humility, poverty, gratitude, and love in the presence of the Lord.

Conchita experienced the fulfillment of all her desires in the Eucharist:

> *How divine you are—you hold in your tabernacle all the delights of heaven that the world cannot appreciate. Oh, my Jesus! I am humbled and confused before this incomprehensible mystery. Only love has made you crush your holy heart to such an extent. That is where our soul's life resides, our heart's only happiness. Heart and soul of all virtues, you have them to share among those who come to you in good will. I am in ecstasy, I can go no further, my reason is lost and confused in such a deep mystery.*
>
> *How can I not see in you, my Jesus, the object of my longing, if when I receive you in Communion, I feel all my desires and wishes fulfilled? The world has never given me the divine well-being I feel in these moments. Yes, my Jesus, you and only you are capable of filling all the recesses of my heart. The soul's desires*

---

[192] Cantalamessa, *The Eucharist: Our Sanctification*, 78.

are infinite, and they can only be met by something infinite like you (T. 55).[193]

And what more do we desire for fulfillment if not Jesus? Yet there are times when Jesus recedes from our hearts while something more transiently entertaining captures the day. We know that our days are numbered, that our breaths are counted, and that opportunities to gain grace for eternity will cease. Frequent reception of the Eucharist empowers us to prefer Christ above all. Conchita wrote, "*Oh! The soul is such a wonderful thing, its value is immense!*"[194] Our souls are to be lovingly nourished by the Eucharist, so they may thrive as God wills.

Jesus: "I Am the Bread of Life"

In prayer, Jesus gave Conchita Scripture passages followed by reflections on them. Here are some excerpts:

John 6:35: "I am the Bread of Life. Whoever comes to Me will not hunger, and whoever believes in Me will not thirst." Jesus spoke, "These words speak to you of infinite humility and love without end, pronounced more by My Heart . . . than by My lips. Bread of Life, that is immortal food, divine substance that will strengthen you to reach your homeland without dying on the way."[195]

John 6:54: "He who eats My Flesh and drinks My Blood has eternal life." Jesus spoke: "This life is the true life, the life of grace that never dies, the immortal life that lasts forever. The Eucharist has the power of converting you into Me. If you could only understand

---

[193] *Irresistibly Drawn to the Eucharist*, 1.

[194] *A Mother's Spiritual Diary*, 138.

[195] Concepción Cabrera de Armida, *I AM: Eucharistic Meditations on the Gospel* (Staten Island, NY: St. Paul's, 2014), 28.

the gift of God. I am the Bread of Life come down from heaven purely out of love! My Flesh and My Blood will give you strength for the battles of life and will communicate to you the celestial fortitude that makes martyrs sacrifice themselves for love. I want to live in you, so that you may live in Me in a divine transformation. I said to My heavenly Father, "I am in them, and You are always in Me, so that they may be brought to perfection as one" (Jn 17:23) because through this intimacy I want to communicate Myself to you. And these will be the effects of the Bread of Life: you will live united, permeated by your Jesus, one with the Father and the Holy Spirit. Come, receive the Bread of love that costs nothing. 'It comes without cost' (Jn 55:1), because it is enough to have purity of heart to come to the Eucharist. Come, 'I am the living Bread that has come down from heaven" (Jn 6:51).[196]

Our participation in the Eucharist should render us more like Jesus. He wants to live in us and love through us. We are called to be His heart for others. The missionary efforts of the Church and the proclamation of the Gospel require witnesses of Eucharistic transformation.

Jesus' Mystical Passion Hidden in the Eucharist

Conchita's diaries contain several astonishing dialogues with Jesus on the Eucharist.

"*I am going to tell you about a secret from my heart,*" Our Lord promised Conchita in one of their conversations, "*and it is this—my Passion has not yet finished . . . .*"

"How can this be, Jesus?" she asked.

---

[196] I AM, 28.

Beautiful Holiness

"*My Passion on Calvary only lasted a few hours,*" He replied, "*but the Passion of My Heart lasted all my mortal life and will last mystically in the Eucharist until the end of the world. Another secret—the Passion of My Body found relief, but the Passion of My soul ...*" (T. 471).

On another occasion, Conchita recalled that, during prayer, Jesus told her:

> *Look daughter, I let myself be seen crucified at Calvary whereas in the Eucharist I am hidden, but that does not mean that I am any less present. The Passion of My Heart continues still because human sin and ingratitude continue still. When I give myself to souls in this Sacrament, I find rest in so few, and so few bring Me down from the Cross.... Study the hidden life in the Eucharist, and in the Cross study the practical life* (T. 926)....[197]
>
> *I have been crucified for centuries for man in the Eucharist, and yet I was only materially crucified for him in a few hours. My Passion has not yet finished, because sin has not yet come to an end, and for as long as there is sin in man there will be sacrifice in Jesus. Sacrifice yourself with me to console me, I am thirsty for sacrifice.... This world only gives me bitterness in its sensuality—so few remember that I am here in the tabernacle the same as on the Cross, praying and offering myself for them to the Eternal Father! Do not forget me ... think of me* (T. 928).[198]

The Passion of Jesus' Heart continues due to human sin and ingratitude. It's difficult for us to grasp the magnitude of the gift of Jesus on the Cross and in the Eucharist. In faith and love, our hearts should be captivated by Christ's gift, which is intimately personal.

[197] *Irresistibly Drawn to the Eucharist*, 37.
[198] *Irresistibly Drawn to the Eucharist*, 41.

We sometimes experience the pain of being rejected, mocked, taken for granted, and simply not being loved. But Jesus experienced these to the point of dying on a Cross. Jesus told Conchita that this is the practical life. Look around you. What would you do to save those you love—to bring friends, family, and even enemies to the Heart of Jesus?

Jesus told Conchita to "study" the hidden life in the Eucharist. Eucharistic life is the risen life. We understand that our sins are forgiven—that Jesus ransomed us and our wounds are redeemed. We know that Jesus lives; that the Eucharist is life. Our lives are practical and hidden, crucified and risen. Our study of the life of Jesus should never cease. In a way, the Church leads us to study the Cross especially during Lent and to study the Eucharist especially during Advent (the Incarnation) and Easter (the Resurrection).

The Purifying Effect of the Eucharist

Another dialogue recorded by Conchita goes like this:

> "My daughter [says Jesus], I wish to possess you, I want to absorb you in myself, in the immensity of my pain and in my infinite joy. I want union, union, an intimate union, that I have been asking you for a long time, and yet I who am Purity itself, I join myself to whatever is pure.... I who am Holiness itself, I join myself to whatever is holy, and I who am Divinity itself, I only join myself to what has been made divine." ...
>
> "But Jesus," I said, "how can You want to be joined to me, I who am neither pure, nor holy, nor made divine, but rather very material. What can I do, Jesus, to bring this about?"
>
> "The Eucharist makes man divine; it purifies him and makes him holy. He will always find everything he needs in the Eucharist, since it is the Nest of all that is holy, pure, and divine. You, my

daughter, have been purified as much as I need you to be. You need me, and you need to be made one substance with the Cross. You have to lose yourself in it, be one with it, so that you can be united to your Jesus. You see my daughter, the eucharistic rays are the ones that purify and unite the fastest, but they only go through souls that have been turned into the Cross" (T. 558).[199]

We ask, "What can I do, Jesus, about being made divine when I'm so very material?" We cannot sanctify or divinize ourselves. That is the work of God. If we look at the lives of the apostles and the saints, we see the practical processes of sanctification. One day they are afraid, insecure, unaware, bound to the flesh and the world. Then they encounter the Person of Jesus, who loves them. They become fearless, confident, free, happy, committed. They become authentic witnesses to Jesus because they have been transformed in Him. They spend their lives for Christ and become holy in the process.

Jesus continued to affirm Conchita's union with His Cross. He told her that the Eucharistic rays are the ones that purify and unite the fastest. It's simple to understand this really. The challenging part of the Lord's message is that those rays "only go through souls that have been turned into the Cross." Perhaps, without grasping the mystery of Eucharistic transformation, we who love Christ are turning into living crosses.

The truly amazing thing is that Jesus urgently, ardently, desires union with you and me. In the Eucharist, having encountered Someone so true and beautiful, we should be amazed. This encounter of love leads to Eucharistic amazement. Are you amazed by the Eucharist?

---

[199] *Irresistibly Drawn to the Eucharist*, 40.

The Eucharist and the Cross:
School of the Saints

Our faith is both-and: love and sacrifice, the Cross and the Eucharist, crucified and risen, suffering and healing, sinners and saints. As Jesus told Conchita:

The school of saints is to be found in the Cross and in the Eucharist. This is where the soul is taught, where it learns, where we suffer, where we love, this is where the soul retreats to from the earth, where it draws near to heaven. Here it is tested and rewarded; here it purified and sanctified, here it dies to come back to life, and live....

You, see, daughter, the Eucharist and the Cross, Love and Pain, are so united that nothing can separate them. I am crucified here at all times, mystically, and the blood of Calvary is the blood on the altar, and the body offered as a victim on the Cross is the wafer of the eucharistic sacrifice.

Love and suffer, daughter, suffer and love. Don't stray from the Cross or from the Eucharist. Bear souls, especially the one I have entrusted to you for perfection. Teach the wealth of pain, of patient sacrifice, of voluntary crucifixion, of living sacrifice, that is, the treasures of the Cross. But teach as well where to find the sources of strength, infinite love, the greatest manifestation of God's tenderness, the Eucharist. Divine substance conquers human nature. May souls love me, my daughter. I want love, but a pure love of purity and sacrifice.[200]

"Don't stray from the Cross or from the Eucharist," Jesus tells us. How could we? Where would we go but into a dark void? We know this void, and many people exist in it without realizing there's

---

[200] *Irresistibly Drawn to the Eucharist,* 44.

something far more excellent offered to them. There are too many who have yet to discover the truth and beauty of Eucharistic life. Let us be better apostles of the Eucharist by becoming what we eat at the Table of the Lord.

We can know intellectually what is required. But often we are like St. Paul: "I do not understand my own actions. For I do not do what I want, but I do the very thing I hate.... For I know that nothing good dwells within me, that is, in my flesh. I will what is right, but I cannot do it. For I do not do the good I want, but the evil I do not want is what I do" (Rom. 7:15-19). Jesus knows that we need the Cross and the Eucharist. "Lord, make me want both, please." The whole divine economy is ordered to our sanctification, through Jesus, the Cross, and the Eucharist.

Holy-Hour Reflections

Then Jesus went with them to a place called Gethsemane, and he said to his disciples, "Sit here, while I go yonder and pray." And taking with him Peter and the two sons of Zebedee, he began to be sorrowful and troubled. Then he said to them, "My soul is very sorrowful, even to death; remain here, and watch with me." (Matt. 26:36-38)

Traditionally, this Scripture is the basis for praying a holy hour. Jesus invited His apostles to keep a vigil of prayer as His agony was at hand. When He returned to them, they were asleep. "So," He says to them, "could you not watch with me one hour?" (Matt. 26:40).

Holy hours are usually prayed during Eucharistic adoration, and this is most appropriate. But they can be prayed at any time, in a church, in a retreat room, or at home to accommodate families. During a holy hour, we place ourselves before Christ Jesus and recollect our hearts. We may remain silent in a gaze of love or meditate on Christ's life or on the Gospel. Conchita's Eucharistic holy-hour meditations are beautiful to ponder, often becoming dialogues with the Lord.

Mary and the Eucharist

Conchita begins a holy hour meditating on Mary and the Eucharist:

> *The cave in Bethlehem, where Mary laid my Child Jesus, was the first of all tabernacles ... and the poor clothes that wrapped Him were the first corporals. O my God, how could I approach the Eucharist, how could I receive it in my heart without thinking about Mary? To whom is it that I owe that treasure of my soul, that divine life, the seed of purity from my heart, if not through the Eucharist given through Mary?*[201]

Mary responds to Conchita:

> *I received Him, my child, being His servant ... and as such, I kissed His feet. ... I received Him as His mother, and then I kissed His forehead. ... I received Him as a daughter and then I kissed His hands ... but always humbling myself ... always disappearing so that He could appear in me. I received Him with an ardent thirst to possess Him. ... I received Him with the whiteness of the lily of the valley in my heart ... with the fire of more than a million Seraphim ... with the greater purity than that of all the angels, and with deeper suffering than that of all the martyrs.*

"*But, with pain, Mother of my soul, why?*" Conchita asks. Mary replies:

[201] *Holy Hours,* 43, 44.

Pain because of the insults that He received ... because of the forgetfulness of souls ... because of the ingratitude of His own people ... because of the longing to possess Him that was killing me. And thus is the preparation you need to receive Him; you must be humble, pure, mindless of yourself, ardent and with suffering and reparation, and with the martyrdom of desiring to possess Him forever.[202]

Conchita promised to think of Mary each morning during Mass—to imagine her at the foot of the altar when the Lord came out of the tabernacle to be adored in the monstrance. Conchita asked Mary for her purity, her fire, her hunger, and her celestial ardor with which to love Jesus.

During our holy hours, we can meditate with Mary. When we feed upon the Bread of Life, we can unite ourselves to the Virgin Mother in whom the Word became flesh. He waits for us, ready to grant us a personal audience.

Sometimes I simply sit in His presence; I enter into stillness so deep that time and space fade. It is exquisite to *be* with Jesus. Let us resist the temptation not to pray, not to go to Mass, not to make holy hours. The devil will persist in distracting us, tempting us to do something else, even good things, rather than keep a vigil of prayer. Protect your prayer time as the most precious hour of your day.

He Hides Himself to Come Nearer to Us

One day, Jesus told Conchita:

I was profoundly hidden in the Incarnation, but it was still not enough.... How could I hide Myself even more? My flesh was already similar to your own flesh, but how could I live nearer to

---

[202] *Holy Hours*, 45.

you ... hiding Myself under the appearance of bread, and making
Myself even smaller than under the likeness of man? And this
other intimate bond that I was yet going to contract with you in
the Eucharist would bring Me even nearer to you, so that I would
constantly be at your side, day and night.

That is why, burning with love, on the night that preceded
My passion, I said, "Take and eat, this is My Body.... Take and
drink, this is My Blood," because I thought of you, because I
foresaw this day, when you would be here at the foot of my throne
contemplating Me.

Child of My Soul, I am in the Eucharist so that I can live
more intimately with you ... to be your comfort, your father, your
friend, your solace, your heaven upon earth. It is My love that
compels Me to cover Myself with these veils ... to keep the secret
of My glory.[203]

Conchita asked Jesus, "Where could you minimize Yourself even
more than in a consecrated Host?"

In your heart, My dearest child, in your heart; and this is the last
step to which the Incarnate Word descends, it is there where I hide
to work marvels in your favor; in the solitary and narrow throne I
repose to transform it, to do it good, by communicating the holy fire
to it, with my own substance. I come down happy and content in
your heart to give you peace ... to make suffering easy for you ... to
form in you a Cross upon which I can rest. When you receive Me
in the Eucharist you become one with Me, another Jesus, but do
you show this in your thoughts, in your words, and in your works?
Do you reproduce me in yourself, being humble, patient, sweet,
attractive, self-sacrificing, obedient, silent, and pure?

[203] *Holy Hours,* 60, 61.

Beautiful Holiness

How are we reproducing Christ in us? The truth is that we are unable to judge for ourselves the true state of our spiritual lives. Like Conchita, we need an objective, trained helper, such as a spiritual director. Early in my reversion, in my mid-thirties, I consumed St. Teresa of Ávila's writings. Then I tried to estimate my spiritual place in her seven mansions. Soon I learned the futility (and pride) of this exercise!

Some evidence of our Eucharistic transformation is seen in the way we love and serve our families, fulfill the duties of our vocation, embrace our crosses, and persist to follow Christ daily. We can ask, "What is the measure of my love for God and souls?"

Blessed Conchita teaches us to prioritize the Eucharistic life. Jesus asks, "Do you reproduce me in yourself," being attractive (among other things). A nightly examination of conscience is a helpful reality check for us. How attractive or loving is my witness: my voice, my words, my countenance, my demeanor?

Here I Am

In one beautiful declaration to Conchita, Our Lord said:

> *I left heaven because I saw you were very far away, My child, and I contemplated you all alone without the Eucharist ... because My love for you, poor little earthworm, impelled me to come nearer, so the Word could take on flesh to give it to you divinized in the Sacrament of Love. I desired to live near and inside of you, and this is the reason that I left My throne of Cherubim, and My pedestal of Seraphim. I have come to occupy, with great pleasure, this, My poor and silent dwelling place upon the earth.*
>
> *I desire to have here simple, poor, hidden and generous souls that have their delight only in sacrificing themselves in My honor. I tell you that I formed this holy place, My tabernacle, for us to be*

here all alone ... nearer to each other ... Heart to heart, communi-
cating to you My innermost being in every heartbeat. I have arrived
so that you may remain in Me, and so that your heart may have life.

... Thus you will imitate Me more easily, crucifying yourself in
union with Me, for there is no other way to become more spiritual
than to mortify oneself.[204]

These words of Jesus are medicine for the soul. Jesus simply will
not leave us starving for His love. In the Eucharist, He stays with
us, never tiring of giving Himself to us. Do we ever tire of hearing
a spouse, a child, or a parent say, "I love you"? These words always
enliven the soul. Jesus speaks the language of love that will quicken
our souls. He wants to stir us to ardor as He did the woman at the
well, Magdalene, Peter, and Paul.

The resurrected Jesus spoke to Peter. "When they had finished
breakfast, Jesus said to Simon Peter, 'Simon, son of John, do you
love me more than these?' He said to him, 'Yes, Lord; you know
that I love you.' He said to him, 'Feed my lambs'" (John 21:15).
Jesus feeds Simon Peter breakfast, sustenance for his physical being. And Jesus feeds Peter spiritual food by inviting him to affirm
his love three times. This overshadows Peter's three denials, now
redeemed by his giving voice to his love of Jesus. Peter would never
again deny Jesus but would give his life for Him. I think Eucharistic
transformation looks something like this.

Conchita's Mission in the Church

Conchita belongs to the Church. Jesus told her:

Each soul bears its own mission on earth. Yours, on account of
my bounty, is the sublime mission of offering yourself as a victim

---

[204] *Holy Hours*, 216.

Beautiful Holiness

for My Church, especially of her Shepherds. You no longer belong to yourself, you belong to the Church, and the Word will make use of you for His sake. Alone you are worth nothing, but in union with Me, God will do great things through you. Repeat often: "I am the Lord's servant" (Diary, February 5, 1911).[205]

Thus, Conchita has been called an apostle of the Eucharist.

Theologians have said that Conchita calls us to a new type of holiness. Blessed Conchita's favorite saint, Thérèse of Lisieux, spoke of a wholly new way, the Little Way, of following Christ. Likewise, without departing from the Gospel, Conchita calls us to a new type of holiness:

Conchita's new type of holiness:

1. *A calling of all, even of the laity, even of married people, to the greatest holiness.*

2. *Through transfiguration of daily life, the sanctification of the profane, divinization by faith, by love, and by the spirit of sacrifice in ordinary life.*

3. *The greatest holiness. Transcendence of the message of the Cross. Even the most banal actions are made of value to the infinite by the offering of love in union with Christ, in imitation of the last years on earth of the Mother of God, in the service of the nascent Church.*[206]

Toward the end of her life, Jesus asked Conchita to begin a new work on behalf of the sanctity of homes:

I want many acts of expiation for the divorces which are the source of so many evils in homes, harmful to spouses, children, and society. I ask expiation for so many hidden sins and for so many

---

[205] A Mother's Diary, 245.
[206] Holy Hours, 244, 245.

sins of omission in the Christian formation of children. I want a crusade of victim souls for the sanctification of homes (*Diary*, Oct. 31, 1935).[207]

Mass and Adoration of the Blessed Sacrament are powerful ways to offer expiation. Jesus asked Conchita for a crusade of victim souls. Is He speaking to us? Is He inviting us to Eucharistic transformation and to the Cross to help save souls? Saints before and after Blessed Conchita attribute to the Eucharist the good that was done in and through them.

Worship and Adoration of the Eucharist outside of Mass

Fr. Domenico explained that in the place and time in which Conchita lived, it was unusual to have Eucharistic adoration outside of Mass. Conchita made a point of finding the tabernacle. Those of us who have easy access to Eucharistic adoration should be grateful, never take it for granted, and adore the Blessed Sacrament for the sake of love.

Cardinal Cantalamessa explains the history of adoration outside of Mass:

Worship and adoration of the Eucharist outside of Mass is relatively new in Christian devotion. In fact, it started to develop in the West at the beginning of the eleventh century as a reaction to the heresy of Berengar of Tours who denied the "real" presence, claiming that Jesus was only symbolically present in the Eucharist. Since then, however, we can say that there has not been a saint in whose life Eucharistic devotion has not been a determining factor. It has been

---

[207] *Holy Hours*, 245.

the source of great spiritual energy, a sort of home fire that is always burning in God's house where all the great sons and daughters of the Church have warmed themselves.[208]

In this chaotic world, there is a refuge, a place of peace and joy that is Jesus in the Eucharist. We should ask ourselves what prevents us from going to Mass and adoration as often as possible. Whatever that thing is, try putting it aside for just one hour a day. You may discover yourself and your life transformed for making the time and effort.

The Eucharist nurtures life and creates nurturing children of God. The Eucharist softens hearts and heals; strengthens soldiers for Christ; equips disciples; and sends forth Christ bearers. Remember Conchita's words about Jesus: "*You hold in Your tabernacle all the delights of heaven.*" Imagine foretasting the delights of Heaven if only we place ourselves in His Eucharistic presence. There are generations of believers who have experienced Jesus in truth, in love, in the Eucharist.

---

[208] *The Eucharist: Our Sanctification*, 60.

Individual or Group Reflection

Ponder

"And they devoted themselves to the apostles' teaching and fellowship, to the breaking of bread and the prayers" (Acts 2:42).

Engage

1. What has Conchita taught you about Eucharistic life?
2. What could you do to honor and reverence Our Lord in the Eucharist more completely?
3. How do the Cross and the Eucharist—suffering and love—impact your vocation?

Pray

Lord Jesus, through our Eucharistic incorporation, grant that I may be a child of the light, salt of the earth, bread for the hungry, water for the thirsty, new wine, and healing oil for others. May people see You in my servant's heart, You in the light of my eyes, You in the warmth of my heart, You in the works of my hands, You in the words of my mouth, You in the incense of my prayer, You in the lightness of my laughter, You in the glistening of my tears, You in the lowliness of Your creature. Hide me, I pray, in the gilded monstrance of Your loving heart so that I can be a living monstrance radiating Your healing rays of love.[209]

[209] Kathleen Beckman, *God's Healing Mercy: Finding Your Path to Forgiveness, Peace, and Joy* (Manchester, NH, Sophia Institute Press, 2015), 133-134.

9

For Love of Priests:
Revelations and Prayers

Like living stones be yourselves built into
a spiritual house, to be . . . a royal priesthood.

—1 Peter 2:5, 9

Priesthood of the Baptized

Christ entrusted to Blessed Conchita a mission for the sanctification of priests. Through her mystical union with Jesus, she possessed a "spiritual vision, which projects a light of particular beauty on the vocation to holiness of ordained ministers."[210] Over the past eighty-five years since Conchita died, priests around the globe have meditated upon "Confidences" from the Heart of Jesus given to Conchita.

In this chapter, we'll reflect on themes found in Christ's revelations for priests. The writings show the international scope of Conchita's charism of spiritual maternity. Evidence of Conchita's charism of spiritual maternity of priests began in 1889, when she offered her newborn son Manuel to Jesus. She nurtured his

---

[210] Concepcíon Cabrera de Armida, *Priests of Christ* (Staten Island, NY: Society of St. Paul, 2015), xvii.

vocation. Years later, living in Spain, Manuel wrote to his mother about his decision to enter the Society of Jesus. She wrote back to her son, who would become a priest:

> *Give yourself to the Lord with all your heart, and do not hold anything back! Forget about creatures and forget especially about yourself! I cannot imagine someone consecrated to God who is not a saint. One cannot give only half of oneself to God. Be generous with him!*[211]

Conchita's writings for priests filled more than a thousand pages in her *Diary*. With all the love of His Heart, Jesus spoke of the exalted dignity of priests, of His singular union with them. Christ entrusts Himself completely into the anointed hands of His ministers. He told Conchita:

> *When I took on human nature, I took on love for man as I bore man's blood and shared brotherhood with man; with both natures, the divine and the human, I deified man through contact with the Word, lifting him up from what is earthly so that he might aspire to heaven. From among all men, I chose those who would be Mine, who would become another Me, men who would continue the mission that brought Me to earth, namely, to take back to the Father what came from Him in the first place; souls to glorify Him eternally.... Each priest is more than any other child, a child of My Mother.*[212]

Conchita's writings for priests were originally titled *Confidences to My Priests* and later called simply *Confidences*. The locutions about priests were scattered among the pages of Conchita's *Diary*

---

[211] *A Mother's Spiritual Diary*, 82.
[212] *Priests of Christ*, 9.

which she originally titled her *Account of Conscience* from 1927 to 1931.[213] Archbishop Luis Martinez was her spiritual director at this period of maturity in her spiritual life. He was a luminous support for this chosen daughter. Reaching a peak in her life, Conchita had serenity that God had fulfilled His promises made in her youth.

> At this time, Conchita was living alone. Her family life consisted of looking after her grandchildren, and sporadic visits from her family. Although illnesses were not lacking either in herself or in others, this was the period of her life with the fewest family responsibilities. She could spend more time praying, writing, remembering and loving.[214]

Although the demands of raising a family were absent, Conchita was occupied with spreading the Works of the Cross through writing numerous booklets and instructing people about the spirituality of the Cross. But she spent extended time in prayer before the Blessed Sacrament, writing, reflecting, and enjoying the company of her Beloved Jesus.

For priests, Conchita was a trusted, wise Marian woman with a reputation for virtue, purity, and simplicity.

Historical Context, *Confidences* to Priests

The Lord spoke to Conchita about His priests during a time of terrible persecution of the Church in Mexico. In 2015, for a book titled *Priests of Christ*, Fr. Carlos Vera Soto, M.Sp.S., wrote a historical introduction about the messages given to priests.

---

[213] *Priests of Christ*, xxii.
[214] *Priests of Christ*, xli.

Beautiful Holiness

Under turbulent political and social conditions, Conchita wrote the *Confidences*. One thing that is surprising in the life of this woman, given the times and the style of the Church at that moment, is that she was a friend to many priests and bishops. What is even more surprising, something that can be seen in her *Account of Conscience*, is that she often went to them to ask for support, advice, spiritual guidance and consolation.

On frequent occasions, however, it was Conchita who helped the "Lord's ministers" with her own words and advice.... Conchita was a privileged witness to the longings, the struggles, the stumbling, the successes, and the sins of the shepherds of her time. Conchita knew the Church "from within." She knew it much better than most other people of her time. Her sensitivity and her profound religious feelings were constantly illuminated or darkened by the qualities or imperfections of those who should have been teachers of holiness.

... Conchita kept in her prayer the martyrdom of the Mexican Church together with the abuses and sins of priests.[215]

The Mexican Revolution (1910–1917) occurred while Conchita was in her forties. The Cristero War (1926–1929) transpired when she was in her sixties. Conchita witnessed the horrific persecution and killing of priests and nuns and the destruction of churches that took a dreadful toll on all her countrymen. Her *Diary* contains gut-wrenching details of these wars.

Dated September 22, 1927, a dialogue between Conchita and Jesus confirmed her concerns about priests:

[215] *Priests of Christ*, lvi.

My Jesus, my Adorable Heaven! What can I tell You? Your sorrow is my sorrow. You know that in all of me I have no will apart from Yours. I will fulfill Your desires and with my soul's blood I will ask the bishops, my spiritual director, and the priests and those who belong to the Works (of the Cross) I can reach, to listen to Your complaints and do something about them. And yet, Jesus, look and take consolation. There is so much that is good in Your vineyard. Many souls long to give You glory, to be crucified for You, longing for You to carry out Your will in them and through them.

Jesus replied:

That is true, My daughter, but you do not know how deeply the sins of those chosen souls, that have cost Me so much, hurt Me. One sin of theirs is for Me like a thousand sins of the common people who have not received such a superabundance of charisms. You cannot measure My love for those souls joined with My love for the Church, the universal center of all My loves. You cannot understand the exquisite torture I feel from their ingratitude (AC, 49:22–24).[216]

Conchita tried to console Jesus. She was pained that the tender Heart of Jesus is excoriated by the infidelity of priests whom He loves extravagantly.

Conchita's idea of priesthood had been influenced by Fr. Félix de Jesús Rougier since their friendship started in 1903. Fr. Félix taught Conchita his high ideal of priesthood—namely, that, due to the greatest dignity of the priesthood, individual priests should mirror the Lord's holiness. But there was corruption in the Church of Mexico at that time, so reform of the priesthood would also

[216] *Priests of Christ*, lvi.

require reformation of society. Fr. Carlos Vera Soto explains that "Conchita and Father Rougier were of the opinion that no sacrifice was too great to eradicate such a great evil, an evil that held the people in misery and that offended Jesus."[217]

Archbishop Ruiz y Flores, Influence, Affirmation

Holy friendships are rooted in God, who, throughout history, united people to support and inspire one another. Conchita had many such friendships. Archbishop Leopoldo Ruiz y Flores believed that the moral life of the laity depended on the holiness of the clergy. He aligned with the French school of spirituality, which included St. John Eudes, St. Louis-Marie Grignon de Montfort, and St. Vincent de Paul. This idea was spoken about with Conchita, so she had similar ideals.

As Fr. Carlos Vera Soto tells us:

Conchita met Ruiz y Flores in 1903, when he was the Bishop of León. The bishop was a true and faithful friend, a man who believed her, admired her, understood her, and loved her with the constancy of a true friend. The letters they wrote to each other are a witness of their friendship from 1903, when they met, until March 1, 1937, two days before Conchita died. Their singlemindedness, their mutual help, trust, admiration, and appreciation of each other can be seen in simple and direct language. The letters are really a manual of friendship between a laywoman and a priest.[218]

In 1913, Archbishop Ruiz y Flores wrote a letter to the apostolic delegate, "In my opinion, Your Excellency, we priests need to

---

[217] *Priests of Christ*, lvii.
[218] *Priests of Christ*, lviii.

make genuine amends to Our Lord, setting out to reform our lives in the ministry based on the inner reform of each one of us."[219]

In 1927, when Conchita spoke to Archbishop Ruiz y Flores about the *Confidences*, he was affirming, asking her to sort out the writings addressed to priests. Then the archbishop confided Conchita's writings discreetly to some bishop friends and asked their opinion about them. Having received many positive opinions, he desired to publish them for priests, and he wrote the introduction to the first edition. He became so convinced of the great good of Conchita's writings for priests that he had them bound in satin, and, as he was now the apostolic delegate, he personally took them to Pope Pius XI (1922–1939) so His Holiness could benefit from the teachings that his friend Conchita had received from God.

The Condition of the Clergy

On their *ad limina* visits to Rome, the Mexican bishops informed the Vatican that "in general ... their priests were honest and upright. They said they obeyed the directives of the bishops and the Holy See. Yet, in every diocese in the country there were some priests, five or six in each diocese, who did not lead lives in accordance with their priestly condition."[220]

In 1908, Bishop José Mora y del Río of León wrote to his counterpart and friend Bishop Juan Herrera y Piña:

The people long for zealous priests, which, unfortunately is not what all our priests are. Some of them forget the obligations of their holy ministry, while others make the most of it in order to act as wolves among their flock, doing

---

[219] *Priests of Christ*, lviii.
[220] *Priests of Christ*, lx.

great damage to souls. I am convinced from experience that a bad priest causes such destruction wherever he is that it becomes exceedingly difficult for people to return to Christian practices. I am at the point of being convinced that people become lukewarm in their faith due to those of us who do not fulfill the duties of their holy ministry.... I turned to the Sacred Heart and asked Him to remedy these needs and free me from such great sorrow. Whenever I found out something for certain, I could not rest until the situation had been remedied. Letting them do as they wish is to be guilty of other people's sins and not to fulfill the shepherd's duty.[221]

The bishop's fatherly heart was with the people who long for zealous priests. The tension between priests and their bishops was no secret. "Persecuted by the authorities, having to work in secret, disguised, hounded by the press and by official opinion, priests' ideals were weakened and loss of heart and the interest for pastoral work was frequent."[222] Much healing and restoration was needed. The Lord matured Conchita's spiritual maternity now.

Spiritual Maternity for Her Priest Son

Manuel was born at the same hour that a priest died. Conchita prayed that Manuel would replace that priest at the altar. Her offering was renewed throughout his life. In 1922, just before ordination, he wrote, "Mother, teach me how to be a priest! Tell me about the immeasurable joy of being able to celebrate Holy Mass. I put everything back into your hands.... As soon as I am

---

[221] *Priests of Christ*, lxi.
[222] *Priests of Christ*, lxii.

a priest, I will send you my blessing, and then I will receive yours on my knees."[223]

On March 23, 1932, Conchita wrote to Manuel:

As for you, how are you? Very brave, very confident, very generous and at peace? I expect this from you and pray the Lord that you profit by these crosses for your soul's sake: why not, if Jesus loves you so that He wished to give you a drop from His chalice, a thorn from His crown? Courage! The Cross carries him who carries it with love. Love Him a great deal. Let Him love you back, boldly ask Him to love you, care for you, embrace you, hug you to His loving Heart, because His delight is being with the sons of men. Become a little child, throw yourself into His arms! It pleases Him that we need Him, that we request, that we confide in His tenderness and in His love! The poorer we are, the more we have a right to His caresses and His graces!

Blessed persecution that opens for you a great horizon to suffer more, to confide more, to love Jesus without measure, because of the fondness of His love! Oh, how good Jesus is! In His arms what can you fear? Inside His Heart, what can you lack? Oh, how good Jesus is! He looks for pretexts to pour out His favors upon us! Who can ever outdo His thoughtfulness and His incomparable sweetness? Can one find a more refined sensitivity than that suffered by a loving heart, a priestly soul? Does love ask for rest, or suffering a pause, since its joy is to suffer for the loved one? Do not measure the height of your Calvaries, nor the weight or the dimension of your Cross: forget yourself, your true sorrow being solely that of seeing

---

[223] Congregation for the Clergy, *Eucharistic Adoration for the Sanctification of Priests and Spiritual Maternity* (Rome: Congregation for the Clergy, 2007), 25, https://www.usccb.org/beliefs-and-teachings/vocations/parents/upload/spiritual-maternity-congregation-fo-clergy.pdf.

Jesus offended, insulted, and persecuted. All our martyrdoms are like shooting stars before the Cross of Jesus.

Be a victim for the guilty, forgive and forget; complete Jesus' passion in your own heart. I envy you, because persecution is a sign of those who are chosen; no wonder Saint Ignatius requested it for his sons.

... Write to me, even if it's only a postcard, so I can hear from you.... Keep praying for your brothers: the time has come for all of us to be put to the test. Blessed be God![224]

If Conchita's advice is put into practice, great strides will be made in the spiritual life:

"Do not measure the height of your Calvaries, nor the weight or dimension of your Cross."

"Let [the Lord] love you back; boldly ask Him to love you."

"Forget yourself; Your true sorrow being solely that of seeing Jesus offended, insulted, and persecuted."

"Complete Jesus' passion in your own heart."

Christ's Passion is a school of love; His Resurrection, the eternal fruit of suffering love. Conchita measured love by the standard of the Cross, and this mother of a priest pushed her beloved son toward the Cross. Is this not like Mary at the wedding feast at Cana, when she encouraged her Son's hour by suggesting that He work His first public miracle?

Conchita wanted to see only Jesus in her priest son because she was preoccupied with his holiness. Mother and son always encouraged holiness through the Cross.

---

[224] *A Mother's Letters*, 38–39.

Holiness attracts, connects, and forms saints. We have examples: St. Teresa of Ávila and St. John of the Cross; St. Clare and St. Francis of Assisi, St. Monica and St. Augustine. Presently Blessed Conchita's cause is advancing, as are the causes of two of her spiritual directors, Servant of God Archbishop Luis Martinez and Venerable Fr. Félix Rougier. The Lord is a masterful weaver of souls.

Spiritual Motherhood of All Priests

As mother of a priest, and a pupil of Jesus, Conchita had unique insights into a priest's soul. She knew the Sacred Heart's ardor for priests. She understood the sacrifices necessary for a virtuous life. Conchita was aware of demonic temptations targeting priests. The devil especially tempts priests to pride, discouragement, doubt, lethargy, futility, and loneliness.

Conchita knew the cost of being a spiritual mother of priests and was willing to suffer for their purification. Jesus told her:

> *There are souls who through ordination receive a priestly anointing. However, there are also priestly souls who do not have the dignity or the ordination of a priest, yet they have a priestly mission. They offer themselves united to me.... These souls help the Church in a very powerful spiritual way.... You will be the mother of a great number of spiritual children, yet they will cost your heart the death of a thousand martyrs.... Bring yourself as an offering for the priests. Unite your offering with my offering, to obtain graces for them.*[225]

Conchita never counted the cost of making sacrifices for priests. Her maternal heart would suffer to give birth to the priests known as Missionaries of the Holy Spirit.

---

[225] Congregation for the Clergy, *Eucharistic Adoration*, 24.

In the vision of the Cross of the Apostolate, Conchita saw the Sacred Heart impaled by a small cross, and she asked Jesus what it signified. Christ explained that the cross that pierced His heart represented the pain inflicted by the infidelities of some priests. Conchita was moved to console the heart of Jesus and to offer reparation.

Years later, the Lord told Conchita how the grace of the mystical incarnation actualized her spiritual maternity of priests:

You are a mother with the image of Mary. A mother mystically of Me and My priests, because, oh marvelous secret that you ignored, when the mystical incarnation took place in your heart, the Holy Spirit, through the fruitfulness of the Father, put the Word into your soul and with Him, My child, He also put His priests. You did not know this origin, nor had you been aware of it, but because of your mystical maternity of the Eternal High Priest, the motherhood of priests was also reflected in your soul, and will never be separated from Him, because they must represent Him, as they are transformed into Him (A.C., Vol 50: pp.176-77, January 6, 1928).[226]

Conchita mystically participated in Mary's mothering of Jesus and His priests since, at the mystical incarnation, the Holy Spirit placed the Word in her soul and in His priests. Mary gives special graces for priests through Conchita's self-offering.

Mariologist Fr. Emile Neubert, S.M., writes, "Mary needs priests. It is especially through them that she can carry out her mission of giving Jesus to the world."[227] Giving Jesus to the world

---

[226] Olivera, *Mystical Incarnation*, 50.

[227] Fr. Emile Neubert, S.M., *Mary and the Priestly Ministry* (New Bedford, MA, Academy of the Immaculate, 2009), 18.

is Mary's mission, into which Conchita was drawn. The mystical incarnation magnified Conchita's Marian character and united her to Mary, Mother of priests.

Conchita's Marriage Contributed to Her Spiritual Maternity of Priests

Jesus told Conchita that her vocation to marriage was necessary for her spiritual maternity of priests:

> *You see, if you had not been married, I would not have given you My priests as your sons; but married and enveloped in the special graces in which My power and My wisdom envelop you, this could be accomplished. Your life had to be so in order to arrive at the end for which My goodness created you; to be a mother through intimate sorrow that you share with Me; to be a receptacle into which I pour the graces of My heart into yours; and with this "third love," to give of what is Mine — to give Me — to scatter upon the priestly souls the perfume and love of your Jesus. The mystical incarnation was the cradle of your motherhood toward priests. As a mother, you pour the divine Son upon your children with all of His treasures and bounties in such profusion that, as it is said, they do not fit in His soul* (December 19, 1931).[228]

When she was twenty-nine, Conchita lamented because nobody ever spoke to her about the possibility of her entering the religious life. "This makes her suffer, since she thinks that like this, married, she belongs *less to God*. Jesus will take care of modifying those ideas in her, and will teach her the reasons for her marriage, her maternity, her laity."[229]

---

[228] Olivera, *Mystical Incarnation*, 50.
[229] Vera Soto, *The Flower of Mexico*, 25.

Beautiful Holiness

Conchita's vocation to marriage and motherhood best suited God's extensive plans for her. Her family was the precise environment to produce the greatest fruit for the holiness of priests. Just because Conchita was a married woman didn't mean that her heart had less ardor for God. Her mystical incarnation enkindled even more zeal for God and souls.

Similarly, our vocation is God's calling to the place and people where He can best sanctify us and produce the greatest fruit for His kingdom. Our vocation is not only where we die to self but where we'll become a new creation in Christ. This is a good thing. "Unless a grain of wheat falls into the earth and dies, it remains alone; but if it dies, it bears much fruit" (John 12:24). Our vocation isn't intended to be the fulfillment of all our desires. Only God fulfills our desires. Conchita learned this, and so shall we.

You Belong to Priests

The call to the priesthood is a call to the Cross. The priest becomes the victim who offers the Victim on the altar. Christ chose mere men to become His other self. This may be the greatest entrustment of divine love. Christ descends into His priest, and a mere man arises to the stature of the Eternal High Priest. This is done for the good of God's people, for you and me.

In 1928, during a retreat directed by Archbishop Martinez, Conchita's spiritual director, Jesus expands her role for priests:

> Even more, it is your duty, insofar as you are able, to lead priests to heaven. Also, the souls of the priests who are in purgatory belong to you, so that you hasten the beatific vision for them. But, look daughter, at My great mercy for you: in each saved priest I will see something of yours which will glorify Me. You don't understand the extent of this divine promise, which will increase your glory,

but your spiritual director does. So do not be afraid. With all the generosity you are capable of, cast yourself toward the only north of your life, which should be My will, glorifying the Trinity. Why should you be afraid if I live in you and will be your strength? Expand your soul and enjoy the painful Cross which My goodness offers you, because to be a mother is to be a living Cross.[230]

Then Conchita inquired, "Lord, so You don't want me for the Works of the Cross anymore, as You have told me many times?"

Yes, you will continue to be for the Works, but in a more perfect and profitable way. From now on, you belong to priests and all your immolations in union with Me will be for priests. Not only this, daughter, but you must also consecrate your life, not only for ordained priests, but also for those in formation, for seminarians, for hesitating vocations and for those whom the devil wants to snatch, because your mission extends to all of them, from the beginning to the end, in those sublime priest races.

Then Jesus spoke about spiritual maternity of the hierarchy:

Look My daughter, the pope, cardinals, archbishops and bishops, parish priests and priests should enter into full acceptance of that spiritual motherhood on behalf of priests. So you must now immolate yourself for their sake because the entire ecclesiastical hierarchy forms one priesthood with the Eternal Priest. But don't be frightened; this is only one way of manifesting My plans in you, accentuating them (Nov. 29, 1928).[231]

---

[230] Concepción Cabrera de Armida, *To Be Jesus Crucified: Retreat Directed by Archbishop Luis M. Martínez* (Staten Island, NY: St. Paul's, 2013), 63.

[231] *To Be Jesus Crucified*, 62.

Beautiful Holiness

Jesus asked much of Conchita, but He also rewarded her beyond anything she could have imagined. He promised to grant Conchita special graces and increased glory for each priest she helped to save! How beautiful it would be to enter Heaven and meet the priests we helped to get home.

Jesus asked Conchita to consecrate her life for the holiness of priests. That required making a solemn dedication to this special purpose. Consecration means "association with the sacred." A consecration to Jesus or Mary is a sacred promise wherein we offer ourselves and our goods to God for His glory. God is always the goal of sacred consecrations. Jesus increased Conchita's capacity to love, to suffer, and to win the prized souls of priests—living and deceased—and seminarians. Christ magnified her offering for priests.

All For Priests? What about My Family?

Later, Conchita told Jesus that she hesitated to offer everything for priests because it was her duty to purchase graces for her children at home.

Jesus replied:

This same sacrifice will be on their behalf too, very much on their behalf, I promise it to you. Besides, I am taking care of them. Anyway, giving yourself on behalf of priests and giving them all does not hinder you from imploring graces for your children, since that is a motherly duty.[232]

Conchita's inquiry was pure and honest. She was a loving mother who prioritized her children. Jesus assured her of the plentitude of divine assistance for her children. Furthermore,

---

[232] *To Be Jesus Crucified*, 62.

Conchita's offering for priests didn't preclude her from praying for graces for her children. The loving duty of a biological mother is to pray and sacrifice for her children. The holy duty of a spiritual mother is to pray and sacrifice for her spiritual children. In this case, Conchita's spiritual children are priests. It is impossible for us to outgive God. There's no limit to the expansiveness of love. Jesus called Conchita to be a Marian apostle to the apostles (cf. John 20:18).

I often lead retreats for spiritual mothers of priests who ask that question about family. Jesus helped me to understand that the goods of the Church are the greatest gift and need of my family. To contribute to the holiness of priests is to contribute to families.

These prophetic messages to priests reveal the Heart of Jesus. We learn to appreciate the plan of God in and through priests. A priest is the Lord's endowment *for the lay faithful.*

Union in the Trinity

Speaking to Conchita, Our Lord made very clear His expectations for priests:

> *A priest must imitate the Father by being a father in the purest fruitfulness and love for souls, showing all the qualities of a father and of the Father who is in Heaven, in whose mind he was begotten.*
>
> *A priest must imitate Me, the Son, the Word made flesh, transforming himself into Me. This is more than imitating Me. He must become another Me on earth, only in order to glorify the Father in everything he does and give Him souls for Heaven.*
>
> *He must imitate the Holy Spirit by being love and spreading love, enabling souls to fall in love with Love, fused in love, deified in love, disseminating, and witnessing to the Word for love of Him*

and uniting all souls within the Trinity, who is love in all of its forms and in all of its infinite consequences.

I want My Church to shine with holy priests, according to My Father's ideal, in the holy and perfect mold of the Trinity.... I thirst to be loved and imitated in this way and I want to present My Father — the delight of My Heart — with model priests, with bishops who have been transformed into Me.[233]

A priest with a fatherly heart is more able to love, gather, protect, counsel, encourage, and heal. Having internalized the Father's love, he is able to extend the Father's heart to others. His identity with the Son is enriched, his ministry empowered. When the priest feeds his people the Eucharist, he is a beloved son of the Father. The Father endows the priest with a heart for sacrificial love — like that of His Son. A priest radiates the Heart of Jesus. A priest loves with the Holy Spirit. Jesus wants His Church to "shine with holy priests," and this should be our daily intention also. We console the Heart of Jesus when we pray for His ministers.

Jesus: God and Man

On another occasion, Our Lord told Conchita:

It is that I am God and yet I am also man, and I wished to take on man's miseries in order to atone for them. I wanted to feel like a man, to weep like a man, to shudder with the same sorrows and joys as a man. Thus, even though I am in heaven, I know how to be grateful, I know how to feel and be moved because I bear every man's refined and deified sensitivity in My soul, in My Heart and in My whole Being.[234]

[233] *Priests of Christ*, 3, 4.
[234] *Priests of Christ*, 9.

Conchita had a great love for the Incarnation, the humanity of the God-Man. It is beautiful that Jesus knows how to feel like a man. He understands human nature since He assumed it to save us. He has a human heart that was fashioned in the virginal womb of the Mother of God. Christ became intimately acquainted with humanity and loved us. He facilitates our transformation from sin to sanctity.

The demands that Jesus makes on priests are holy demands that He took upon Himself. The challenge for priests and laity is to center our lives on Jesus when the world shouts, the devil attacks, and the desires of the flesh eclipse God. Jesus understands our human nature. "Little children, you are of God and have overcome them; for he who is in you is greater than he who is in the world" (1 John 4:4). Priests are on the forefront of the spiritual battle for souls. We pray for their strength, sanctity, and protection.

"I Saw a Legion of Souls in My Priest"

Likewise, Jesus told Conchita:

> The life of a priest is not like that of any ordinary man, just one life and that's all; no, in the life of a priest I see many lives (in a spiritual and holy sense), which derives from his life and many hearts that will give Me glory eternally. Each priest, eternally conceived by the Father, participates in a kind of eternal generation united to the Word.
>
> The life of a priest is not just something of little importance; it has a divine and spiritual origin, a heavenly seed; it is the object of the Trinity's intervention; it participates in something of the infinity of the Father, and His fruitfulness for souls. This is why a priest's vocation is so sublime, so holy, so superhuman, and his mission on earth is so divine. The material and intellectual world has no idea of the greatness of the priest.

Beautiful Holiness

... Yet he is a man, marked out for heaven, he is on earth, and as a man, he is subject to human misery. But the divine vocation defends him and inclines him to what is pure and holy, and if he loses his way and tramples his sacred vocation underfoot, it is his own fault, his own grave fault—because a priest has more means, more grace and double the power to conquer the temptations of the enemies of his soul.

He was born for the Sanctuary, and the Sanctuary has powerful means for liberating him.... If he is a soul of prayer, an interior soul, pure and crucified, without any doubt, rays of divine light will bathe him.[235]

Christ's tenderness, patience, and designs for priests are as high as the heavens and as enduring as flint. The priest is born for the Sanctuary. In the Sanctuary, a priest most resembles Jesus in His perfect sacrifice and experiences the deepest union with Him. Jesus states that if the priest fails to experience the love of the Trinity, it is because he has closed his eyes, his mind, and his heart intentionally. May no priest or layman be guilty of that.

Whenever People Hurt My Priests

But if Our Lord was demanding of His priests, He was hardly less demanding of those they serve. His message to the laity is just as important:

I love My priests so much that whatever is done to them is done to Me. What does this mean? When I said this, I was thinking about their transformation into Me, as thus it should—I in them and they in Me—and whenever people hurt them in anyway, they hurt the apple of My eye and the most delicate fibers of My Heart. I have

---

[235] *Priests of Christ*, 20.

even imposed grave punishment upon those who are unfortunate enough to injure them, to mock them, to despise them and yes, even to lay hands on them for evil purposes.

… What denigrates, dishonors, or makes them suffer in any way, in thought, word or deed, hurts Me deeply. I have not treated anyone else with such delicacy. And even more, this inconceivable love and tenderness comes from My Father, from My beloved and loving Father, who sees all priests in Me and loves them in Me and cares for them in Me and watches over them in the unity of the Church, and He is indignant when someone that is Me or that represents Me is offended, no matter how slightly.[236]

It pains the Lord whenever we hurt, insult, or misjudge a priest. Jesus wants us to resist temptations to speak ill of priests or gossip about bishops. Our awareness of the failures of priests should lead us to pray more, to offer reparation to the hearts of Jesus and Mary. Aware of scandals (caused by both priests and laity) in her time, Conchita imitated Mary's custody of the tongue, her fasts, and her ardent prayers. We know that God is able to work all things for the good of those who love Him. We hold priests to a higher standard. I believe we should hold ourselves to the same.

Mary Sees Priests in Her Son

Our Lady, too, had a message for the clergy:

It is a great consolation for the priest — that the more they are transformed into Me — the more they will become sons of Mary, more deserving of her tenderness, her caresses, and her pure and motherly love.

---

[236] *Priests of Christ*, 24.

... The Immaculate Heart rests her gaze with pleasure upon pure priests. She looks for the fragrance of her Jesus, the Lily of the Valley, in priests whose mission is to represent Him on earth; she takes pleasure in the purity of their souls, in their unstained hands which touch the Lamb, ... because Mary delights and focuses her entire soul on the transubstantiation.

Mary is the shortest way to reach the Holy Spirit, to grow in love that transforms, assimilates, unites and sanctifies! Mary is the sweetest, the tenderest, the purest and the most delicate means to attain Him![237]

No one deserves so glorious a gift as Mary our Mother. But she is ours. She especially belongs to priests, who are sacramentally configured to her Son. Mary *mothers* priests to grow in virtue and live the Beatitudes. She aids priests in their receptivity so that they may let God love them boundlessly. Mary protects priests from demonic and human enemies of the priesthood. She is always at the service of priests—always a Mother for priests. What she did for Jesus, she does for priests until the end of time. Mary needs priests to perpetuate Jesus on earth.

The Devil's Principal Weapon against Priests

And just as surely as Jesus and Mary love His priests, the devil hates them with all his might. Priests are the foremost targets of the fiery darts of the evil one. But Jesus expects His priests to be the foremost guardians of their personal sanctification according to His message.

What I'm about to say is very sad, but there are priests who are harsh because their hearts are not purified of the world and of the

[237] *Priests of Christ*, 27–28.

flesh, because there is nothing that petrifies a priest and prejudices him as much as secularization and the contact with what is not pure.

These sins harden the heart of the priest and kill what is spiritual in him. With these sins he loses faith and, as the immediate consequence, the lack of trust in My great mercy takes possession of him. The lack of confidence in priestly souls is the devil's principal weapon to obtain the triumph of his malice that is final impenitence on the part of the priest.

At the terrible and decisive hour of the priest's death the two spirits, the Holy Spirit and the evil spirit, engage in battle. I am there and My tender and loving Heart is offended by the most cruel and painful sin: the sin against the Holy Spirit, that of the lack of confidence in God, which is not forgiven. To this point the evil one propels him; this is his goal in the sinful priest who has gradually become lukewarm in My service and negligent in watching over his own soul. There the devil waits to give him the mortal blow and finally to snatch him out of My arms and My Heart and to cast him to hell.

The priest begins by becoming lukewarm; and then comes discouragement and lack of sacrifice, which provided incentive for his spiritual works. The faith, which gave life to them, becomes extinguished, hope dies, and that soul becomes overwhelmed with distrust, the last weapon which the evil one wields and with which he snatches many souls from My loving arms.

The priest, more than anyone else, should watch over his own sanctification, frequently checking the pulse of his fervor, the purity of his heart and love for Me and for Mary. Every day the priest should reinforce his enthusiasm for prayer by mortifying himself, above all, in the fulfillment of the duties of his ministry.

Tell all priests to come to Me and I will cure their ills, wipe away their tears and heal their wounds, to unite them to Me, to transform them into Me, and to surrender Myself to their trust. I want to break the distrust that pierces My soul. I want to have done with that enemy who snatches priestly souls from Me. I want to show the world My triumph over hell, to give more splendor and glory to My Church, and to satisfy the yearning of My loving Heart for holy priests, all in the bosom of the Father, without leaving a single one outside of the refuge of My Heart.[238]

Jesus implores His priests to trust Him and to allow Him to minister to their every need. Imagine a mother or father whose beloved child doesn't trust him or her. It hurts the heart.

The temptation to distrust God is the ancient demonic tactic that caused Adam and Eve's fall. Priests and laity should immediately resist, reject, and renounce this temptation when it arises. Distrusting God leads to the folly of self-reliance. Pray to deepen trust in the Lord; pray for dynamic faith, determined hope, and untiring love. In His hands we are exceedingly safe. If we don't feel safe with God, if we're paralyzed by distrust, how can His love enter to heal us?

Christ's Church Will Shine with Holy Priests

Love, says Jesus, is the key to a healthy and holy priesthood:

Love is the driving force of the Church and the sacraments. It is Love that begot priests in the Father, because the Trinity is one essence and will without beginning. Love forms priests.... I want My Church to shine with holy priests, according to My Father's ideal, in the holy and perfect mold of the Trinity.[239]

---

[238] *Priests of Christ*, 244–245.
[239] *Priests of Christ*, 3.

"It is ... Jesus Christ, whose sacred person his minister truly represents."[240] In Gethsemane, Jesus said to Peter, "Watch and pray that you may not enter into temptation; the spirit indeed is willing, but the flesh is weak" (Matt. 26:41). Stay awake; beware of enemies of your salvation; pray because the flesh is weak. Prayer strengthens the spirit so it can subdue the flesh. Jesus prayed for and with the apostles. His vision of a Church *shining with holy priests* is realized in the commitment of ardent daily prayer and fasting, that of priests and laity.

A Vatican Initiative: Foundation of Prayer for Priests

Twenty-five years ago, a priest friend introduced me to Conchita and presented me with her book *Priests of Christ*. Years later, at a church luncheon, a visiting Missionary of the Holy Spirit priest gifted me with a third-class relic of Conchita. A decade later, my path crossed with Fr. Domenico Di Raimondo, M.Sp.S., my collaborator on this book.

In 2007, inspired by the Congregation for the Clergy's initiative "Eucharistic Adoration for the Sanctification of Priests and Spiritual Maternity" and with encouragement from then-Prefect Cardinal Mauro Piacenza, I wrote the book *Praying for Priests*[241] and cofounded the Foundation of Prayer for Priests. The book and the foundation are means of building an army of intercessors for priests. In thirteen countries, thousands of spiritual mothers and fathers of priests offer Eucharistic adoration, rosaries, and fasting

---

[240] CCC 1548, quoting Pius XII, encyclical *Mediator Dei*: AAS, 39 (1947) 548.

[241] Kathleen Beckman, *Praying for Priests: An Urgent Call for the Salvation of Souls* (Manchester, NH: Sophia Institute Press, 2018).

for the holiness and protection of priests. I invite you to please join our apostolate for priests.[242]

The Congregation for the Clergy published an intriguing statement about Conchita:

> Maria Concepción Cabrera de Armida (Conchita) was a wife, and mother with children. Over the course of many years, Jesus prepared her to live a life of spiritual motherhood for priests. In the future, she will be of great importance for the universal Church.[243]

I believe the hour has come when Conchita is of great importance for the Church. Jesus told Conchita that He desires a new priestly Pentecost. Priests are leading a Eucharistic revival now. We pray that a priestly Pentecost will follow. Jesus told Conchita, "*The world needs to be regenerated, respiritualized, and saved. But the only way to arrive at this end is the transformation of priests into the eternal, pure, holy and only Priest and Savior, who wants and promises to return to earth in His priests in order to bring about a new era of salvation and sanctification in the world.*"[244]

A priest friend, Msgr. Stephen Rossetti, shared that Conchita's writings have had a profound effect on him. He keeps a copy near his bed, and before going to sleep, he often reads a few paragraphs from her book *Priests of Christ*.

Cardinal Raniero Cantalamessa wrote, "The Lord today is calling the faithful in ever-growing numbers to pray, to offer sacrifices, in order to have holy priests. A concern, a passion, for

---

[242] Foundation for Priests: www.foundationforpriests.org.
[243] Congregation for the Clergy, *Eucharistic Adoration*, 24.
[244] *Priests of Christ*, 64.

holy priests has spread as a sign of the times throughout today's Church."[245]

The Holy Spirit and a Priestly Pentecost

Conchita received these prophetic words from Jesus:

> *The Holy Spirit with divine anxiety searches for vessels into which to pour His infinite treasures. He wants priestly souls who, enlarging themselves, call Him, invoke Him, receive Him, transmit and give Him. He, in fact, is the gift of God, the gift of gifts, the only one capable of renewing souls and worlds. He wants to cleanse and purify souls so that they may be reborn in the Holy Spirit.*
>
> *A new period, which belongs especially to the Holy Spirit, is coming into the world for its renewal; but He wants to make Himself felt especially in His priests transformed into Me. He wants to lift them up ... to sanctify them so that with Him, through Him and in Him they may give new impetus to His kingdom in the Church, which will then move souls and hearts....*
>
> *A new Redemption will come, not through My human passion, but through My passion in crucified souls. And a new Pentecost, brought about by the living dynamism of the Holy Spirit, will come to honor the Father and this new Pentecost is the goal, which the Holy Spirit and I have proposed.*
>
> *But, in order to save souls, to set souls ablaze and to perfect them, we have to start at the root, that is the Church, beginning with My priests, as a powerful aid to the saving work that is going to come, that is already at the doors.*[246]

---

[245] Raniero Cantalamessa, O.F.M. Cap., *Sober Intoxication of the Spirit, Part Two: Born Again of Water and the Spirit* (Cincinnati: Franciscan Media, 2012) chap. 3. Kindle ed.

[246] *Priests of Christ*, 56, 81.

Beautiful Holiness

Through the intercession of Blessed Conchita, let us implore the Lord for a new infusion of the Holy Spirit, starting with Eucharistic revival and a priestly Pentecost. These are two key movements for renewing the Church and world.

Lord, may the Church shine with holy priests!

Individual or Group Reflection

Ponder

"For we have not a high priest who is unable to sympathize with our weaknesses, but one who in every respect has been tempted as we are, yet without sinning" (Heb. 4:15).

Engage

1. What have you learned about spiritual motherhood or fatherhood of priests?
2. How can you encourage your loved ones in their growth in holiness?
3. What act of service can you render your priest(s)?

Pray

Mary, with what love you must have inflamed the hearts of the apostles so that they might spread the Church; so that they might joyfully shed their blood and give their lives to uphold Jesus' cause: the truth and the faith! You, who were the light of the apostles, the fire who caused them to burn, thirsting to communicate the doctrine they had received to souls. Help priests—that chosen portion whom Jesus loves so much—and unite them to yourself. Console them, fortify them and daily teach them—in ever greater depth—what Jesus is like and how He wishes them to be other Christs. Amen.[247]

[247] *What Jesus Is Like*, 108–109.

10

Loving with the Holy Spirit

*But the Counselor, the Holy Spirit, whom the Father will
send in my name, he will teach you all things and bring
to your remembrance all that I have said to you.*

—John 14:26

Conchita's genius is her *dependence* on the Holy Spirit, her *docility*
to the Breath of God, her *love* for life in the Spirit. "*If the Cross is the
center of Conchita's spiritual doctrine,*" Jesus told her, "*the Holy Spirit
is at the summit. It dominates the Cross and illumines it from above.*"[248]
In this chapter, we'll reflect on how Conchita *loved with the Holy
Spirit.* We'll learn how to refine the way we love God and others.

Conchita's life, vocation, missions, and apostolates were permeated by her ardent love of the Holy Spirit. This beautiful flower of
Mexico drank deeply of the Spirit's living water. Conchita wanted
to be a worthy little "nest" for the Holy Spirit, whom she sometimes
called "divine little Dove."

The Cross at the center of Conchita's spirituality was much
more than a pious emphasis or devotion; it was her lived experience of Love Crucified. She was transformed by the Cross of

---

[248] *A Mother's Spiritual Diary,* 129.

Jesus, which formed in her, splinter by splinter, in the crucible of agonizing sorrows, imprinting itself on her soul. Yet this Cross is not the summit, says the Lord. The Holy Spirit is the summit because He is divine love. The Third Person of the Trinity illumines everything from above.

Conchita is in the school of the Holy Spirit; with Jesus as her Teacher, she explains:

There exists a hidden treasure, a wealth remaining unexploited and in no way appreciated at its true worth, which is nevertheless that which is the greatest in heaven and on earth: the Holy Spirit. The world of souls itself does not know Him as it should. He is the Light of intellects and the Fire which enkindles hearts. If there is indifference, coldness, weakness, and so many other evils which afflict the spiritual world and even My Church, it is because recourse is not had to the Holy Spirit.

His mission is heaven; His Life, His Being, is Love. On earth His mission consists in leading souls toward this hearth of Love which is God. With Him, there is possessed all that can be desired.[249]

Ponder Christ's words: "With Him, there is possessed all that can be desired." Jesus refers to the deepest desires of the heart. The desire to be loved, known, cherished, and safe is fulfilled in the Holy Spirit. Human love, necessary and beautiful as it is, will not suffice; it cannot fulfill the desire of the soul because we are made for the Thrice Holy One.

The Holy Spirit was alive in Conchita, and she was alive in Him. She was held in divine love even when she was deeply pained, as in preparing her beloved husband for his death or burying four cherished children. That same Holy Spirit is ours.

[249] *A Mother's Spiritual Diary*, 30.

At Baptism, the Gift of God is poured into our soul. The Holy Spirit takes possession of us. We possess the Sanctifier to the degree that we desire and commune with the Sacred Guest of the soul. All the baptized who possess grace are temples of the Holy Spirit (see 1 Cor. 6:19). We are indwelt by the Spirit of God. He speaks to the heart, inspires the mind, strengthens the intellect, enlivens the memory, and animates our ability to love and to be loved. Amazing grace!

The Holy Spirit Dominates the Cross

During Conchita's vision of the Cross in January 1894, the very first thing she saw was the Holy Spirit in the midst of great light. Then the vision developed, and she saw the Cross with the pierced Heart of Jesus at the center. The Holy Spirit formed Conchita into Love Crucified.

In March 1894, at the age of thirty-two, Jesus taught Conchita about the importance of the Holy Spirit:

> *The Holy Spirit is He who governs the world and the Church, after I departed. After the Ascension, I sent Him. Yet if you only knew how little He is honored and little known!... He is not given the glory He merits as a divine Person. I hide Myself within the Cross of the Apostolate in order that He reign and be adored.... Without Him this work would crumble, but with His divine breath He will communicate the Spirit of the Cross. Tell all this to your director in order that he reflect and that the first ejaculatory prayer in this Apostolate be an invocation of the Holy Spirit. He will cover with His wings this Apostolate of the Cross and His divine influence is of the greatest importance* (Diary, March 1894).[250]

[250] *A Mother's Spiritual Diary*, 129–130.

Conchita's apostolate would crumble without the help of the Holy Spirit, said the Lord. We're reminded of the psalmist's words: "Unless the LORD builds the house, those who build it labor in vain" (Ps. 127:1). The five Works of the Cross were consecrated to the Holy Spirit. Christ prophesied, "The apostolate of the Cross will erect temples to Him [the Holy Spirit] throughout the whole world. In these churches, a cult of perfection will be rendered to the Holy Spirit."[251] When the Holy Spirit is invited, He intervenes in surprising ways.

God Is Love

Our perception of the Cross and view of a God crucified out of love for us must be illuminated by the Holy Spirit. Jesus told Conchita that the Cross is truly dominated by the Holy Spirit. This makes Love the center of all. The victory of the Cross is the triumph of Love.

Central to our redemption, the Cross is sometimes met with fear and anxiety rather than appreciation and love. I've learned more about divine love by gazing at the crucifix above the altar than by thirty-five years of reading books, taking courses, and listening to preachers and teachers. There was a time when I'd prefer an image of love that is nice and neat, without pain. But when my heart was broken and I thought I'd die from pain, gazing at the crucifix was the only thing that made sense of suffering. My pain had value united to Christ's Cross. A part of me died, but it was to give birth to a better version. Love suffers, dies, and rises; it is messy and doesn't fit into nice, neat boxes. Love crucified unleashes the heart to soar. Saints are prime examples of transformation through the Cross. All of this is the work of the Holy Spirit.

---

[251] *A Mother's Spiritual Diary*, 129.

Fr. Philipon distinguishes Conchita's hallmark:

St. Augustine's God is the "Supreme Good" drawing all things to Himself. St. Thomas Aquinas' God is the God of Sinai: "I am who am." St. Thérèse of Lisieux's God is "Merciful Love." Conchita's God is "Crucified Love" which brings us to "Infinite Love."[252]

Conchita wrote of her experience of the Holy Spirit:

I saw how every legitimate and holy love, filling man's heart, is a drop from this soundless Ocean, a luminous ray from this immense light! I experienced how love flares out from this infinite hearth of charity which You Yourself are and how You are pleased to set in the heart of man this insatiable thirst for loving, which neither the perishable or the finite can quench but only the imperishable and the infinite. I felt how souls are as it were a particle of God Himself, a gentle breeze from His divine essence, a breathing of His Holy Spirit.[253]

Our soul is a particle of God Himself. Our soul is a breathing of His Spirit. Conchita saw how love flares out from the infinite hearth of charity, which is God, and then gives man's heart an insatiable thirst for loving. Our thirst for God is imperishable and infinite. Ponder the beauty of your soul and how you are caring for it. Ask the Holy Spirit to breathe, cleanse, enliven, and empower you to love with His love.

The Holy Spirit Stays Close to Souls

The Third Person of the Trinity is not the kind of lover to keep a distance! As Conchita explains:

---

[252] *A Mother's Spiritual Diary*, 137.
[253] *A Mother's Spiritual Diary*, 138.

Beautiful Holiness

Some souls think that the Holy Spirit is very far away, far, far up above. Actually, He is, we might say, the divine Person who is most closely present to the creature. He accompanies him everywhere. He penetrates him with Himself, He calls him, He protects him. He makes of him His living temple. He defends him. He helps him. He guards him from all his enemies. He is closer to him than his own soul. All the good a soul accomplishes, it carries out under His inspiration, in His light, by His grace, and with His help. And yet He is not invoked, He is not thanked for His direct and intimate action in each soul. If you invoke the Father, if you love Him, it is through the Holy Spirit. If you love Me ardently, if you know Me, if you serve Me, if you imitate Me, if you make yourself but one with My wishes and with My heart, it is through the Holy Spirit.

He is considered inaccessible, and He actually is, but there is nothing that exists nearer, more helpful to the creature in his misery than this Being of a supreme transcendence, this most holy Spirit who reflects and who constitutes one and the same holiness with the Father and the Son.[254]

Perhaps you've been tempted to think that God is far away, somewhere above—not close to you, not interested in your ordinary or messy daily life. But the Holy Spirit is very close to you: calling, protecting, accompanying, and loving you every moment of your life. If we could see ourselves and others through the eyes of the Holy Spirit, we'd be amazed by the dignity that God has conferred upon man. Nothing about us is unimportant or meaningless in the divine drama. We're created for a divine purpose that unfolds moment to moment. The Holy Spirit enables us to

[254] *A Mother's Spiritual Diary*, 138.

live each moment with God. With the Holy Spirit, we discover that life has eternal meaning.

The Soul of Christ Moved by the Holy Spirit

Jesus spoke these words to Conchita on January 29, 1915, when she was fifty-three years old:

> *Every movement of My soul has been inspired and carried out under the movement of the Holy Spirit. He it is who animates My faculties, My senses, My will, holding them in His possession for the glory of the Father to whom I return everything. The Holy Spirit loves My humanity with an incomparable predilection. . . . If you only knew with what delicacy, with what tenderness, with what splendor the Holy Spirit adorns My soul. My faculties, My feelings, My body, and My heart! Even more than a mother He is all love. He displayed all His might, all His riches to form Me in Mary's womb, as a perfect model of all that is beautiful, pure, and holy. All the riches and treasures which adorn My Heart, I owe to the Holy Spirit. I do not like devotion to My Heart to be regarded as an end but only as a means of being raised up to Divinity, as a step for reaching the Holy Spirit since it is He who created, formed, and enriched my human heart, who poured on it all the delights of His love as well as all the interior sufferings and the manner of undergoing universal expiation for the pardon of culpable mankind. The heart of man and his body had sinned. There was need of another heart and another body united to the power of a God to give satisfaction to this Other who is God. This plan, this action, this salvific purpose, glorying my humanity and for the salvation of the world, are owed to the Holy Spirit.*[255]

---

[255] *A Mother's Spiritual Diary*, 135.

See how Jesus Christ loves the Holy Spirit! Jesus wants Conchita to know that He and the Spirit are *one* Love. He highlights how the Spirit formed Him in the womb of Mary. Imagine! Conchita had a profound appreciation of the Incarnation of the Eternal Word. She encouraged everyone to "fall in love with the Incarnate Jesus." She shared this characteristic of Teresa of Ávila, who lived 350 years before her. Jesus told Conchita that the Holy Spirit enriched His Heart and His faculties. We can ask the Holy Spirit to do the same for us: *Come Holy Spirit, permeate our imagination, memory, understanding, and will with Your divine light and love.*

Loving with the Holy Spirit, 1926 Retreat

Conchita committed to making retreats throughout her lifetime, and she greatly benefitted from them. In July 1926, when she was sixty-four, Archbishop Martinez, who had been her spiritual director for three years, led her retreat in Morelia. The theme of the retreat was "Loving with the Holy Spirit." Thirsting to grow closer to God, Conchita made this retreat and received illuminations on the Holy Spirit.

Commenting on Archbishop Martinez's spiritual formation for Conchita, Sr. Clara Eugenia Labarthe, R.C.S.C.J., wrote:

> Bishop Martinez recognized throughout the years of his direction the spiritual and doctrinal depth and thread of Conchita's reflections, which he fostered by directing her to the very themes of Catholic doctrine which her own prayer life and spiritual experiences had brought her, adapting them to her capacity as a layperson of her times, her spiritual style and cultural heritage. Conchita's insights were never mere abstractions, but arose from her person to Person encounters in prayer, encounters with God in Three Divine Persons: The

God of Creation in the Person of the Father, who created us from nothing; the God of Salvation in the Person of the Son, who entered human history as the obedient and suffering Servant; and the God in the Person of the Holy Spirit, the gentle nesting Dove, who causes the salvation wrought by the Son to bear fruit in the ordinary lives of His children.[256]

At the start of the retreat Archbishop Martinez chose the theme "Simply Your Life in Love," and this was an exhortation to begin "loving with the Holy Spirit, the mystical way of loving God and neighbor from deep within God Himself."[257]

Her *Diary* entry from the first day of the retreat reveals a very human side. Conchita was authentic. She didn't hide weaknesses in her writings: "*This afternoon I start my retreat. I am scared, but it is probably the devil that wants to disturb me. Holy Mother, help me! What may Jesus ask of me?*"[258]

We can relate to the lurking fear of what Jesus will ask of us. Sometimes we're reluctant to move from the place where we've grown comfortable in the spiritual life, especially if we're in a good place with the Lord and our prayer life is on track. But comfort doesn't reconcile with growth in Christ. More will be asked of us because God desires us to experience more of Him and His wondrous works. When we let Jesus move us from one stage of love to the next (this is the spiritual life), we discover yet another level of beautiful possibilities we had not dreamed of. The Holy Spirit helps us to discover God's dream for us. We simply can't dream as big as God.

---

[256] Concepción Cabrera de Armida, *Loving with the Holy Spirit* (Citta del Vaticano: Libreria Editrice Vaticana, 2007), 13, 14.

[257] *Loving with the Holy Spirit*, 15.

[258] *Loving with the Holy Spirit*, 24.

Beautiful Holiness

As Conchita suspected, her fear at the start of the retreat was likely a demonic temptation. The devil would be threatened when Archbishop Martinez led Conchita's retreat since incredible grace would flow to both souls.

The bishop gave Conchita a meditation in which he recalled a series of graces given to her as signs of God's exquisite love. This is the foundation—remembering that God chose her because He loves her. These Conchita recounted in her *Diary*:

> *First Meditation. God loves you. He Himself has told you this, and He has told you in so many ways.... Remember with what tenderness, ardor, and perseverance the Lord has reiterated His love for you. Is there anything more beautiful and delightful than hearing from the mouth of the Beloved His word of love?*
>
> *Second Meditation. God has proven His great love for you with awesome deeds including:*
>
> *The divine calling (First directed retreat, 1889). The apparition of the Holy Spirit (1894, the Holy Spirit appeared in the form of a Dove). The spiritual betrothal (January 23, 1894). The spiritual marriage (February 9, 1897). The mystical incarnation (March 25, 1906). The Works of the Cross (Founded 1895). The martyrdoms (desolations). The fruitfulness (her love for Jesus feeds many souls).*[259]

God was extravagant in giving Conchita proofs of His love. Perhaps you and I should list graces that we've received in our lifetime as proofs of God's love for us.

Conchita was in awe; her heart stirred with gratitude. Jesus told her:

> *Loving with the Holy Spirit requires countless degrees of transformation. Look how each degree of transformation prepares for and*

---

[259] *Loving with the Holy Spirit*, 28–31.

draws to the next if the soul corresponds. But the plentitude of this
love can only be reached in Heaven. Only there is it fully possessed.
Only there is My Heart, which is Love, satisfied.[260]

Jesus speaks of countless degrees of transformation when we *love with the Holy Spirit*. Each stage of transformation will have its purpose, leave its mark, beautifying and refining the soul. Jesus told Conchita that He is the Holy Spirit's masterpiece. Perhaps the Holy Spirit considers us little masterpieces in the mold of Jesus, the Masterpiece.

The Holy Spirit helps us to perceive ourselves in the light of truth. It's difficult for us to see ourselves as God sees us. There seems to be a universal struggle with self-worth (too low or too high). Jesus told the Samaritan woman at the well, "If you knew the gift of God …" (John 4:10). If we truly believed that we are indwelt by the same Holy Spirit who indwelt Jesus and Mary, might we soar to new heights like the saints we venerate.

On the first day of the retreat, Conchita wrote, "*I have dwelt on the incomparable tenderness of Jesus for my poor soul and am so moved by it. Still, I have not entered deeply enough into myself. It is as if I wander upon the rooftops. Today's Mass and Communion is offered for the intention that the Lord guard me against obstacles in His grace and that He make and unmake me as He pleases.*"[261]

Then Conchita spoke to the Lord, "*You have begged for souls, living crosses, children, priests, bishops, souls that are pure, chaste, filled with light, on fire, zealous, souls which love sacrifice. This is the type of love which You have always sought! This is why the Father gazed upon me and communicated His divine fruitfulness to me. For the sake of*

---

[260] *Loving with the Holy Spirit*, 36.
[261] *Loving with the Holy Spirit*, 32.

Your design, for the Love You had for me, You revealed the Holy Spirit to me."[262] Jesus will always reveal the Holy Spirit to us if we ask Him.

Bishop Martinez's Reflection on Characteristics of Divine Love

On the second day of Conchita's retreat, Bishop Martinez gave a reflection: "How does God love you?" "God loves you with the same love with which the Father and the Son love one another; *God loves you with the Holy Spirit* (May 23, 1926)."[263]

The bishop presented seven characteristics related to loving with the Holy Spirit:

1. God is purity because He is He Who Is, and there is not and cannot be any admixture in Him of what He is not.... This love is selfless, without deficiencies and eclipses. It is divinely transparent love.... One very simple love, which is, at the same time, infinitely rich.

2. It is love which is all light! It is real, deep, profound, and intimate love! Have you ever contemplated God's familiarity with your soul?

3. It is eternal love. The Father and the Son have always loved each other.... It is their ineffable ecstasy of love that has neither beginning nor end. God loves you in this way. The love He has for you has no beginning, and it will have no end. God's love for you, on His part, is an eternal ecstasy into which you are already being drawn and into which you will fully enter in Heaven, where you are sure never to fall out of love.

---

[262] *Loving with the Holy Spirit*, 34.
[263] *Loving with the Holy Spirit*, 37.

4. It is the blazing love of the thrice holy God. Imagine that you are all ablaze within it and will be total and eternally ablaze with love!

5. It is powerful and fruitful love, an endless font of the divine mysteries. This is the love which brings redemption, the forgiveness of sins and the eternal reward of souls.

6. This love is an ineffable effusion, delightful and incomprehensible to angel and man alike, and it is only conceived and perpetuated by the infinite God Himself.

7. Think of the candor of the love ... of the sublimity of this love ... of the depth and fire of this love that pervades the Father and the Word without consuming them and which unified them as One God.[264]

These are beautiful words used to describe divine love: pure, selfless, simple, rich, light, infinite, ecstatic, blazing, holy, powerful, fruitful, sublime. The Holy Spirit gives us a taste of this love, and by it we are transformed.

Conchita Hears from Mary

On day two of the retreat, Conchita wrote, "*I was about to begin when I felt the Blessed Virgin say to me*":

Jesus desires to sweep away what is dirty and to increase virtues in the hearts of those who belong to Him. Worse days are to come, but the response in the Church and in the hearts of the faithful will be very pleasing to Him. God does not allow anything by which He is not glorified. Even though human understanding may fail, the Lord is glorified in all things.

---

[264] *Loving with the Holy Spirit*, 38–39.

Conchita replied, "*But how can this be, given that there are so many sins and offenses committed against Him?*"

Mary continued:

He detests sin, but forgives the sinner. He is always glorified, either in the reward or in the punishment of souls, for His mercy and justice always triumph. These persecutions cleanse and purify. Mexico has much to expiate, even in the Church, but religion and faith will triumph.

Immediately following, Jesus spoke:

Daughter, . . . would that all the pure of heart, all those who are Mine, united to Mary, be a bulwark against so much wickedness. So will My offended Heart be consoled. Cry out to the Father who is ready to forgive but remember how He desires victim souls. May the Holy Spirit, adversary of Satan, reign. He alone can transform what is earthly into what is heavenly, and what is stained into what is pure, for the glory of the Blessed Trinity.[265]

Jesus continued this message speaking about how "the bishops are sustained in their suffering"; "the head suffers for the sick members"; and "leaders will be abundantly rewarded for their expiatory suffering." He reminded Conchita that "the Works of the Cross must be imbued with the real spirit of the Cross."[266]

Mary speaks of sweeping away what is dirty. And how is this done? In the same sentence, Mary says there's a need to increase virtues in those who belong to Jesus. Vice is overcome with the practice of virtue. The sacrament of Reconciliation is Christ's provision to sweep away what is dirty.

---

[265] *Loving with the Holy Spirit*, 39, 40.
[266] *Loving with the Holy Spirit*, 40, 41.

Mary reminded Conchita that everything will redound to God's glory. Conchita asked, "How can this be?"—an echo of Mary's words at the Annunciation. Mary responded by assuring her the God is glorified in the "reward or punishment of souls" and that Mexico has much to offer in expiation due to her grave offenses to God.

These prophetic words given to Conchita in 1926 echo some of Mary's messages to the Fatima seers in 1917, nine years earlier. The Holy Spirit sanctifies, unites, purifies, and does the Father's will. The Father is preoccupied with the salvation of souls. This is Conchita's mission also. Finally, the Lord beseeched His daughter to "cry out" for the reign of the Holy Spirit—calling the Spirit the "adversary of Satan."[267]

How Has God Loved You?

On the third day of the retreat, the bishop gave a reflection on how each Person of the Holy Trinity loved her uniquely.

How does the Father love you?

With boundless tenderness. The infinitely generous Father has given His Son to you in so many ways! Consider in particular that He has given Him to you as Son, allowing you to participate in His paternal fruitfulness, in Jesus and in souls.[268]

How does the Son love you?

... Reflect on how Jesus has obediently fulfilled His obligations as Son: He respects you, elevates you, and showers you with graces. He shares the secrets of His heart

---

[267] *Loving with the Holy Spirit*, 39, 40.
[268] *Loving with the Holy Spirit*, 46.

with you. He stays near you, with continuous gestures of filial tenderness.... He shares His riches with you. He gives you His beauty as your own possession. He transforms you into Himself.[269]

How does the Holy Spirit love you?

He is a loving Teacher, who has guided you, and continues to guide you, with wisdom and charity. He is a sensitive and extremely close Friend. He is an Artist, who molds you with exquisite skill. As the divine Dove, who has made of your soul His nest, He delights you with soft cooing. He is a faithful Spouse who places His glory in your hands and makes of you an instrument for establishing His Kingdom.[270]

We may think that Conchita had one continuous mountaintop experience during the retreat. No! Interspersed among exquisite graces, she experienced interior battles and temptations. It's typical during spiritual exercises and retreats to get discouraged or tempted since these are occasions for hearing God's voice and renewing our love.

Conchita noted how she struggled through parts of the retreat:

- *I feel spiritually cold and indifferent; I simply give thanks to the Holy Spirit for His gifts, fruits, sensitivity, teachings, caresses, predilection, and love.*
- *I recall these things, but without enthusiasm which should attend to His blazing fire.*
- *No matter how hard I tried to meditate on the points, to pray with my arms outstretched as if on the Cross, no matter whether I stood or*

[269] *Loving with the Holy Spirit*, 46.
[270] *Loving with the Holy Spirit*, 46, 47.

knelt, I could not shake my coldness. I praised God's will, accepting my powerlessness, and prayed that He be glorified in my weakness.

- *Nothing extraordinary; I gratefully contemplated the sensitivity of Jesus in the mystical incarnation. But afterward spiritual dryness, sadness, confusion.*

- *The other day I was tempted to think that Bishop Martinez should not be my spiritual director. Satan proffered thousands of reasons.*

- *Now I struggle with this retreat. What am I doing so far away from my obligations at home? I must be exasperating and boring to others. What a torment of stupidities.*

- *Among these temptations were spiritual frigidity of glacial proportions, mental darkness, and confusion.*[271]

What Is Loving with the Holy Spirit?

On July 20, 1926, day three of the retreat, Archbishop Martinez gave a reflection on what it means to love with the Holy Spirit. He began by reminding Conchita what the Lord told her: "*I love you, my daughter, the way I ask you to love Me, with the Holy Spirit.*"[272] Archbishop Martinez explained *loving with the Holy Spirit* in five points:

1. God, in His ineffable Love, sends forth the Holy Spirit into souls so as to achieve a kind of proportion. This loving condescension obtains that the Holy Spirit, who by essence is the Spirit of God, becomes by participation the spirit of the soul. In this way the soul can claim, in a certain sense, to love as it is loved, that is, with the Holy Spirit.[273]

---

[271] *Loving with the Holy Spirit*, 52.
[272] *Loving with the Holy Spirit*, 53.
[273] *Loving with the Holy Spirit*, 53.

2. Loving with the Holy Spirit requires: (A) That the creature lose itself totally, in the sense that the creature's
   own spirit must disappear so that the soul there is but
   the Spirit of God, according to the words of St. Paul:
   "But who is joined to the Lord becomes one spirit with
   Him" (1 Cor. 6:17). (B) In order attain this love, one
   needs to be united very closely to the Holy Spirit.…
   One should regard everything with His eyes, think with
   His thoughts, seek with His will, love with His Heart,
   speak with His mouth, act with the strength of His
   arm, and live with His life. (C) The love of the soul
   that loves with the Holy Spirit is characterized by the
   same characteristics as God's love, but always in proportion: most pure, universal, total, singular, holy, fruitful,
   ardent, most sweet, most joyful, and most sorrowful.
   Thus was the Love of God in our Lord Jesus Christ:
   brave, courageous, peaceful, etc.[274]

3. Loving with the Holy Spirit means loving the Father as
   Jesus loves Him, because the Holy Spirit is the one Love
   of the Father and the Son. Think how Jesus loved His
   heavenly Father: With what tenderness! With what ardor! With what constancy! With what adoration! With
   what self-denial! With what longing to glorify the Father
   and offer Himself in sacrifice! With what fidelity to His
   designs! With what passion for His will! With what
   eagerness to please Him! This is how He asks you to
   love the Father.[275]

---

[274] *Loving with the Holy Spirit*, 55.
[275] *Loving with the Holy Spirit*, 56.

4. Loving with the Holy Spirit means loving Jesus as the heavenly Father loves Him: With the ineffable tenderness of the Father. With the same delight. With the Father's gaze upon Him. With an open heart totally devoted to Him. With the Father's ardor. With the Father's constancy. The Father so loves Jesus that He gave Him His life. And in the same way the soul should love Jesus.[276]

5. Loving with the Holy Spirit means loving this personal Love as He loves Himself, as the Father and the Son love Him. How much the Father and the Son love their Love, the bond of their unity, the source of their joy, and the strength of their action![277]

We pray, "Lord, I desire to love with the Holy Spirit."

Throughout the retreat, Jesus spoke to Conchita about the Holy Spirit:

> Even as there are many loves, all love coalesces in the one love of the Holy Spirit. Infinite Love pours itself out in every form of love – paternal, filial, and so on. God is charity. God is Love. The Father and the Son do not merely experience love, but rather they are love. The sun, though it remains one sphere of light and source, diffuses countless rays of light and color. Similarly, God is always one Love in the Holy Spirit, from whom radiates every form of love on earth and in Heaven.[278]

On another occasion, Jesus spoke about sin:

> It might be said that sin, the obstruction of God's vehement desire to do good and the ingratitude of man, are God's only martyrdom.

---

276 *Loving with the Holy Spirit*, 56.
277 *Loving with the Holy Spirit*, 57.
278 *Loving with the Holy Spirit*, 48.

Beautiful Holiness

Sin douses the flames of divine Love which can melt a thousand worlds. Sin is a horrible dam that stops streams and oceans of Love, which would otherwise bring such joy to the earth, to the entire universe, and to human hearts, The one sin on earth, man's ingratitude, is his lack of love!

In response, Conchita asked, "*What can we do, my Jesus?*" "*Allow the Holy Spirit to reign,*" said Jesus. "*That was all He told me.*"[279]

The Immaculate Virgin: Loving God with the Holy Spirit

On the fifth and sixth days of the retreat, Bishop Martinez gave reflections on how the Blessed Mother is the perfect model of *loving God with the Holy Spirit*. We learn beautiful insights on the heart of Mary.

The soul of the Virgin Mary is like the purest atmosphere, fragrant with the Holy Spirit, and like the most beautiful spring breeze. How does the Virgin Mary love God?

- With singular piety.
- With supernatural love.
- With heavenly gentleness.
- With perfect generosity.
- With purity that mirrors the purity of the Holy Spirit for she is Immaculate.
- With recollection. The soul of Mary dwelt in the silence of adoration and love.
- With love that seeks the likeness of love in souls, that they may vibrate in unison with Him.

[279] *Loving with the Holy Spirit,* 51.

- With perfect docility that opens the soul to the Holy Spirit's inspirations.
- With suffering that is the face of Love on earth, and Mary is the Queen of Sorrows.
- With sweet dialogue, heavenly harmony. From Mary's childhood the Holy Spirit experienced her docility to His attentions.
- Mary loves Jesus with a love very near to the paternal love of the heavenly Father.
- Mary loves the Father as Jesus loves Him, with the same tenderness, passion, and fidelity.
- Mary's song of love to the Father is her Magnificat hymn.
- Mary offered Jesus on the Cross to the Father in a "wondrous holocaust of ineffable love"—her Mother's heart joined intimately to the priestly heart of Jesus.
- Mary courageously moved Jesus to the start of His public ministry when, at Cana, she asked Him to work the miracle of the wine.
- Mary's love for Jesus most reveals itself in His passion and on Calvary, where she offers her Son, and herself along with Him, in sacrifice, sharing in His suffering.
- Mary loved with the Holy Spirit. The last full and definitive outpouring of the Holy Spirit upon the soul of the Virgin Mary was so ardent, so intense, so powerful, that even Mary, accustomed to the most prodigious divine outpourings, could not bear it and she died, she died of love, she died in an unspeakable outpouring of the Holy Spirit.[280]

Archbishop Martinez recalls the life of Mary guided by the Holy Spirit. Espoused to the Holy Spirit, Mary is the exemplar

---

[280] *Loving with the Holy Spirit*, 63, 64, 72, 73.

of loving with the Holy Spirit. The Sanctifier is Mary's mystical Spouse and her spiritual director throughout her life. In light of this, how docile have you been to the love and promptings of the Holy Spirit?

Conchita's Retreat Reflections on the Holy Spirit

During prayer following Mass, Conchita reflected on how the Father, the Son, and the Holy Spirit love each other. She wrote some of the most beautiful points:

- *One can only perceive and love the Holy Spirit. One cannot penetrate Him with understanding.*
- *The soul needs Him. He is its breath, and life, and for this reason, once the soul has tasted Him, the heart, the soul, and whole being of the creature cry out: Come!*
- *The Holy Spirit communicates Himself in many ways.*
- *He told me one day that He had five ways of reaching the soul:*
  Through His touches.
  Through His repose.
  Through His quiet.
  Through His possession.
  Through His union.[281]

Conchita's heart was deeply stirred at the end of her meditations. She wrote:

I have meditated on so many ways of loving with the Holy Spirit, all of them so perfect. I will strive ever to study, experience, and live them. Gratitude, fidelity, the commitment to spread His glory,

---

[281] *Loving with the Holy Spirit*, 66.

and the consummation of the virtues—my God, what heights! But they are not impossible if the Holy Spirit, with the Father and the Son, be my companion and my all. Everything through Mary![282]

Then Conchita struggled and wondered what she was doing far away from home and family.

Jesus told Conchita that during the retreat, Bishop Martinez was examining the inmost recesses of her soul: "*The more your soul is examined, the more I will be found within, and what will be discovered is not what is yours, but rather what is Mine, which you can neither understand nor appreciate.*"

Conchita replied, "*Lord, let my director see deep down into my defects, please. I beg this of You. Not only what is Yours and beautiful, but what is mine and ugly.*"[283]

Again, Conchita honestly wrote about her faults:

+ *I seem docile, but deep down within my soul there is a dam that seems to be humility, but which in truth is an obstacle, a thread, which thwarts my flight to the heights to which God is calling me.*
+ *I hear His voice, and I flee from it. I am drawn by His charm, and then I withdraw from it. I welcome the invasion of the Holy Spirit, and then I trifle with Him. I block my ears and stoop to make clay bricks rather than allowing myself to be airborne.*
+ *I often feel that He is sad and disappointed. My God, how much You love! And I pretend not to notice.*
+ *So many times I preferred the company of creature to His company. I fear heights. I find the ordinary way of donkeys more secure. My God! I do not let myself be loved.*

---

[282] *Loving with the Holy Spirit*, 66, 67.
[283] *Loving with the Holy Spirit*, 75.

• *I do not respond in the depths and totality of my spirit but only by half measures.*[284]

Many relate to Conchita's sentiment: "I do not let myself be loved." For many people, receiving love is more difficult than giving love. Mary is the Mother of "receiving love" and helps with our receptivity of divine love.

Conchita shared her sentiments with Bishop Martinez, who decided to prepare for her an Act of Oblation to God. This solidified the grace of the retreat in a formal gift of self to God. At the end of my retreats, I do the same. This is a fruitful exercise because each act of oblation reinforces our commitment or consecration to God.

Conchita's Offering Prayer

Near the end of her retreat, Conchita made this offering to the Godhead:

> Oh Most Holy Trinity, Father, Son, and Holy Spirit, You are all Love. You have loved me eternally with sweet predilection, and You have filled me with the ineffable wonders of Your love throughout my life!
>
> Oh God of Love! You desire that I be all Yours, and out of the abundance of Your Love, You desire to be all mine. Sweetly surrendered to Your Love, and with all the love of my poor soul loving with the Holy Spirit, today I offer myself, totally and forever, to Your Love, to the sovereignty of Your Love, to the tenderness of Your Love.
>
> I desire that all the rights You have over me as God be a mutual expression of our love; that You treat me, with all due

[284] *Loving with the Holy Spirit*, 76, 77.

proportions observed, as You treated the Blessed Virgin and the Sacred Humanity of Christ; that You deal with this poor creature according to Your will, to accomplish Your designs of Love, with no consideration of my will, which belong to You. From now on I shall not be preoccupied with my misery, which will be the immense void opened to the ocean of Your Love.

From now on, my most sweet Love, my eyes will see Your wonderful graces directly, because Love will keep them open, that You might fill the inmost recesses of my soul. May my love become a lyre vibrating in unison with Your Love, reproducing, without losing a single note or tone, the song of love of the Holy Spirit; and even my body, which You will sanctify more each day, will become assimilated to the bloodstained body of Christ. Along with my body may my soul become Your tabernacle, Your Cross, Your throne, on which You reign as King of Love.

I offer myself, through the immaculate hands of Mary, ceaselessly renewing this prayer of offering with every beat of my heart, with every breath, to the glory of the Father, who with the Son, in the unity of the Holy Spirit, lives and reigns for ever and ever. Amen.[285]

To close the retreat, Conchita noted the following resolutions.

1. *Renew daily my gift of self and offering.*
2. *Continue to strive to simplify in love.*

And to achieve these, she added:

- *I should seek deep and constant intimacy with the Holy Trinity.*
- *I should have no other will than God's will.*
- *I should love everyone with the Holy Spirit.*
- *All in Mary.*

[285] *Loving with the Holy Spirit*, 84, 85.

Beautiful Holiness

Prophecy: The Reign of the Holy Spirit

Jesus gave this prophecy regarding the Holy Spirit:

> *"It is time that the Holy Spirit reign." Very moved, the Lord told me this. But it is necessary that He reign here, right close, in each soul and in each heart, in all the structures of My Church. The day on which there will flow in each pastor, in each priest, like an inner blood, the Holy Spirit, then will be renewed the theological virtues, now languishing, even in the ministers of My Church, due to the absence of the Holy Spirit. Then the world will change, for all the evils deplored today have their cause in the remoteness of the Holy Spirit, the sole remedy.... There is no virtue without the Holy Spirit. Let His place be given Him, that is, the first in intellects and wills! No one will be lacking anything with this heavenly wealth. The Father and I, the Word, We desire an ardent and vitalizing renewal of His reign in the Church (Diary, Feb. 19, 1911).[286]*

These words remind me of the timeless messages of Pope John Paul II (May 31, 1998), Pope Benedict XVI (May 27, 2007), and Pope Francis (May 19, 2013) during Pentecost events in Rome. In 1998, I was among the five hundred thousand pilgrims gathered in St. Peter's Square in response to the pope's invitation to the ecclesial movements. In 1998, St. John Paul II declared a Year of the Holy Spirit in preparation for the Jubilee Year 2000. Subsequently, at respective Pentecost events in St. Peter's Square, Pope Benedict XVI and Pope Francis spoke words similar to Conchita's messages received eight decades earlier! Each pope invited us to open our hearts and lives to the Holy Spirit. They beseeched us to invoke the Holy Spirit continuously

---

[286] *A Mother's Spiritual Diary*, 131.

for the Church and the world: *Veni, Sancte Spiritus!* St. John Paul II told us, "Let us pray to Mary, sanctuary of the Holy Spirit, a most precious dwelling place of Christ among us, so that she may help us to be living temples of the Holy Spirit and tireless witnesses of the Gospel."

I have grown to trust, adore, rely on, invoke, and commune with the Holy Spirit throughout each day. I have the greatest confidence in the Holy Spirit. He has never failed me.

Nearly a century before these popes urged the intervention of the Holy Spirit to renew the face of the earth, Jesus told Conchita why the Holy Spirit's reign is essential for the salvation of souls:

> *Here is why I want His glory to be shown to the end of time....*
> *One of the cruelest interior sufferings for My Heart was this ingratitude of all times, this worship of idols of other times, and today man's self-worship, forgetful of the Holy Spirit. In these latter days sensuality has set up its reign in the world. This sensual life obscures and extinguishes the light of faith in souls. That is why more than ever, it is necessary that the Holy Spirit come to destroy and annihilate Satan who under this form penetrates even the Church* (Diary, Jan. 24, 1915).[287]

We need an intervention of the Holy Spirit and Our Lady to illumine humanity with truth. Let us be brave cooperators with the work of the Paraclete and the Immaculata. Like Blessed Conchita, we can be God's instruments for the cure of spiritual sickness that plagues humanity. As Jesus told Conchita, the reign of the Holy Spirit begins in our hearts. Are we living Spirit-filled, Spirit-led lives? Do we know and love the Person of the Holy Spirit?

---

[287] *A Mother's Spiritual Diary*, 134.

Beautiful Holiness

DAILY CONSECRATION PRAYER TO THE HOLY SPIRIT,
WRITTEN AND PRAYED DAILY BY BLESSED CONCHITA

Holy Spirit, receive the perfect and total consecration of my entire being; be in every instant of my life and in my every action my Director, my Light, my Guide, my Strength and all the Love of my heart. I abandon myself without reserve to Your divine actions and want to be ever docile to Your inspirations. Holy Spirit, transform me with Mary and in Mary into Jesus Christ for the glory of the Father and the salvation of the world. Amen.[288]

---

[288] *Priests of Christ*, 361.

Individual or Group Reflection

Ponder

"Do you not know that your body is a temple of the Holy Spirit within you, which you have from God? You are not your own; you were bought with a price. So glorify God in your body" (1 Cor. 6:19–20).

Engage

1. How is the Holy Spirit working in your life, in your prayer, and in your relationships?
2. How has God revealed His love to you?
3. How can you better "love with the Holy Spirit"?

Pray

Holy Spirit, since you are ineffable Repose and infinite Peace, console our suffering hearts, and sweeten the burden of our crosses. Give us the simplicity of the truth in all our words! May we speak without concern for others' approval, act without duplicity, and work with perfect charity.

O Eternal Love, how we need You in our society, in our families, and in our hearts! You have always been needed in all of our lives, but now more than ever in these times of cold selfishness and crass materialism that cause faith to agonize in the human soul. You are indispensable more now than ever! You, who are the joy of heaven itself, pour into our hearts a happiness that will not fade away, that of a pure conscience, and of a soul that is at peace even in a time of suffering.

Come, come Holy Spirit! Renew the face of the earth: "create in me a pure heart and renew within me the right spirit" (Ps 51:12).

Only then will all things be renewed in Christ, and Christian homes will be multiplied to the honor and glory of the Most Holy Trinity. Amen.[289]

[289] Concepción Cabrera de Armida (Conchita), *Open to the Holy Spirit* (Staten Island, NY: Society of St. Paul, 2017), 38.

11

The Mystic: Spiritual Direction, What Jesus Is Like, Spiritual Battles

Abide in me, and I in you.

—John 15:4

Blessed Conchita has already acquired an importance in the spiritual formation of thousands of Catholics in many countries. In this chapter, we'll approach Conchita as our spiritual mother who shares what Jesus is like and gives us insights on spiritual direction and spiritual warfare.

If we imitate the heroic virtues of saintly souls such as Conchita, we'll be on the path to becoming today's saints, the ones God has chosen for the renovation of our era. And if not a saint, what then? If not holiness, what am I choosing? If God isn't worth my time, my love, or my life, what is? If we desire to become the mystics the Church and the world need, Blessed Conchita shows us how.

Conchita's Mysticism

Throughout these pages, I have said, "The Lord said to Conchita" and have used terms such as *mystical*, *locution*, and *vision* to describe Conchita's spiritual life. Mystical theologians such as Réginald Garrigou-LaGrange, O.P., say that such expressions almost always relate to "intellectual visions" (infused knowledge imprinted upon the intellect), which are the least likely to be illusions or contain errors.[290] Rather than present what theologians have written about mystical grace, I chose to present what Jesus teaches about the way that He bestows mystical graces upon Conchita. In her *Diary*, Conchita details how she receives them:

> *Sometimes He dictates to me, more or less, with phrases or words; other times not so, but all at once He imprints a stream of things inside of me, sometimes very briefly, but leaving in me a clear intelligence of what has come through, of what is to come ... sometimes little by little, or other times, all of a sudden. My senses quiet themselves as a signal that the Lord is coming and so do my faculties, leaving me as a blank paper, as though emptying of myself and of every worldly noise. Thus, without coordinating ideas, I receive an inference of interior words, or already ordered concepts; let us say that I understand all of a sudden.*
>
> *I do not hear a voice with my corporal ears, except perhaps a few times. Sometimes I am tempted to believe that I am inventing it all, that I am deceived, but when I am at peace, I cannot doubt that these things come from God.*
>
> *Besides that, in my experience, when the Lord does not give, I may spend hours in prayer, yet I cannot even write a line by myself; I am without juice, all dried up, without being able to invent, even if I desired to do so.*
>
> *Sometimes months go by, and the Lord does not speak to me, and others, I hardly have time to write all He says to me. Another way in which the Lord communicates with me has been*

---

[290] Ignacio Navarro Alfaro, M.Sp.S., *Conchita's Spiritual Journey* (Staten Island, NY: St. Paul's, 2019), 115.

my writing. Many times, when I am praying or at another time, I have heard his voice say to me, "Write." At the beginning, I resisted and instantly I was filled with dryness – such aridity – until I began to obey; at the very moment of taking up the pencil, the Lord started to spill Himself out, dictating sheets and sheets, sometimes about lofty theological items, they say, which I never could have invented myself.[291]

Jesus then offers a little catechism on mysticism that provides a beautiful reflection for prayer:

Also, the manner of communicating Myself to you involves the aspect of unity because, in God, everything is one. For example, I reflect Myself in the mirror or crystal of your soul. Those divine rays remain there and you, experiencing yourself touched by them, start to see, to contemplate and to understand.

And afterwards, with the help of your mind, you give them form with the words that you more or less suitably adapt, that of which I Myself, without your realizing it, have left the substance. In the first streak of light, you trace the essence, the photograph of the communicated thing in your soul, to your intellectual facilities, and from there to the paper.

In this manner of communication of God with the creature there is almost never a mistake, except if human passions come to involve themselves; then they obscure and twist and even erase the signs of God in the soul.

When a soul receives this communication humbly and lends itself to it with purity of heart, which is essential, without mixing in any passion, God's impression is clear, clean, and luminous, and there is no danger of mistake.

[291] *Conchita's Spiritual Journey*, 115.

Surely, when the divine comes through the human, it takes a form or color of the receptacle receiving these communications, but this is secondary. The essence, the substance and even the form remains the same that God was willing to communicate.

My daughter, thus because of my goodness and for My high goals, I have made of you an instrument or an aqueduct. Never stain the mirror of your soul, because now I need you more than ever clean, clear, and transparent, to communicate the outpouring of the Holy Spirit's graces. Do not lift up your glance and do not ever be proud; lower it always. Look for Me in the hidden mirror of your soul, and you will find Me there, and there will you listen to Me, and there you will understand the marvels of your only unique God that has His delight in making Himself known to humble souls that will give Him glory.[292]

This little catechism on mysticism provides a beautiful reflection for prayer.

Conchita's Small Plan of Spiritual Direction[293]

Conchita deeply appreciated her chosen spiritual directors throughout her life. On one occasion, she prayed to Jesus to ask if He would give her a simple plan for spiritual direction. The Lord said that she already had such a plan within her soul. Conchita, thinking of her volumes of writings, responded that she was seeking a simple plan, something practical. Jesus responded, *"Then here is a simple*

---

[292] *Conchita's Spiritual Journey,* 118.

[293] Conchita Cabrera, *Spiritual Direction according to the Small Plan of Concepción Cabrera de Armida,* (Modesto, CA: Sisters of the Cross of the Sacred Heart of Jesus, 2007). The English translation has been edited and abbreviated in these pages.

plan: Lead souls to love and honor My humanity, My heart, the Holy Spirit, the Eucharist, and the Cross."

Later, eighteen points of spiritual direction were composed. Fr. Félix Rougier wrote the first commentary for the novices of the Missionaries of the Holy Spirit. Then they developed this expanded version as a practical application for spiritual direction.

1. *Encourage directees to fall in love with Jesus' humanity, and to love and honor His Heart, the Holy Spirit, the Eucharist, the Cross, and Mary.*

   Holiness consists in following Someone, falling in love with Someone; it means dying to our self in order to experience a new life in Someone else: Jesus Christ.[294]

2. *Lead directees to total consecration to Jesus: to total surrender to the Lord.*

   This total surrender and self-giving is proper to perfect love. Total surrender doesn't happen all of a sudden. This unconditional surrender begins from our imperfect love which needs to develop into perfect love.[295]

3. *Help directees to grow in hunger and thirst for Jesus. Urge them to entrust themselves to Him.*[296]

4. *Help directees to detach themselves from worldly affections. Help them to transform their affections through purity.*[297]

5. *Help directees to constantly practice the offering of their thoughts, words, and actions to the Lord.*

   We need to develop something like a natural reflex that is conditioned by our desire to become more like

---

[294] *Spiritual Direction*, 5.

[295] *Spiritual Direction*, 7.

[296] *Spiritual Direction*, 9.

[297] *Spiritual Direction*, 11.

Christ every day. We need to react according to the will of God. If we try in faith, we will find ourselves reacting supernaturally under any given stimuli.[298]

6. *Help directees to become aware of Jesus' abiding presence so they realize that it is impossible to live without Jesus by their side.*

   If we do not incarnate our aspirations, they become just one more illusion in our lives. The practice of abiding in the presence of Jesus greatly enhances spiritual life.[299]

7. *With the help of the Lord, uproot the tendency to venial sin. Guide directees to love transparency of their soul, but without falling into scruples.*

   "Without scruples" is to say "with common sense" because common sense is the basis of a life of holiness. This is not an invitation to have a life of constant violence or of psychological tension. When love is true, it sees and asks for the presence of the beloved. This presence is that of a God who wants to be close to us, not as our judge but as our tender, faithful lover, a God who is compassionate and tender. This is something very real, deep.[300]

8. *Teach directees how to fly with freedom of spirit; with expanded hearts, without limiting God.*

   What does "to fly" mean in the language of Conchita? It means taking initiative in responding to the Lord's voice. Teach directees to be very responsible in their spiritual life, and to practice the initiatives of the Holy Spirit.[301]

---

[298] *Spiritual Direction*, 14.
[299] *Spiritual Direction*, 15.
[300] *Spiritual Direction*, 17–18.
[301] *Spiritual Direction*, 19–20.

9. *Teach directees to pray and mortify themselves for love of God.*

    Prayer according to Conchita is above all the acceptance of the loving will of God. To pray is not something that causes me to enclose upon myself. Mortification must be practiced above all in the fulfillment of our daily duties. Our daily lives are filled with opportunities to act according to God's will.[302]

10. *Teach directees that the most secure way to unite to Jesus is not by the sweet experiences but by the Cross.*

    The Cross of Jesus is a sure tool to create virtues. Patient endurance is the only road to solid virtue.[303]

11. *Help directees to become courageous and untiring in making effort to practice solid virtues. Help them not to be fearful of any cross.*

    This rule leads to Christian maturity wherein spiritual life is no longer subject to the whims of our will, or our psychology, or the variation of moods, or temperaments. Sometimes if we are in a good mood, we say, "I will do my best to be a saint." If we are in a bad mood, we say, "Today, I do not have any time for holiness." We need to free real virtue from human fluctuations.[304]

12. *Help directees to love the virtue of humility under any form. Help them to practice it constantly.*

    What does humility mean? It supposes an invaluable grace of self-knowledge, not only for the complete acceptance of our own limits, but it involves a light coming from God to see very clearly our own misery.

---

[302] *Spiritual Direction,* 21–23.

[303] *Spiritual Direction,* 25.

[304] *Spiritual Direction,* 27.

It is only God who is able to take us to the depths of our nothingness. The result of true humility is better knowledge of ourselves and better knowledge of God.[305]

13. *Lead directees to complete trust in Jesus; to be secure in Him.*

First, we find humility and then we find trust. This is a logical sequence. Once we've accepted our limitations and His omnipotence, we are ready to place all our trust in Him to the point of abandoning ourselves into His hands.[306]

14. *Guide directees to always choose willingly to take up their cross.*

This is a difficult task! This is something superior to what we presented in rule 9. There we spoke of mortification. This principle supposes a deep action of the Holy Spirit in our souls. He is the only Person who is able to give us an impulse to choose the cross. Discernment is important at this stage.[307]

15. *Invite directees to walk through the divine field of every perfect virtue.*

There is a difference between the practice of virtue that is of human volition versus God's volition. The latter is a gift from God that comes to crown our humble efforts.[308]

16. *Encourage directees to wrap their whole life in holy purity until they fall in love with it.*

Purity equals authenticity. Christian life is pure when there is no mixture of any alien reality or motivation

---

[305] *Spiritual Direction,* 28–29.
[306] *Spiritual Direction,* 30–31.
[307] *Spiritual Direction,* 32–33.
[308] *Spiritual Direction,* 34–35.

in it. The absence of foreign elements makes a thing completely pure. In a life which is pure, everything is clean and transparent.[309]

17. *Help directees to respond to the Lord on the foundation of the virtues, simplicity, and clarity.*

Psychology has discovered in us a very deep turmoil; complications in our way of being. We impersonate others, wear masks, like disguises under different motivations. We see ourselves so lacking in good qualities of any kind, we need to appear different, we take on attitudes that are different from our own. That is to say, we lack simplicity. There is a certain disguise that we wear. When we have God present in us, what is the use for the disguise? Our soul is under His loving gaze as it is. There is no need of anything else. If I do not manifest my own truth, then spiritual direction is worthless.[310]

18. *Form directees in the virtue of obedience to God.*

Obedience is the virtue that conforms us to Jesus because obedience is the soul of redemption. Obedience is Jesus' seal of authenticity. He did not come to do His will but the will of the Father.[311]

Mystical Writings: What Jesus Is Like

We have said that Conchita is considered one of the most prolific mystical writers in the Church. She wrote for the sole purpose of inspiring us to fall in love with Jesus. The following reflections

---

[309] *Spiritual Direction*, 37.
[310] *Spiritual Direction*, 39.
[311] *Spiritual Direction*, 40–41.

and prayers composed by Conchita are found in her book *What Jesus Is Like.* During the Holy See's process of canonization, the censor wrote that these are genuine meditations on Jesus Christ, approved by several bishops, and *also granted indulgences.*

I composed the testaments that follow Conchita's reflections and prayers to convey a practical application of her principles.

His Physical Appearance

Reflection

How handsome Jesus was and is! What beauty, what clarity, what transparency, what an infinite depth of all perfection! There is not a single divine ardor that does not come from that central point, nor a single drop of heavenly joy that is not derived from that Font. Knowing Him, studying Him, and feeling His presence, who would be capable of offending Him? One must manifest Him, taste Him, penetrate Him, but more than anything else, one must love Him, because love draws us closer to Him. Love is a light that illuminates, transforms, and unites. To be united to Jesus is to have surrendered to the will of the Father.[312]

Prayer

O Mary, who in this world has known the beauty of Jesus as you have? Show Him to me. Give Him to me. For He is also mine. Cause me to imitate Him, to love Him, to sacrifice myself for His sake, in order to give you many souls who might glorify Him here on earth, and eternally at your side.[313]

Testament

"He is so beautiful!" These words were spoken by my beloved mother, now deceased. For a time, she had a fear of death. Then,

---

[312] *What Jesus Is Like,* 1.
[313] *What Jesus Is Like,* 2.

in a dream, she saw Jesus approaching her with His hand out-
reached. His face was radiant with a gaze of love that invited trust.
His beauty drew her to Him. She understood that the next time
Jesus came for her, she would go with Him. She stated that her
passage from this life to the next would be like stepping out the
front door of her home into His home. "I'm not afraid. He is so
very, very beautiful." Thus, Christ draws us to Himself because
we are made for the Beautiful One.

His Name

Reflection

*Jesus' Name is a Name of love, of suffering and of hope! But what a price
Jesus paid to receive this most sweet Name which means Savior! Jesus is a
Name of peace which calms all storms. A Name of light which illumines
the nights of the spirit. A Name which embraces and consoles. Which
sustains and gives one the strength for sacrifice. A Name which penetrates
even to the inner recesses of hearts and purifies them. A Name of glory
and splendor. A Name that tastes of heaven. Adorable Name!*

*At times I see Him as a child. The first thing you ask a child is,
"What is your name?" Let us do this often with Jesus. He will answer
in the depths of our soul. He will tell us what we need to hear. "I am
the Resurrection and the Life" (Jn 11:25). His Divine Lips will tell us
over and over that our faith will be illuminated and our hope for future
happiness will expand the breadth of our soul, anguished at the thought
of the death of those we love. "It is I. Do not be afraid" (Mk 6:50). We
shall hear, be touched, and feel ourselves relieved of a great weight that
oppresses us as we become aware of His Compassion, His Charity, and
His Infinite Love.*[314]

---

[314] *What Jesus Is Like*, 12, 13.

Beautiful Holiness

Prayer

O Most Holy Virgin, why did you give Him to us if not that we should constantly try to love Him as you loved Him? Thank you, Mary, my Mother. We beg you to place in our hearts, on our lips, and in our souls that precious imprint, that Divine Seal that is ever saying to us: Jesus, Jesus, Jesus! Amen.[315]

Testament

St. Paul writes that the name of Jesus Christ is a powerful name that is above every other name (see Phil. 2:9-11). Matthew writes, "You shall call his name Jesus, for he will save his people from their sins" (Matt. 1:21), assigning salvific power to the Name. In Luke's Gospel, we hear the apostles say, "Even the demons are subject to us in [Jesus'] name" (Luke 10:17), assigning exorcistic power to the Name of Jesus. In speaking or praying the Name of Jesus, we echo these inspired sentiments since the Word of God is alive. Powerful is the utterance of the Holy Name of Jesus!

His Heart

Reflection

Everything about Jesus is to be admired. His words, His gazes, His smile, His thoughts, and actions, but most of all His incomparable Heart, Center and Fount of those allurements! In Him are encompassed all virtues and perfections: His holiness and His love. His Infinite, Ardent, Pure and Divine Love. Nothing is more demanding and yet more tender and precious than that Heart in which every holy affection could be seen to radiate. But that which is most admirable in the Heart of Jesus is His serenity in His intimate sufferings, in that interior cross which tormented His soul

---

[315] *What Jesus Is Like,* 12.

from the instant of the Incarnation until His death. In His Most Sacred Heart, Jesus felt the piercing thorns of all our suffering and the bitterness of all our tears.

This Divine Heart wants to unite Itself to us in an intimate embrace and to fuse our soul into His Own. He loves us in order to reveal His secrets to us. To grant us His Spirit. To give us that which is His. To inebriate us with His love and to communicate to us His very life, His heartbeats, His martyrdoms, and His happiness.[316]

Prayer

Dear Jesus, I want to help You with your interior cross. I want You to share with me some of those intimate, bitter sufferings that hurt You so much. I want to be pure for those who are not pure. I want to sacrifice myself for those who do not sacrifice themselves. To be grateful for the ungrateful. To be Your victim on behalf of Your beloved Church.[317]

Testament

The Sacred Heart of Jesus is and always will be a gift of divine love, a safe refuge, a furnace to warm ourselves, an ocean of mercy, an icon of holiness, a pillar of the priesthood, a personal invitation to the wedding feast of the Lamb.

On practically every wall or table in my childhood home, the image of the Sacred Heart was present. He was among our family as Lord and friend. At times, my parents walked up to the image and gazed intently at it, pouring their heart out to His. There were bills to pay, many kids to feed, repairs needed for the house or the one family car. Whatever the intention was, it was presented to the Heart of Jesus with faith that His Heart was concerned for our needs. The

[316] *What Jesus Is Like*, 15, 16.
[317] *What Jesus Is Like*, 17.

Sacred Heart never let my parents down. The Heart of Jesus has never let me down. His is the Heart that provides what is needed.

His Loving Complaints

Reflection

"Have I been with you for so long a time, and you still do not know Me, Philip?" (Jn. 14:9). From His monstrance, from His Tabernacle, He speaks to us. "For such a long time I have been with you, living by your side, coming to you daily in Holy Communion, never leaving you, being even closer than I was to My disciples. Still you do not know Me. Have you not contemplated My virtues? Have you not entered into My Sacred Heart? Have you not shared My very Life? I love you so much, so very much, beloved soul who is listening to Me." … Jesus was deeply moved, and He was speaking to all the cold and indifferent souls of all the ages with the emphasis of the heart.

Again, Jesus, whom we so frequently forget about, complains with a sadness that tears the heart about that which hurts Him most: our ingratitude![318]

Prayer

Mary, my Mother! I know that the one who is best able to love is the one who best knows how to voluntarily suffer, the better in order to console you. Mother of my soul, grant that I may never bring sadness to Jesus' Heart by my forgetfulness of Him and my ingratitude. Grant that I might know Him, meditate upon Him, penetrate Him and that He may never be able to complain about my not loving Him enough. I do love Him very much! Amen.[319]

---

[318] *What Jesus Is Like*, 29, 30.
[319] *What Jesus Is Like*, 31.

The Mystic

Testament

To my surprise, my husband came home in the middle of his workday to present me with two dozen perfect long-stemmed red roses arranged in a beautiful vase. Exquisite! He pointed to the handwritten presentation card, "One rose for each of the past twenty-four months in which I caused you pain. I'm sorry. Thank you." I was speechless. I didn't realize how much I needed to hear that. An acknowledgment, an apology, and gratitude are hallmarks of genuine love. These hallmarks heal the heart and strengthen human relationships. They matter to us. They matter to Jesus! His Heart is pierced by our ingratitude, indifference, and lovelessness toward Him. Pray that we never bring sadness to Jesus' tender Heart. If we do, apologize to Jesus and begin again.

His Words

Reflection

Heavenly words of mercy, of justice, of sublime charity and of holy love fell from the divine lips of Jesus as gentle dew falling upon a parched earth. His words were and continue to be the great Splendor, the great Light for all mankind. His lips always spoke piety, sweetness, and confidences. He was and is Goodness, Mercy, and Kindness personified. If we were to allow His words to penetrate our heart, how rapidly we would begin our transformation into Him. Whoever said that the presence of God in His actions and His words has to be felt? Sometimes God grants that sensation. At other times, He doesn't. The words of Jesus enthrall us and fill us with love. In them we find all that is pure, luminous, and beautiful and they take the soul beyond one's possible dreams of holiness. Those words of Jesus are food, light, perfume, life, delight, strength, and love![320]

---

[320] *What Jesus Is Like*, 36, 37.

Beautiful Holiness

Prayer

O Jesus, Your gospel is Your very life among us! Your doctrine is my breath, my drink and the light that brings joy to my eyes. You words are my strength in my struggles. My rest, my peace, my best companions, and my reward. This is because You are there. The Doctor who knows me and who cures my every ailment. The Shepherd who guides me as His beloved sheep. The Friend from whom I hold nothing back. The Husband whom I worship. He who has the remedy for every disorder. The Divine Word Himself. The Splendor of the Father, of His holiness and His beauty. Amen.[321]

Testament

At his rectory, my priest friend poured himself a cup of coffee and drank it. Immediately, his esophagus constricted, his throat and mouth burned; he had difficulty breathing. Calling the paramedics first, the housekeeper explained that she had poured lye in the coffee pot to clean it. Father made coffee in a pot with poisonous lye. Inside the paramedic van, Father silently prayed from memory, "They will pick up serpents, and if they drink any deadly thing, it will not hurt them" (Mark 16:18). At the hospital, his stomach was flushed, and he recovered. A brilliant priest of charismatic faith, he memorized much of Scripture. When he proclaimed Scripture interiorly, he believed that the Word of God would be effective. There is power in God's Word! Scripture is a living reality, a sword against harm.

His Mercy

Reflection

We do not need a great deal of thinking to appreciate what Jesus has been for us. We need only recall some of the happy memories of our lives, and, full of gratitude and love, we shall realize some of what we owe Him! How

---

[321] *What Jesus Is Like,* 38.

much He has loved us at every stage and at every moment of our lives! With what ineffable gentleness He has treated us! With what patience, He has endured us! With what solicitude He has cared for us! With what tenderness He has led us, not by the hand, but in His arms and in His Heart! What finesse He has shown us! This is how Jesus is! This is His infinite Charity. This is why He knows how to love us: unmindful of our sins, casting our infidelities into the sea, drowning our unfaithfulness in the wellspring of the Love of His Heart, consuming even the straws of our imperfections in the fire of His bosom. How different earthly love is when compared to the love Jesus![322]

Prayer

And you, Mary, who are all pure, loving, and indulgent, whose Heart burns with love for souls, obtain for us the grace to be truly grateful to your Son. This we beg of you, our most loving Mother of Mercy.[323]

Testament

As I was kneeling before the Blessed Sacrament a few days after an unspeakable family trauma, the Lord spoke to my heart: "I simply ask that you repeat My words from the Cross, 'Father, forgive them; for they know not what they do' (Luke 23:34). Will you do this for Me?" The Lord asked me to forgive the murderer of my beloved father-in-law, who was beaten to death. I wanted only justice. Jesus knew that the poison of unforgiveness would eat away at me. How could I adore the Blessed Sacrament and not do His will? I told Jesus that I'd say the prayer but needed special grace to mean it. Then Jesus flooded my soul with Divine Mercy. No matter how heinous the murder, I wouldn't desire eternal damnation

---

[322] *What Jesus Is Like*, 58, 59.
[323] *What Jesus Is Like*, 60.

for anyone. Unfathomable divine mercy, be merciful to me, and to the whole world.

His Eucharist

Reflection

The Eucharist is the compendium of all the marvels of God and the consummation of all the mysteries that He brings about in souls. The Eucharist perpetuates all the mysteries of Jesus and makes them present to us who were not alive when He was on earth. Let us live with Jesus in Holy Communion and He will live within us and will communicate to us all that He is. Let us cast far from us tepidity and indifference. Let us come to the altar with our soul on fire, with an insatiable longing to receive Jesus. Let us offer the Incarnate Word unceasingly to the Heavenly Father within our hearts. Let us unite ourselves to all His immolations on behalf of His beloved Church and in thanksgiving for the Gift of gifts, the Holy Eucharist. Let us make reparation to the most Holy Sacrament of the altar for the times we have forgotten Him. [324]

Prayer

Undoubtedly, it was particularly for you, Mary, that Jesus instituted the Sacrament of Love. If He was not willing to leave us orphans when He ascended into heaven, how could He abandon you in exile without living at your side? Without leaving you His Body, His Soul, His Heart, and His Divinity during the years of your solitude on earth? Obtain for us today, from Jesus, that he might pour out, over those of us who love Him so much in the Eucharist, all the blessings that He sends to the world by means of the consecrated Host. Amen. [325]

---

[324] *What Jesus Is Like*, 104.
[325] *What Jesus Is Like*, 105.

The Mystic

Testament

In the shadow of France's Pyrenees mountains, the hospital doors opened. Long rows of patients on gurneys emerged and were wheeled to the Grotto of Massabielle, the place of the 1858 apparitions of Our Lady of Lourdes. Against the Grotto walls were hundreds of crutches and wheelchairs no longer needed by the countless people who had been healed at Lourdes. The priest emerged walking with the Blessed Sacrament. Silence veiled the crowd of thousands. I gazed at the Blessed Sacrament as the priest carried the monstrance among the sick patients, their eyes full of hope. "Only say the word, and my soul shall be healed." Jesus in the Eucharist touches and heals His people, the sick, the weary, the oppressed, and the frightened. The Eucharist heals because it is the Lord who physically touches us with His Body and Blood.

His Priests

Reflection

What is it that Jesus loved with the greatest preferential love? His mother and His Church, the depository of His doctrine and His Heart, of His very self in the Eucharist. In the plan of salvation, the Church was the fulfillment of Jesus' ministries on earth, because Jesus entrusted not only His teachings and His salvific and sanctifying power, but He Himself remained in it until the end of time. Jesus built His Church upon Peter. Without priests, how would God's blessings be applied to us? The priest has the key to the heavenly treasures. He opens that door for us. He is the administrator of all its goods.

What an obligation we the faithful have to sacrifice ourselves in union with Jesus for His priests in order to shore up their spiritual strength, since we owe them so much and we have cost them so much. What little gratefulness we show these souls who sacrifice themselves for us, who offer up their lives, who no longer belong to themselves. This is Jesus the

Beautiful Holiness

Eternal Priest: the One who has made His priests a continuation of His very self on earth.[326]

Prayer

Mary, with what love you must have inflamed the hearts of the apostles so that they might spread the Church! So that they might joyfully shed their blood and give their lives to uphold Jesus' cause: the truth and the faith! You, who were the light of the apostles, the fire who caused them to burn, thirsting to communicate the doctrine they had received to souls. Help priests, that chosen portion whom Jesus loves so much, and unite them to yourself. Console them, fortify them and daily teach them in ever greater depth what Jesus is like and how He wishes them to be other Christs. Amen.[327]

Testament

A priest friend invited me to meet him at the hospital to pray with his parishioners. The young father of the family received a dire prognosis. The wife was told to take her husband home and enjoy his presence while she and their two little sons could. I entered the hospital room where the family and the priest stood in a circle of prayer. I silently joined. Father beseeched Jesus to grant healing to the man's brain. Father beseeched Jesus for a needed miracle. The atmosphere in the room changed from fear to hope. Gone was a spirit of death. The priest proclaimed healing in Jesus Christ. The Lord honored the prayers of His priest. Discharged from the hospital, the man lived, with some limitations, but he lived for his family. To pray daily for our priests is our imitation of Mary, Mother of Priests.

[326] *What Jesus Is Like*, 108.
[327] *What Jesus Is Like*, 109.

The Mystic

His Love for Mary

Reflection

How Jesus must have loved His Holy Mother! He was so loving, so tender and so grateful to her! It was to her, through the action of the Holy Spirit, that He owed His human life. To her that He owed His body that would be crucified, His blood that would nourish us! Jesus, would You like to tell us Your thoughts and feeling at the side of Your most Holy Mother?[328]

[Jesus speaks:] "For thirty years I witnessed, in our hidden life in Nazareth, the heroic virtue of My mother. Her care and solicitude for My every want, giving up sleep and totally sacrificing herself to help and please Me. Mary was able to read My soul like an open book. She saw concerns that used to absorb My thinking and the suffering that tortured Me. She used to see Me pray to the Father and offer Myself over and over to be sacrificed in order to save fallen mankind.

The Holy Spirit enabled her to conceive all of her future children in love and in sorrow. These children, who participate in My life through grace, would imitate her here on earth until the end of time. The final outpouring of the Holy Spirit in the soul of My beloved mother was so intense and ardent, so impetuous and divine, that Mary, although she had previously experienced God's love, was unable to withstand it. She died in love, because of her love, and so actually died of Love itself."[329]

Prayer

My Mother! Is not this the word that expresses all of your dignity, all of your graces, your special gifts, and your mission in heaven and on earth? Mother of God! Mother of mankind! Mother, the word and the name that speaks of your ineffable and maternal love for Jesus and us, for Jesus in

328 *What Jesus Is Like*, 115.
329 *What Jesus Is Like*, 116.

His human body and in His Mystical Body. Mary, our heavenly Mother,
look upon us with compassion, and we beg your never to leave us. Amen.[330]

Testament

I was inconsolable. In the brief time that she was alone, my beloved
mother died of a heart attack. The family was terribly grief-stricken
as we planned the funeral for our mother. We were blessed to
have seven priest friends concelebrate the Mass. At the end, the
grandchildren slowly wheeled their grandmother's casket from the
altar. Suddenly the seven priests harmoniously filled the Church
singing the Salve Regina as they accompanied mom's casket to the
awaiting limousine. In hearing the Salve Regina sung, Heaven and
earth touched for me. My broken, mystified heart experienced the
consolation of Heaven. I just knew that Mary was near my mother
and my family. She and her beloved priest sons lowered Heaven
for a moment of grace to minister to a grieving family who had
lost their mother.

Family Witnesses: Conchita's Spiritual Battles

I inquired of Conchita's living relatives, whether she experienced
demonic attacks like many other saints. Maria Teresa Madero,
granddaughter of Conchita's daughter Lupe, provided some personal accounts.

> My grandmother Lupe who, at this period, was the only
> daughter at home with Conchita, slept in the same room
> and witnessed the following. She told me that her mother
> often woke up with bruises. My grandmother Lupe knew
> that her mother had physical struggles with the devil

---

[330] *What Jesus Is Like*, 115, 116.

because she felt his movements. At times she felt the devil pulled Conchita out of bed, dragged her around, and physically assaulted her.

On one occasion, while she was in a hotel in Rome, waiting for a papal audience to request permission for the Foundation of the Missionaries of the Holy Spirit, she awoke with bruises on her face and a black eye. When Ignacio, her son, who slept in another room, came to greet them and saw his mother, he began to admonish Lupe, believing her to be the cause. My great-grandmother (Conchita) stopped him, saying, "Don't reproach her for anything. Lupe is not the cause. They are my concerns. Don't ask questions."

Another time, it was attributed to the devil that, on one of the first oil paintings of Conchita's Vision of the Cross of the Apostolate on which was written "love and suffering," the word "suffering" was burned away so it couldn't be seen.

My grandmother Lupe tells that when my mother [Teresa, granddaughter of Conchita] was in her crib, when she was six months old, she heard a roar in the baby's room. They went to see what was happening and found the baby crying, very scared. The lamp with glass beads was on and shaking by itself. Conchita arrived, put her hand on the child's forehead, and made the Sign of the Cross.

Another occasion: The servants of the house had their rooms on the rooftop level. There were problems with boys from the neighboring house, so they built a brick and cement wall to avoid problems. The construction was complete. Then, one day while the family was in the living room, they heard a loud noise on the roof. My grandfather and Conchita's son Ignacio went upstairs to see what happened. They found all the construction materials for the wall, bricks and cement, as if they'd never been used for construction. That is, the bricks were in neat piles, and the cement was back inside the bags, unused.

The grandchildren called Conchita "Mane," short for "Grandmother." Mane would tell them not to consider such strange things. She simply blessed them and did not give them explanations.[331]

A Soldier for Christ

The testimony of Conchita's relatives who witnessed some of the external spiritual warfare that she experienced is consistent with the lives of other saints. Conchita reacted to demonic attacks with courage and wisdom. She rightfully deprived the devil of attention, and she turned to Jesus. She immediately made the Sign of the Cross, which is considered a prayer, a blessing, and a sacramental. Conchita's humility empowered her to overcome the spiritual battles described by her family. The proud devil despises humility.

In her spiritual *Diary*, Conchita wrote about interior demonic temptations, including doubt, discouragement, lies, and fear. The Lord allowed Conchita's faith, hope, and love to be tested so that she would grow in virtue. She was sanctified through trials of human suffering and spiritual warfare. This spiritual battle included interior struggles and the exterior attacks of the devil. The book of Job provides a good example of a person who underwent demonic oppression as allowed by the Lord for the sanctification of his soul.

---

[331] Maria Teresa Madero, granddaughter of Conchita's daughter Lupe, personal notes translated from Spanish by Fr. Domenico Di Raimondo, M.Sp.S., 2021.

"Resist the devil and he will flee" (James 4:7). Conchita did as this Scripture verse teaches, and so can you. There is nothing to fear if you are in the state of grace. Bless yourself and your family with the Sign of the Cross. Sprinkle holy water on yourself and on your loved ones, around your home, and on your possessions. Faithfully dress yourself in all of God's armor (see Eph. 6:10–18). Frequent the sacraments, especially Holy Communion and Confession. Sacraments and sacramentals have powerful exorcistic grace.

In Maria Teresa Madero's account, the devil gives a vital clue: the word *suffering* was burned away from the oil painting of the Cross of the Apostolate. In Mark's Gospel, a Roman soldier speaks thus, "Save yourself, and come down from the cross!" (Mark 15:30). This is the perennial temptation of the evil one to reject the Cross and to reject suffering as meaningless. We know that the Cross is Christ's victory over sin and evil. Therefore, we can do as Conchita did and be credible witnesses to the power of the Cross with its saving grace.

Prophet and Spiritual Mother

Through Conchita's prophetic voice, Jesus addresses three areas in the heart of the Church:

1. Clergy: He desires complete transfiguration (communion) through the Cross (sacrifice), heroic virtue (sanctity), that the Church shine with holy priests (witness), and that priests experience a priestly Pentecost (abundant life) and lead the Church to the reign of the Holy Spirit and Eucharistic renovation.

2. Religious sisters: He desires transforming union with His consecrated brides through the Cross (sacrifice) and the Eucharist (communion), Mary's solitude (love), perpetual adoration (worship), spiritual motherhood of

souls (fruitfulness), and intercession for the salvation of souls (reparation).

3. Laity: He desires mystical transformation through His Heart (love) and Cross (sacrifice); the universal call to holiness of life (virtue); that marriages witness to love (fidelity); and that laypersons bring souls to Christ (intercession) and be Mary's ambassadors (reparation).

What would Blessed Conchita say to us now? Perhaps she would say that life with Jesus is worth every sacrifice; that we should heroically fulfill the duties of our vocation as witnesses to Christ's love; that we should pray, "Save them, Jesus, save souls."

Conchita would tell us: You are privileged to enter the Holy of Holies. Be an apostle of the Eucharist. Love with the Holy Spirit. Have expectant faith in the God of miracles. Jesus is the fulfillment of your desire. Do not fear the Cross. Love requires sacrifice. Suffering is already here. Don't waste the opportunity of this precious moment. Let the Lord love you. And love Jesus Christ with all your heart. Stay engaged in His Church. Love and serve your family with tenderness and courage. Your gift of self makes a difference to God and souls. God has planted seeds of greatness within you. Do not doubt your calling.

Finally, this poor author echoes Conchita's words to Jorge Treviño during the miracle: "*Do me a favor: receive Communion daily and pray for priests.*" Not only will doing these two things console the heart of Jesus and sanctify us; these spiritual offerings can lift this falling world. "Rise! Let us go!" (see Mark 14:42). Let us fall in love with Jesus again and radiate to the world His beautiful holiness. The world aches for God in His saints.

Blessed Concepción Cabrera de Armida, pray for us please.

INDIVIDUAL OR GROUP REFLECTION

Ponder

"Blessed are the pure of heart, for they shall see God" (Matt. 5:8).

Engage

1. What was your favorite reflection on *what Jesus is like?*
2. How have you profited from the lessons on spiritual direction?
3. When you experience spiritual warfare how do you respond? What lessons have you learned from Conchita?

Pray

O Mary, there was not a single moment of your precious life that you did not remain in Jesus' love! Most faithful Virgin! Without equal in your correspondence to the inspirations of the Holy Spirit! You were always faithful to the Eternal Father in your obedience. Faithful to Jesus in every circumstance of your life. Obtain for us the grace to remain always in the love of Jesus, that we may please Him and fulfill His desire in that which He asks of us today as the finishing touch of this series of meditations. "Remain in My love" (Jn. 15:9). Amen.[332]

---

[332] *What Jesus Is Like*, 113.

Appendix

Timeline of Blessed Conchita's Life

1862   Born in San Luis Potosí.

1863   Lives in the haciendas of her wealthy family.

1867   Sees Jesus in a dream.

1869   Homeschooling begins.

1872   First Holy Communion.

1879   Falls from a horse and has a spiritual conversion.

1883   Experiences the tragic death of her brother Manuel; matures quickly.

1884   Marries Francisco and is deeply drawn to God.

1885   Her son Francisco is born.

1886   Her uncle Luis, a priest, dies; she sees the Heart of Jesus.

1887   Her son Carlos is born.

1888   Her father dies.

1889   Her son Manuel is born; spiritual exercises: her mission to save souls is told by Jesus.

1890   Her daughter Concha is born.

1893   Her son Carlos dies; Fr. Alberto Mir, S.J., becomes her spiritual director; she is told to choose the most perfect.

1894   Her husband becomes ill.

1895   Her son Pablo is born; she begins the Apostleship of the Cross.

1896	Her son Salvador is born.
1897	Begins the Sisters of the Cross of the Most Sacred Heart of Jesus; receives the grace of the mystical incarnation.
1898	Her daughter Lupe is born. Jesus says that Conchita will be a victim for the Church.
1899	Her son Pedro is born.
1901	Her husband dies.
1902	Suffers several illnesses.
1903	Her son Pedro dies; she encounters Fr. Félix Rougier.
1905	Her mother dies.
1906	Her son Manuel joins the Society of Jesus.
1908	Her daughter Concha joins the Religious of the Cross.
1909	The Covenant of Love is established.
1913	Her son Pablo dies; audience with Pope Pius X.
1914	Visits son Manuel in Spain; begins the Missionaries of the Holy Spirit priests.
1916	First religious vows of her daughter Teresa; Archbishop Ibarra stays at Conchita's home for her to assist him in his illness.
1917	Her first grandson is born.
1918	Sorrows of her children; a life of solitude like Mary's.
1919	Ignacio marries.
1920	Sorrow with her children; spiritual desolation.
1921	Sorrows within the family; spiritual exercises with Fr. Guadalupe Treviño, M.Sp.S.
1922	Grave personal illness.
1923	Her brother José dies; spiritual desolation.
1924	Her daughter Lupe marries; Conchita in solitude.
1925	Her daughter Teresa dies; Archbishop Luis Martinez becomes her spiritual director.

1926   Her daughter Lupe becomes very ill; retreat on loving with the Holy Spirit.

1927   Businesses of her children fail; religious persecution.

1928   Brother Octaviano very ill; her spiritual maternity of priests grows.

1929   Sorrows within the family; her union with the interior suffering of the heart of Jesus.

1930   Financial situation worsens; her spiritual motherhood of souls expands.

1936   Becomes very ill; spiritual solitude.

1937   Dies at the age of seventy-four; she dies configured to Christ, in total abandonment to God's will.

About the Author

Kathleen Beckman is the author of several books on the spiritual life, an Ignatian retreat director, and an evangelist who has spoken in thirteen countries, addressing seminarians, clergy, religious communities, and laity. She is often featured on Catholic television and radio.

She is the president and co-founder of the Foundation of Prayer for Priests (www.foundationforpriests.org), an international apostolate of prayer for the holiness of priests and a movement of spiritual motherhood and fatherhood for clergy.

Kathleen serves as the lay administrator of healing, deliverance, and exorcism ministry in her diocese and is a member of the exorcist's team. For six years, she was on the faculty of the Pope Leo XIII Institute, which trains priests for the ministry of exorcism. She completed the International Association of Exorcists course at the Pontifical Regina Apostolorum University in Rome in 2017.

In 2002, Kathleen was invested in the Equestrian Order of the Holy Sepulchre of Jerusalem. She and her husband live in California and have two married sons and a granddaughter.

Sophia Institute

Sophia Institute is a nonprofit institution that seeks to nurture the spiritual, moral, and cultural life of souls and to spread the gospel of Christ in conformity with the authentic teachings of the Roman Catholic Church.

Sophia Institute Press fulfills this mission by offering translations, reprints, and new publications that afford readers a rich source of the enduring wisdom of mankind.

Sophia Institute also operates the popular online resource CatholicExchange.com. *Catholic Exchange* provides world news from a Catholic perspective as well as daily devotionals and articles that will help readers to grow in holiness and live a life consistent with the teachings of the Church.

In 2013, Sophia Institute launched Sophia Institute for Teachers to renew and rebuild Catholic culture through service to Catholic education. With the goal of nurturing the spiritual, moral, and cultural life of souls, and an abiding respect for the role and work of teachers, we strive to provide materials and programs that are at once enlightening to the mind and ennobling to the heart; faithful and complete, as well as useful and practical.

Sophia Institute gratefully recognizes the Solidarity Association for preserving and encouraging the growth of our apostolate over the course of many years. Without their generous and timely support, this book would not be in your hands.

www.SophiaInstitute.com
www.CatholicExchange.com
www.SophiaInstituteforTeachers.org

Sophia Institute Press® is a registered trademark of Sophia Institute.
Sophia Institute is a tax-exempt institution as defined by the
Internal Revenue Code, Section 501(c)(3). Tax ID 22-2548708.

Notes

Notes

Notes

Notes

Notes

Notes

Notes

Notes

Notes